Intuitive Intelligence

MAKE LIFE-CHANGING DECISIONS WITH PERFECT TIMING

Paul O'Brien

Foreword by **John Gray, Ph.D.**

BEYOND WORDS
Hillsboro, Oregon

BEYOND WORDS

8427 N.E. Cornell Road, Suite 500
Hillsboro, Oregon 97124-9808
503-531-8700 / 503-531-8773 fax
www.beyondword.com

Managing Editor: Lindsay S. Easterbrooks-Brown
Copyeditor: Jenefer Angell
Proofreader: Ashley Van Winkle
Interior design: Devon Smith
Composition: William H. Brunson Typography Services

First Beyond Words paperback edition September 2019

BEYOND WORDS PUBLISHING and colophon are registered trademarks of Beyond Words
Publishing, Inc. Beyond Words is an imprint of Simon & Schuster, Inc.

For information about special discounts for bulk purchases, please contact Beyond Words Special Sales at
503-531-8700 or specialsales@beyondword.com.

Manufactured in the United States of America

10 9 8 7 6 5 4 3 2 1

Library of Congress Cataloging-in-Publication Data

Names: O'Brien, Paul D., author.
Title: Intuitive intelligence : make life-changing decisions with perfect
    timing / Paul D. O'Brien ; foreword by John Gray, PhD.
Description: Hillsboro, Oregon : Beyond Words, [2019] | Includes bibliographical references.
Identifiers: LCCN 2019003858 | ISBN 9781582706986 (pbk.)
Subjects: LCSH: Intuition. | Decision making.
Classification: LCC BF315.5 .O27 2019 | DDC 153.4/4—dc23
LC record available at https://lccn.loc.gov/2019003858
ISBN 978-1-58270-724-2 (ebook)

The corporate mission of Beyond Words Publishing, Inc.: *Inspire to Integrity*

For my grandson, Bryce,
and all future decision-makers.

Contents

Foreword

Synchronicity is a term that the psychologist Carl Jung coined to describe the phenomenon of meaningful coincidence. When something happens that feels like an amazing twist of destiny, perhaps providing a turning point in our lives, we intuitively sense that events are not random. A common fruit of synchronicity is meeting the right people at the right time. The term provides extra irony for me with regards to Paul O'Brien, because it describes our first meeting in more ways than one.

It was 1992 and I was on a book tour after *Men Are from Mars, Women Are from Venus* was published. Paul had just taped an interview with me for his *Pathways* radio show in Portland, Oregon. I thought he was an excellent interviewer and asked if radio was what he did for a living. He smiled and told me that he was a volunteer host for the community radio station (a public service he has continued for over thirty years). He also shared that he had recently left a position as a high-tech executive to start a "quirky" Macintosh software company. Being an early Mac user, this intrigued me, and I inquired as to the type of software he was developing.

When I learned that his program was an interactive version of the I Ching for the Macintosh that he named Synchronicity, I almost fell out of my chair. "*You* developed the Synchronicity program?" Surprised by my reaction, he replied, "You've heard of it?" I said, "Yes, I own it, and my wife and I love it. I can hardly believe that I am meeting the guy who developed Synchronicity!" Paul replied, "Well, it's amazing for me to realize that I have been listening to your cassettes on relationships for years—not knowing who *you* were . . . and now I discover that you are one of my first customers. . . this is almost *too much* synchronicity!" We shared a good laugh over it.

My wife, Bonnie, and I had used different versions of the I Ching as an aid to decision-making since the 1970s and found the Taoist divination system to be a source of wisdom. Around 1991, we tried out Paul's new software and found it an engaging new way to consult the I Ching. In addition to taking all the busy work out of casting a reading (the recording and calculating of six lines based on how three coins land six times, and so forth), the program contained an elegant, modern, and nonsexist version of the ancient text, composed by Paul.

The program's combination of poetic text and multimedia was groundbreaking in 1990, but Synchronicity would only prove to be the opening act in Paul's entrepreneurial adventure. Focusing on a mission to provide universal access to authentic divination systems, he eventually gave the world do-it-yourself I Ching and tarot readings via the internet. In the process he also created what turned into the largest astrology and numerology website, which became the exclusive provider of horoscopes and divination features for AOL, Yahoo, Google, Beliefnet, MySpace, and other large websites.

Part memoir, part how-to, and part philosophy, *Intuitive Intelligence* includes the story of how Paul made the strange but ultimately strategic decisions that led to fascinating business success based on staying true to his unique creative vision, against all odds. Beyond the highly entertaining personal anecdotes, the book provides an unconventional tool kit grounded in timeless wisdom, designed to help you improve your odds at finding success in your own way by upgrading your decision-making and improving your timing. His visionary approach to decision-making revolves around Jung's synchronicity principle, which Jung discovered based on his own fascination with the I Ching, and which describes the essence of perfect timing.

I have long noticed how synchronicity plays a huge role in relationships, especially for people who are destined to become partners. It certainly played a prominent part in my connecting with my wife, Bonnie, over thirty-five years ago. In an amazing twist of fate that occurred a couple of years before I met her, I was assigned the task of taking care of her needs—specifically some health needs—under the direction of our spiritual teacher. She was pregnant and needed special things to be procured, errands to be run, etc. I was a monk at the time and had not even met her. But as a result of synchronicity, I was helping provide for my future wife's needs years *before* we even met!

If life is elegant, synchronicity explains why. As Paul puts it, from the synchronistic point of view, there are no accidents. The way Bonnie and I came together is just one example of the mystical ways that people who are destined to be together can and do find each other. In thirty years of relationship counseling, I have heard so many simply amazing stories of how long-term partners have met. More often than not, a meaningful coincidence—or synchronicity—is at the start of it.

Timing has also played a major role in my career as an author and teacher, but as this book explains, synchronicity doesn't operate in a linear fashion. This is where two key components of Paul's Visionary Decision Making approach—self-discovery and intuitive intelligence—come to the forefront.

In 1983 I was a relationship counselor and starting to speak about the ideas that would later coalesce in *Men Are from Mars, Women Are from Venus*. I wrote my first book in 1989, entitled *Men, Women, and Relationships*. It revealed a way of approaching and enriching relationships between men and women, based on appreciating our differences as well as our similarities. To highlight any differences, real as they may be, was "politically incorrect" in the 1980s. As timing would have it, my first book came out one month after Deborah Tannen's bestseller, *You*

Just Don't Understand. Although her analysis was quite different, it was academically grounded. The popularity of her book created a wider discussion around the different ways that women and men communicate.

Her book overshadowing mine seemed like a setback at the time, but it turned out that a scientifically oriented, academic book was necessary to launch a serious discussion about the reality of gender differences. A year later, *Men Are from Mars, Women Are from Venus* came out and went on to become one of the biggest best sellers of all time. In the inscrutable way that synchronicity operates—as Paul describes in the profound book you have in your hands—what ended up looking like perfect timing was aided by a setback that seemed terrible at the time, but which turned out to be a blessing in disguise. As we adopt new beliefs around intuitive intelligence and cultivate what Paul calls a "synchronistic lifestyle," we can better hold on to our visions. We will know there is a reason for everything—including frustrated plans and apparent setbacks—even if we don't understand those reasons right away.

In this book, Paul O'Brien shares his hard-won wisdom along with timeless principles on how to awaken intuitive intelligence to improve your results in any area of life. Over the past twenty-nine years, Paul's modern version of the I Ching has helped hundreds of thousands of people—via software, the internet, an ebook version, and a smartphone app. Now *Intuitive Intelligence* lays out a more expansive tool kit to put the knowledge of synchronicity, the power of archetypes, and an elegant mindfulness of intuitive intelligence to work for you. If you give them a chance, the principles and practices taught in this book will help you manifest happiness, success, and, of course, love!

John Gray, PhD

Introduction—
Author's True Story

At times you have to leave the city of your comfort and go into the wilderness of your intuition. . . . What you'll discover will be wonderful. What you'll discover is yourself.

—Alan Alda

Ask yourself—have you ever passed up something good, hoping something more perfect might come along? Did you ever miss a great opportunity because you were too busy or your timing was off? Have you ever found it difficult to tell the difference between wishful thinking and a risk worth taking?

Making the right moves at the right times is not always easy, and you are not alone if you have suffered from professional missteps and bad timing. I know, because I have made all these mistakes—and many more. But there is another side . . . for me, for you, and for all of us. The surprising tale of my unlikely success as an entrepreneur—resulting from much introspection, a passionate search for meaning, and the cultivation of intuitive intelligence—vividly illustrates how risks worth taking arise in our lives at the right time. Taking those risks and succeeding wildly depends so much upon developing an intuitive sense of timing.

Back in 1988, I had an established career as a software marketing specialist in the high-tech sector, having advanced from a job as a secretary at a computer center to VP of marketing for a well-funded startup within fifteen years (framing a two-year sabbatical in meditation centers around the world in the middle). During that time, I developed considerable direct marketing skills and achieved executive status and pay, but I was not a happy camper. I longed to make a living promoting something more meaningful to me. I dreamed of creating software that would provide "experiences" that could help people on a personal level—as opposed to making a well-paid living peddling sterile high technology for profit.

I had never produced software, let alone multimedia—which was only then becoming feasible with graphical computers like the Macintosh. I understood the young software industry and found its unfolding potential fascinating and inspiring. I was particularly enthused by visions of how computer-coded interactive multimedia might be used to educate and enlighten, as well as entertain, having had visions of multimedia for twenty years before CD-ROMs were invented.

The other fascination of my youth was the Taoist *Book of Changes*, or *I Ching*, a reflective aid that I first learned to appreciate as a nineteen-year-old college student, when I set out to study the Taoist philosophy behind my martial arts training. This oracular system was developed in China some three thousand years ago to help emperors and military leaders activate intuition so they could make better strategic decisions.

One day, inspired by a reading from the *Book of Changes*, I decided to spend my life savings to produce a multimedia version of the I Ching, which had existed only in book form for thousands of years. I thought that by developing an interactive version of this tool that was so special— even sacred—to me, I could bring intuitive decision-making support to others via a more engaging presentation. I had no reason to believe an interactive program based on a system of Taoist wisdom would ever become highly profitable, but the idea fascinated me so much I didn't concern myself with potential profitability. It all started out as an experiment driven by intense curiosity, a labor of love.

Obviously, I knew that a computer-assisted I Ching product was too esoteric to attract a publisher or investors. It was the kind of investment opportunity that would have gotten laughed off *Shark Tank* for all kinds of good reasons—yet I couldn't bring myself to set the idea aside. I was enthralled by the intersection of two personal fascinations—the ancient Taoist oracle and the potential of interactive media.

So, inspired, the urge to create an interactive version of the I Ching took on a life of its own. I couldn't help myself. I had to try, even if it meant spending my life savings. Unbeknownst to me, the outcome would be the first divination program ever published and one of the first multimedia titles for consumers, some five years before CD-ROM technology became available. It was certainly a novel product, but at the time it was probably one of the dumbest business ideas ever. If it was ever going to be viable, it wasn't now; it was probably too far ahead of its time. And my peers in the software industry told me so, as kindly as they could.

Nevertheless, with the help of a grad student programmer and an artist friend, I spent my entire nest egg on the creation of a prototype while I continued my day job. A few months later, when the prototype was marginally functional, I was so pleased with how well I thought it was going to work I decided to complete development, package it, and take it to market, even though it required the rest of my savings and risked my career. I also was faced with the daunting need to come up with my own I Ching text, the equivalent of a hundred-page book. Not totally happy with the ancient versions, which were so patriarchal and arcane, I set out to compose a modern version with the help of a Taoist writer friend. A lot more work for no pay!

I could only hope the result would appeal to enough people to keep a small startup afloat until I could figure out how to more widely market such an offbeat product. Or develop more popular product ideas that appealed to me. All of it started in my basement.

Now, I know the story of a guy with an idea starting a company in his basement (or garage) sounds familiar. What made this situation different was the extraordinary degree to which the plan was driven by personal fascinations, not to mention a lack of resources and utter absence of investors. This was extreme "bootstrap" territory, and mere survival depended on an agile intuition, a willingness to make bold decisions, some savvy, and a lot of luck. Instead of taking on the seemingly impossible task of raising money to capture market share (aka "eyeballs"), my approach depended on noticing subtle signs and trusting my intuitive sense of timing and selling things for profit as soon as possible. Since I was so totally driven by a creative vision that inspired me, I called the company Visionary Software.

As a bootstrap entrepreneur, I knew it was critical to make the right moves at the right time. If the enterprise was to survive, exceptional decision-making would be mandatory. With no credit other than the mortgage on my house, I faced the looming possibility of running out of cash and going bankrupt for years. Everything was on the line and there was no room for major missteps. It wasn't easy to sleep. Fear of failure and bankruptcy kept me awake. In the beginning, I just tried to stay focused on the product creation side, while I continued to bring in some money moonlighting as a consultant.

I named the first I Ching software Synchronicity, after the famous principle that the great psychologist Carl Jung coined to explain how divination systems like the I Ching work (hint: it's all about intuition and timing). Though the English translation of the Chinese *I Ching* is *Book of Changes*, it is more of a system than a book. In fact, it is a book in service of a divination system (which we shall explore in chapter 8). The traditional book form comes with a set of coins designed to stimulate intuition for strategic decision-making and change management.

Ironically, even though Jung's synchronicity principle is about timing (as we shall explore in some depth in chapter 3), it is entirely possible for a visionary to be ahead of his or her time—and my timing in producing I Ching software in June of 1989 proved that. As much as I desired such an app for my own enjoyment and use, people familiar with the I Ching didn't buy software in those days, way before email and the world wide web. And there was no real market for multimedia either, since CD-ROMs were not yet in use. This meant anything with graphics or sound required a cumbersome installation process involving multiple floppy disks. To make matters worse, the only people who bought software were engineers or accountants, almost entirely men with little awareness of or interest in Taoist wisdom or intuitive decision-making. A book about intuitive intelligence had not come out yet.

Despite being fifteen years ahead of its time, Synchronicity managed to become a minor cult hit in Macintosh circles, if only because it was aesthetic and unusual. And it had a sense of humor. The front of the first box read, "Warning: Repeated use may lead to feelings of superiority." Synchronicity was never going to be a bestseller, but it was unique and our direct marketing worked well enough to give the company a bit of positive cash flow for a couple of years. I wasn't getting paid most of the time, but I was holding it all together. (I even poured some energy into creating a new product for flashing customized affirmations across the Macintosh menu bar, which I called Mindset. We launched it, but due to some technical hurdles it never got much traction. I still think it was a good idea!)

Even with all my fervent marketing efforts, it became clear that the survival of the new business would require reaching a much broader audience than such products could attract. So, I hustled to keep my startup afloat by quickly developing programs in the more mainstream area of scheduling and time management. Curiosity and enthusiasm propelled my first product, but I had a larger vision for myself, which I characterized as *creative freedom*. My modest definition of creative freedom was to make a living producing software that I thought was cool and good for people. I wasn't dreaming of making a fortune. I wasn't expecting to pay off my mortgage. I just wanted to make a decent living in a creative way that was authentically me. At the same time, I didn't want to take myself too seriously. Our original company motto, printed on the back of the first Synchronicity box, was "Creative freedom through vision and humor."

A bit of an Irish gambler at heart, I've always been fascinated by good timing. That partially explains why my foray into mainstream productivity software was for a priority management program. First Things First filled a need for personal information management programs in those days, and FTF did pretty well in the marketplace, realizing broader popularity than Synchronicity ever could. Cash flow from sales was better than ever, but there was never much cushion. To have any hope of really making a hit, we would have to develop an MS Windows version of the program, a huge development challenge.

After a couple of more years of struggling month-to-month and a growing desire to focus my creative energies on the category I had invented—divination software—a team of three MBAs who loved First Things First approached me to take over and raise money for a Windows version. Ultimately, I handed management of the company over to this team, three business "experts" who invested their own money and vowed they would raise much more to make the product a world-class time-management program. As it turned out, their failure to raise money and their lavish spending bankrupted the company, which had been profitable enough to sustain itself until they took over. In the process, I lost everything I had built—except I retained the legal ownership of Synchronicity and Mindset, which they didn't care about. In a prescient move, I had previously had the company legally assign these to me as the author, and honoring that became part of the settlement agreement.

The failure of my first entrepreneurial company was disheartening, but at least I still had the rights to my original creation. Approximately ten thousand people had used Synchronicity; many had even sent heartfelt thank-you letters. For years I would occasionally bump into people who, when they found out that I was its author, confessed they had pirated the program, and some even handed me a twenty-dollar bill on the spot. The appreciation from such people encouraged me to hold on to other visions of such products and my dream of creative freedom in producing them.

When CD-ROMs and then the world wide web came into popular use five years after the demise of Visionary Software, I saw a new opportunity to resurrect my original vision. This new delivery platform made it possible to deliver a much richer multimedia experience, and for both Mac and Windows. So, for the second time around, I used every dollar I had socked away (as a product and marketing consultant in the meantime) to turn Synchronicity into a graphically and musically rich CD-ROM. Soon after, I happened to interview a tarot scholar on my *Pathways* radio show (which I have been hosting on KBOO FM radio in Portland, Oregon, since 1984). Through that interview, I came to understand that authentic tarot (not the psychic mind-reading variety) operates on the same synchronicity principle as the I Ching, only using a different set of archetypes, in the form of the seventy-eight cards. With her scholarly help, I spent a year and a half compiling a database of tarot interpretation text and another year developing a media-rich, do-it-yourself tarot reading CD-ROM to double my new company's multimedia product line.

Within a year after we had put up a website to market the two new CD-ROMs (for I Ching and do-it-yourself tarot), we noticed that people were seriously banging on a little animated sampler clip of casting coins that we had put on the website to help market the CD-ROMs. Any kind of online animation was rare in those days and this little sampler became a popular feature, even though it didn't deliver a reading or do much. But the animation was unusually cool.

In spite of the sampler's click-through popularity, our CD-ROM sales hardly increased at all. This was confusing, since that little interactive bit on the internet was going viral, with thousands of people playing it over and over and showing it to others. I took this as a signal that our new company was meant to be in the interactive website business rather than just using the web for e-commerce to market CD-ROM products. Therefore, we strategically needed to build a "pay-to-play" e-commerce gaming-type website. In 1999, this was a novel and unproven business idea and would be quite an expensive proposition to develop from scratch.

Through a most unlikely sequence of synchronicities (there's that word again)—and after being laughed off by two banks, including the one I'd had a great relationship with for twenty years—a gnomish middle-aged banker with a comb-over, wearing a polyester suit, and driving a Ford Pinto was willing to believe in me. He did all the paperwork to get us an SBA loan from Key Bank to build a website to sell do-it-yourself readings on a one-off basis. Who would have ever imagined a large regional bank—or any bank, for that matter—financing an I Ching and tarot reading website in 1999? Faith and perseverance paid off, because everything was in sync!

Once we had that critical seven-year loan, building the pay-to-play e-commerce site took almost a year, during which time I invented a new form of web currency, which I called "Karma Coins," to allow people to make micropayments (amounts too small for a credit card). Karma Coins were like tokens at an arcade or county fair that allow access to various amusements. Our virtual arcade consisted of various types of I Ching and tarot card readings, followed in a couple of years by numerology and astrology features. Karma Coins made intuitive sense to me, because I envisioned how we could use them: as a bonus to attract new members, as an awards program for good customers, as a way to sell volume discounts, even as a holiday or birthday gift to registered members throughout the year. Micropayments were a new and revolutionary concept at the time and, considering that e-commerce was the only way we had to monetize our website, a highly risky concept to bet the farm on. But my creative juices were flowing and the timing felt right, as I brought my creative and marketing skills to bear as a bootstrap entrepreneur once again.

Its implementation was the fruit of a visionary decision that came along with a huge financial risk of failure. We had no way of knowing whether selling Karma Coins would work out or only prove to be a costly distraction that alienated users and made our e-commerce effort—which was risky enough—more confusing and difficult to pull off.

We unveiled our innovative e-commerce website one month before the end of the year 2000, and I decided that we should test the power of Karma Coins on New Year's Day by depositing fifty Karma Coins into each of our registered user's accounts and emailing them an announcement and wishes for a prosperous new year. We only had about a hundred thousand users at that point—and only 1 or 2 percent were paying customers—but we were financially dependent on every customer we could get.

After the Karma Coin launch, I remember predicting to my small staff that we were going to take a revenue hit for at least a few days, because we were essentially giving product away. How wrong I was— our sales actually tripled almost immediately with lots of new customers! People spent their free Karma Coins on our unique, high-quality product offerings and many were inclined to buy more. This was a great sign for us and a good lesson about the power of generosity.

After a few more years of plugging away and again managing to keep it all together (at one point taking out a second mortgage on my home to make payroll), I had added astrology to the mix and tried to negotiate syndication deals with the largest internet portals—America Online (AOL), Yahoo, MySpace, and Google Gadgets among them— who wanted the "fresh daily content" of a well-written horoscope on their home pages.

Big deals entail big risks. The largest and most significant business deal I ever made was winning the right to provide AOL our new daily horoscope in 2003. They appreciated the quality of our offering, which made sense because we had procured the services of the finest horoscope writer out there—Rick Levine, one of the top astrologers in the world. There's no way to automate a daily horoscope; its ongoing production is laborious and expensive. One might naturally assume that any publisher would want to pay a fee or royalty for publishing it. After all, we were! But not the likes of AOL or Yahoo—au contraire! Having the privilege of providing a free horoscope on the home page of a huge portal like

AOL is like garnering a plum corner booth at the Saturday Market or the endcap at a huge supermarket. It's going to cost you, except a lot more! The terms of the deal seemed outlandish and gave me serious pause: We would have to guarantee AOL 50 percent of revenues resulting from the sale of reports on our site or pay a minimum fee of $500,000 per year—whichever was greater. This would be the cost for the privilege of giving away expensive content for free. In return, all we would get was trickle-down traffic from a small "Powered by Visionary" link on AOL's homepage, which we could only hope to sufficiently monetize.

To put the deal in perspective, our little company was making an annual profit of less than $200,000. The guarantee demanded by AOL, therefore, would be two and a half times our entire annual earnings. If we were going to win the deal, I would have to bet that we would make at least $500,000 in profits off that tiny link. Much less than that and our company might have to file for bankruptcy. I ran some spreadsheets with projections, but having had no experience at that level—and still nervous about the viability of Karma Coins—there was no way to confidently project results. The pressure of having to compete combined with the uncertainty caused me to lose sleep over the prospect of risking our company, which had finally become profitable. At the same time, if we were to have a chance of benefitting from such a deal, I had to maintain a confident posture in the bidding war against our competition—the world's two largest astrology websites at the time. Believe me, this was nerve-racking. I was scared. I had never been so stressed out by a strategic decision in my life, but I my intuition told me I had to go for it. And, somehow, I was able to summon the confident-seeming composure needed to convince the VP at AOL that we were big and stable enough for them to partner with.

As a result of successfully closing the deal and having our little link on AOL's homepage alongside the daily horoscope, sizeable traffic began flowing to our fledgling e-commerce website, which in turn needed to expand—and keep expanding—fast. Just keeping things running became a hugely stressful challenge because in a syndication deal with the largest portals even 1 percent downtime is cause for instant termination. The additional stress of monitoring things 24/7 for the next few years probably took some years off my life, but with constant tracking and a lot of very late nights, we kept the servers up and running during continuous expansion.

Luckily, AOL allowed us to pay the guarantee quarterly. With the help of Karma Coin sales, we ended up successfully monetizing the traffic, managing to bring in more than the required $500,000 guarantee the first year, and considerably more in following years. Thanks to strategic relationships with other huge partners, within a few years our site acquired millions of registered members and became the world's largest astrology website. Approximately 2 percent of our members bought a reading or report product—a notable direct-marketing feat in itself, and a highly profitable one. Ever averse to being in debt, I paid off the entire SBA loan within two years.

By this time, my original Synchronicity app from fourteen years earlier had evolved into a divination website offering astrology, numerology, and tarot, as well as my original I Ching. These online experiences were not only creative and authentic, but also wildly popular—especially with women who, following the advent of the world wide web and email services, had started to use computers for email and the web in larger numbers. After fifteen years of pursuing my entrepreneurial vision, and struggling to make ends meet, my creative endeavors began to produce exceptional returns. Nobody, including myself, ever believed an esoteric program like Synchronicity could morph into a profitable business. It seemed foolhardy enough to imagine that such a niche product could support me and my son—let alone a staff of people—but this enterprise was becoming downright lucrative!

Even though accumulation of wealth had not been my goal, this second time around, my startup was growing fast and far exceeding my original concept of creative freedom. I was receiving vastly more income than I had ever made as an executive or consultant, and our interactive products were touching the lives of millions. This felt like success both financially and creatively: my career and my purpose had intersected beautifully.

Even before our website was generating over fifty million internet pageviews a month, the company began winning growth awards. Using web metric tools, large media firms like Disney and Barnes & Noble began to notice that we had massive traffic and came sniffing around. They could sense the high profit margins and were interested in acquiring the company. Such attention was flattering, but at first, I politely waved it off. I loved this little business I had created, which had grown to support twenty-five employees, ten million registered members, and hundreds of thousands of customers. We had no debt...or nervous investors. I felt pride that the business was serving so many people and winning awards, as well as making millions of dollars. I was having fun developing new products and running a prospering business. After so much grueling labor, I felt a strong affection for my "babies," the products and services that were the offspring of my creative imagination. The last thing I wanted was to sell them off now that they were amply repaying my sacrifices and labors of love.

However, the company's success had more than fulfilled my vision of making a living doing something I found fascinating and cared about. I had succeeded beyond my initial dream of creative freedom, gutting it out by moonlighting as a consultant and the help of a serendipitous small business loan. I had never had an "exit strategy," nor any perceived need for one. The goal of creating a sustainable business had provided enough motivation for me to work extreme hours for many years, but those days of killer stress were in the past.

As I entered my fifties, with a couple of decades of 70- to 80-hour weeks, I began to tire. It was also draining to have to stay ahead of copy-cat competitors who were duplicating almost every creative move we made. Although I was sleep-deprived and fatigued from years of long hours, I still felt young and strong, and the traditional idea of retirement held no meaning for me.

My imagination began to consider how I could enjoy even more creative freedom if I could sell the business for a good price and be able to let go of the pressures of running a business—with all the burdens of taking care of employees, customers, budgets, and deadlines. I had worked for nonprofits in the past and was interested in how I might spread new ideas, books, and interactive media to promote personal and cultural evolution. I knew that I liked to write and speak publicly; I enjoyed consulting and mentoring—talents and interests I didn't have time to develop while building and running a business. If I were able to sell the company for a high enough price, I could have the freedom to pursue creative endeavors at my own pace in a nonprofit format for the rest of my life. A new vision was incubating within me.

The year was 2006. After the implosion of the dot-com bubble, the markets had begun to restabilize. The number of new companies going public with an IPO—which had dropped 90 percent since 1999—was starting to rise again. My intuition told me that if I could sell the company during this window of opportunity, the timing might be right to fetch a great price. It was certainly an option to consider. On the one hand, my emotional attachment to the company and our millions of subscribers made letting go a difficult decision. Plus, the company was making serious profits and there was no need to sell it. On the other hand, I knew my strongest passions were becoming ever more philosophical and philanthropic than acquisitive or managerial, so I stayed open to considering a huge change.

Even though I was conflicted, I felt called upon to make a pivotal decision that would have monumental consequences for the rest of my life. I knew from experience that windows of opportunity don't stay open long and that timing is always a critical factor. Fortunately, I had some help for making major important decisions. After meditating on my dilemma, I cast an I Ching reading on the subject and got the reading "Breakthrough," which pointed to deliberately making a big move. After meditating on this for a couple of days, I decided I would accept if I could get my "number"—the right offer for an amount large enough to support creative freedom for the rest of my life. With the stipulation that no employees would have to move or lose their jobs, I envisioned letting go of my attachment to the company and giving it over to new owners who could send my beloved creations into even wider distribution.

Retaining an investment banking firm to find a compatible buyer was the first order of business. I wanted an outfit that understood new media, one that could locate a buyer who could realize the future potential of what I had created and put its resources behind continuing growth. Because of the esoteric nature of my products and services, I knew that finding the right match would take a minor miracle. But it would only take one, and after years of studying the I Ching, I had come to appreciate the seemingly miraculous power of synchronicity.

To further complicate the process, I felt that I needed to personally negotiate the terms of the deal—a horrific idea to investment bankers. In fact, they were shocked and practically livid when I didn't back down. But this was going to be the biggest deal of my life, and I would not allow a broker to negotiate the price or the terms. In spite of intense pressure from the bankers I had retained—who, like all brokers, were more worried about no deal rather than the best possible deal—I had to summon my inner rebel warrior to stand up to these hard-driving experts. This turned out to be a visionary decision too.

Drawing upon internal resources, feeling strong in my position as a nondesperate seller, trusting intuitive guidance, and sticking with my decision to be the one who negotiated the deal, in the end I managed to get twice my number! Much to the bankers' happy surprise and benefit, their commissions skyrocketed beyond what they had been shooting for. The sale of the company took place in January 2007, which turned out to be excellent market timing—with corporate valuations as high as they had been since the dot-com era, just months before the financial crash of 2008.

Creative freedom, my dream for decades, had come home in a much bigger way than I had ever imagined. Faced with an abundance of creative opportunities I was now free to explore, I realized how limited my original idea of creative freedom had been. And I was entirely grateful for it. My first act after selling the company was to set up the nonprofit

Divination Foundation (DF) to enjoy this greater creative freedom, producing good works without the need or pressure to make a profit.

The Greatest Takeaway—
The Visionary Decision Making Approach to Success

While my story may seem like a fluke—perhaps the result of exceptional luck or "good karma"—there is more to it than that. Forty years of personal trial and error went into developing what has become the Visionary Decision Making (VDM) approach presented in this book. The art of more conscious decision-making, informed by greater access to intuitive intelligence, has been central to my unfolding destiny, and it can work wonders for you too. Any motivated person can learn and master the concepts, skills, and philosophical approach of VDM and apply them to achieve success and happiness on their own terms.

With this book, I hope to share the valuable lessons and skills that I mastered over decades, so that you may more easily achieve your own definition of success—whatever it is—in any area of life. My particular success involved an entrepreneurial venture. Yours might pertain to some other important realm—relationship, family, spiritual development, or artistic expression. No matter what you are trying to achieve or attain, skillful decision-making and timing will be critical.

Understanding your strengths and weaknesses is an unending process of self-discovery and personal evolution. Real success depends on being true to what fascinates you. Living authentically and learning to access creative powers will help you better manage change, feel the confidence to take risks that can grow you, and open to greater grace, creativity, contentment, and wisdom.

Intuitive Intelligence is intended to help you take note of those make-or-break moments when using your intuition can help you decide your next best move. Learn to reawaken and tune up your intuitive sensitivity and to harness new beliefs that change the way you approach situations, opportunities, and relationships. Once you learn how to activate intuitive intelligence when you need it most, you will more quickly realize visions that align with who you are. The secret to achieving the abundance and joy you deserve is twofold: becoming clear about what your heart desires and making the right moves at the right time.

On a practical level, VDM philosophy and techniques can help you decide when to have a difficult conversation, what financial or emotional risks are likely to pay off, and how to invest wisely, get that dream assignment, or create the lasting relationship you've always wanted. Learn how to prioritize decisions so you know what you should take up now and what to put on the back burner. By learning to recognize fruitful turning-point opportunities and identify when they are ripe for decisive action, you can approach them with clarity of vision and greater self-confidence.

There is no formula for strategic decision-making, because you can't force intuition or make creative decisions through willpower alone. To do your best, you need to know how to produce the conditions in which the intuitive sense is able to receive clear signals. You also need to master the skills that you will call upon when a turning point arises.

This book is divided into three parts. Part I explores the real meaning of success, the problem of poor decision-making, and the key psychological forces that support intuitive intelligence. Part I also shows how we have access to creative resources that may seem hidden but are always available to us—when we learn how to tune in to them.

Part II describes the techniques and practices that comprise the Visionary Decision Making process: focusing on a strategic vision, understanding how our "triune brain" affects decision-making and how to work with it, activating your intuitive antenna, utilizing the power of archetypes, tapping collective wisdom via an authentic divination system, executing a plan at the right time, persevering in your pursuit of results, and achieving levels of mastery. These skills are reliable pathways for cultivating your intuitive intelligence.

Part II also contains short practices designed to increase your self-knowledge, activate your intuition, or approach your choices. These exercises will help you develop VDM skills and become more aware of psychological resources at your disposal. With practice, these skills become habits that support you and provide stability on the road to a more meaningful, harmonious, and abundant life. Perform the exercises as you encounter them, or come back to them at any time. For your convenience, the exercises and practices are also compiled in appendix B.

Part III explores the philosophy of intuitive intelligence, which includes upgrading your belief system, experimenting with new "visionary beliefs," and ultimately enjoying a synchronistic lifestyle. Here we entertain a new perspective and experience of life—marked by the grace, confidence, and wisdom that flow from an empowered and creative way of approaching change while staying true to what fascinates and inspires you.

Although developing good habits is vital, developing intuitive intelligence requires more than following a formula or set of rules. This VDM skillset is more like learning how to dance. When it comes to making the right moves at the right time, your dance partner is life itself, leading you to fulfill your calling and your destiny. Your role is to do your best to follow its lead and stay in sync. The more you pay attention and cultivate intuitive intelligence through the practice of VDM skills, the more you will sense the unique rhythm of your unique life, in order to make big moves with exquisite timing.

Ultimately, this is a book about manifesting what you want, about giving and receiving what your heart desires. In various parts of the book, I reference my Creative Manifestation Treatment, a meditation that leverages the law of attraction as well as Visionary Decision Making, calling into play your personal vision (in chapter 5) and the archetype of Creative Power (in chapter 7). The entire treatment is laid out as a template for your editing and personal use in appendix A.

It is my wish and hope that this book will help you cultivate your intuitive intelligence and, as you become more sensitive to this exquisite faculty, improve your judgment and timing around the manifestation of what your heart desires.

Part I

Context and Resources

1

The Challenge of Success

I arise in the morning torn between the desire to improve (or save) the world and to enjoy (or savor) the world. This makes it hard to plan the day.

—E. B. White

Life is the sum of all your choices.

—Albert Camus

I was voted "Most Likely to Succeed" in high school. The acclaim was flattering, but I didn't know what success meant—to my classmates who voted . . . or myself. It's safe to assume they were thinking in worldly terms. As it turned out, in the realm of business they were at least partly right. Worldly success is generally measured in terms of how much money a person makes or how much property they accumulate. But life has taught me that success has a much broader meaning, and that it can—and should—mean different things for different people. If you let others define your success, you can end up very unhappy—no matter how much material wealth or fame you accumulate. The suicides of the rich and famous amply demonstrate this point.

Unless you play competitive games for fun, success worth having never comes at anyone else's expense. Although money is a medium of exchange and a measure of wealth, true success cannot be measured by the number of digits in a bank account or a never-ending accumulation of material goods—fueled by our social epidemic of always comparing ourselves and craving more. In general terms, success might be defined as accomplishing your goals and attaining whatever you value most highly. The pathway to authentic success becomes clear when you come to terms with who you are and what is most meaningful to you. Success is a natural result of finding and developing whatever aligns with your temperament and feeds your spirit. As Maya Angelou put it, "Success is liking yourself, liking what you do, and liking how you do it."

There is no right or wrong to wanting anything—as long as your desire isn't harmful. Your desires and fascinations are good for you—if only because they serve as signposts that point the way. You deserve to have what your heart desires—and many people don't realize for a long time that no substitute will satisfy you until you have tasted it. No matter how much of anything else you enjoy or accumulate.

As someone who was raised to feel guilty about even having wants and needs—who was taught to believe all my needs were selfish—I keep a reminder note on my bulletin board to this day: "I deserve to have what I want and what I want is good for me." Whatever you want, go for it. Experience how it feels to have it, if only to learn that you don't really want it that much, which is in itself a valuable lesson. Ultimately, happiness and success come from consciously choosing to do whatever reduces suffering and/or increases joy in yourself and those around you. Bessie Stanley described a successful person as someone "who has left the world better than he found it, whether by an improved poppy, a perfect poem, or a rescued soul . . . who has always looked for the best in others and given the best he had; whose life was an inspiration; whose memory a benediction."[1]

Property's Shadow

Our modern world equates success with money, because money can get us so many of the things that we desire—security, status, power, freedom, luxury, pleasure, and property. In reality, money is just a technology and, as such, is sterile if made into a goal. It is a useful system using numbers and symbols to provide a medium of exchange that makes it easier for humans to trade possessions, time, energy, and labor for things they need or want to use or consume. Money that is saved up or accumulated can be thought of as stored labor—a way of compensating its owner for strategic and determined efforts already made or for risks successfully undertaken.

By turning valuable labors into a symbolic commodity that can be spent later (in exchange for what's produced by somebody else), we need money, or something like it, as a unit of value and medium of exchange. It's a useful technology to facilitate transactions, but not properly an end in itself. It needs to flow. I sometimes characterize money as being like manure. Hoard it and it's toxic and stinks to high heaven. Spread it around, on the other hand, and it can be a fertilizer that helps things grow. It's interesting to note that Freud drew a connection between the covetousness of money and babies' obsession with their own excrement during the process of toilet training.

For a million years before the agricultural revolution transformed the way humans lived, our hunter-gatherer ancestors neither had nor needed a monetary system. Anthropologists estimate that nomadic tribes consisted of no more than 150 individuals who shared everything communally (perhaps even sex and parenting). To compete with cohorts for special status or to hoard resources was much worse than bad form. Such self-centeredness might mean ostracism from the tribe, which in those days would mean an early death.

Between five thousand and seven thousand years ago, the first farmers organized permanent communities and built dwellings based on familial relations. Living in one place with an allotted amount of space and a store of provisions necessitated a new social invention—private property. Money is an offshoot of private property, which did not make sense until we learned to domesticate food and animals, moved out of the forests, and settled down.

The notion of private property gave us a way to manage an accumulation of resources that, to begin with, could keep members of a community fed and warm through a winter. Property was an important concept for protecting and dividing vital resources. Beyond its utilitarian aspect relative to food and housing, however, the idea of private property took over human consciousness and monumentally changed the course of cultural evolution.

With the advent of personal possessions, owning and protecting one's property became important. We invented writing to codify rules and laws pertaining to property rights ("Thou shalt not covet . . ."). We invented arithmetic to account for the distribution of resources (unequal from the very beginning) and track who owned what. Competition between communities and the need to protect against raiding bands led to a need for weapons technology. Even now it seems the resulting arms race will never end, despite the fact we can already destroy the planet many times over.

Inequality was baked into the social equation from the beginning of civilization. Just imagine the first bully of a developer who stood on a hill and declared, "This land is mine. Anyone who says otherwise is going to have to fight me and my men." This dynamic of domination by the strongest member of a community immediately took hold. And the power elite—the so-called 1 percent—have ruled society ever since, reducing others to subordinate status, as serf, soldier, wife, and so on.

City-states gave rise to empires, deadlier technologies, and large-scale wars. Monotheistic religions sanctioned those wars and the inequality of wealth they enforced. Thus, patriarchy took hold only five thousand years ago, and its new monotheistic male "God" not only sanctioned warfare but also banished female deities (and, in the case of Judaism and Islam, the active expression of the right brain—pictorial art itself).

In the span of humanity's existence on this planet, five thousand years is recent, but that is as far back as the age of writing and recorded histories go. As a result, we have no real perspective on the impact of civilization and have come to take society and monetary systems that were constructed around property and its unequal distribution for granted, as if it were the way it always was or has to be. But all of it bears review because it was so monumental and to this day continues to shape our culture.

In addition to material assets and resources, women and children needed to be protected. Monogamous marriage was invented, primarily as a property agreement between men. For thousands of years—until a hundred years ago—women's property and political rights were mandated to flow through husbands, fathers, and brothers. Riane Eisler, author of *The Chalice and the Blade*, referred to a "dominator culture" that took over the world, demoting women and children to the status of property—men's property.

One might think that patriarchs would award themselves as many wives as they could afford—and, indeed, in many societies that has been the case. But, according to one theory, monogamy was made the general law in slightly more modern cultures to give male serfs some dominion of their own—authority over a wife and children—while the men themselves served as fodder for bloody raids, wars, and other dangerous expeditions on behalf of the ruling class. Except for the "nobility," normal life meant backbreaking work, lack of natural weaning for children, and subsisting largely on an imbalanced grain-based diet of gruel. It was not a healthy or long life. Archeologists note that, based on archeological digs, the hunter-gatherers of ten thousand years ago were a foot taller, much healthier, and lived longer lives than the agricultural peasants of five thousand years ago.

Interestingly, some credible theories of prehistoric culture suggest that there was social and political equality between males and females during the eons that humanity worshipped feminine deities, including creativity and fertility goddesses. In a profound book, *The Fall: The Insanity of the Ego in Human History and the Dawning of a New Era*, Steve Taylor reveals how the paradigm shift of agriculture and settled civilization reversed the status of females, who had been equals, if not leaders, during the hunter-gatherer period that had prevailed since the rise of our species. Although the hunter-gatherer period preceded the invention of writing (so, obviously, there is no written record), strong evidence from excavated eight-thousand-year-old burial sites and observations of modern hunter-gatherer behavior show that women played some of the most revered roles in the community (as evidenced by the largest and most highly decorated graves such as those of Catal Huyuk in Asia Minor)—serving as priestesses to the great goddess, to whom the community built shrines.

This monumental transformation of human social organization may have started seven thousand years ago and taken place over a span of some one or two thousand years, but considering that modern *Homo sapiens* has been around for over two hundred thousand years, the change happened extremely quickly in the grand scope of things. The result of the agricultural revolution was that, in the process of this "fall from the garden," the patriarchal society that has prevailed ever since has been marked by a predominantly ego-driven, power-hungry, materialistic, and possessive value system.

In our media-saturated world, you don't have to look far to see legions of miserable rich people who never feel they have enough power or security. What good is that kind of success? Again, for the sake of your own happiness, remember that success is a fluid term and not synonymous with the accumulation of property or power over others. Who you are and what fulfills you—your values—are what ultimately will define true success for you. If you increase happiness for yourself and others, you are a success, even if you are performing a humble service that few people notice, pay you for, or give you credit for.

Taoist sages who understand the flow of yin and yang in the cycles of nature and culture know this in their bones. True sages are modest and do not feel the need to call attention to or aggrandize themselves. Such masters of balance are not trying to prove anything, so they have no need to solicit "Likes" on social media. In their humility and voluntary simplicity, they are fine being nobody special—ironically so, since this attitude is precisely what makes them valued and revered!

Their decisions and timing are effortless and skillful, free from stress. Let us salute those who find contentment in a peaceful harmony with the rhythms of nature! In terms of peace, personal satisfaction, and freedom from suffering, such people—a rare breed these days—are the ultimate success stories.

Arguably, the ancient sages had an advantage, living in slower-paced times and in a far simpler world that could not support the appetite for possessions and attention that our culture constantly stimulates. Because resources were limited and survival a real concern, they could not afford to be so superficial or addicted. They depended on each other, extended family, and a close-knit community. Real connections, not virtual or fake ones, were the best security. This dynamic of interdependency can still happen. In his own way, my cousin Lennie is a modern example.

Cousin Lennie—A Counterculture Success Story

Before he retired, my first cousin owned a barbershop, and he still occasionally cuts hair for a bit of extra cash. Otherwise—with the help of his tightknit community, on which he can depend and which can depend on him—Lennie has figured out how to live off the grid as much as possible. He hunts, fishes, and gardens for food around his solar-assisted house and trout ponds that he built with the help of friends. He makes guitars, writes songs, and performs at events, often for free. I visit him every other summer in Lake Leelanau, Michigan, a freshwater wonderland peninsula surrounded by Lake Michigan. All four of my grandparents and both of my parents were born on the shores of Lake Leelanau. Lennie lives his simplified life there with passion; he's doing what he has chosen to do, and he loves a radically independent life. It wasn't easy for him to liberate himself to follow his calling—his bliss—but he did it. If accomplishing the life of his back-to-nature dreams is not a true success, I don't know what is. Real success depends upon fulfilling your own personal values and top priorities. Multiple desires are operating at the same time with new ones ever arising, so there is no shortage of things that have the power to distract the mind. Just hold on to your clarity about what is most important to you, including your grand vision for yourself if you have one.

As Lennie's story and my own story demonstrate, if you put energy into passions that align with who you really are, you will be rewarded with success, in one form or another. If you have been trying to live up to the expectations of others, let that go. You are the director, the CEO, of your own life. As the saying goes, "I don't care what other people think . . . they don't do it that much anyway!" It's time to know yourself and start making decisions that align with your personal values no matter what you think others think.

Getting Clear about Your Personal Path

You are unique. When it comes to doing what will make you happy, you need to be clear about your highest values—the ones that reflect what you want the most.

The social philosopher Eric Hoffer observed, "When people are free to do as they please, they usually imitate each other." Amusing as this is, it's also true—which makes it almost tragic. Compared to any other nation or past civilization, citizens of the modern world have tremendous freedom. But with so many choices, we find it that much harder to form a clear idea of what we want.

It's much easier to rule out what we don't want. As philosopher and spiritual author Ken Keyes Jr. once put it, people can easily say, "I don't know what I want, but I'm damn sure this isn't it!" While it's easy to identify with such a sentiment, this approach doesn't help you move forward in manifesting your heart's desires or goals. Critical analysis can provide some useful information, but to succeed you must go beyond determining what you *don't* want to identify and target what you *do* want. To manifest your vision, first commit to gaining clarity on what that is, and then take the risk of going for it, asking for it, and, finally, achieving it.

To this end, desire is a central stimulus. It's a natural and necessary stimulant for movement and growth. The etymology of the word is the Latin *sideris*—or "of the stars"—which reminds us that desire is a signal that comes from above—nudges from what I refer to (and define in chapter 4) as "Infinite Intelligence," toward a new direction or higher calling. But the positive nature of desire is widely misunderstood. Like me, many people grow up thinking that desires are selfish, something to be ashamed of. Certain religions are often perceived to teach that personal desire is inherently wrong or evil, or at best a source of temptation. In Buddhism, for example, the second of the Four Noble Truths is often misconstrued as, "Suffering is caused by desire." But the original word *tanha* has a much more nuanced meaning than the English word "desire." In the ancient Pali language, *tanha* referred to an intense yearning for the continuation of pleasure or the cessation of pain. It implies a kind of emotional demand that is much more compelling than a desire or preference. The word "craving" or "addiction"—a desire connected to an emotionally-backed demand—is a more precise translation.

The Buddha's teaching, therefore, was not that we should live a detached life, free of desires. On the contrary, wisdom means knowing what to care about and making skillful decisions to cultivate what we care about most. Without desire, progress toward anything—including the state of mental freedom called "enlightenment"—is impossible.

Before we go further, I want to clarify that the desires I refer to here are more about doing and producing than about having and consuming. Often, when I ask people what they desire, their answer involves acquiring a thing or an experience. Of course, there is nothing wrong with shopping or travel or other pleasure-oriented consumption. But for the sake of personal fulfillment, we need to focus on our desire to be and to do rather than to have. We grow ourselves and live fulfilling lives when we contribute something that aligns with who we are and our desire to be our authentic selves.

So how do we go about identifying our most authentic desires— the ones that can truly inspire and guide us on our journeys? It helps to remember that a deeply meaningful desire engages both the mind and the heart. If a desire engages only the head, it is invariably ego-driven. This is not categorically bad, just never deeply satisfying. On the other hand, purely emotional desires are out of balance in the opposite direction. We have to "feel it," but we also need to avoid letting emotion completely override common sense. Beware of granting strong emotion a decisive leadership role it isn't qualified to fill.

A synchronized, coordinated intersection between head and heart allows intuitive intelligence to operate in a context that makes sense. For example, if the desire to practice law is based on a talent for argumentation (a logical alignment), combined with a desire to defend victims of violence (a heart alignment), the chances of feeling deeply inspired to become a lawyer will be much higher. Can you think of one or two things you do, have done, or might do that represent an intersection between your heart and your head?

The heart is not just a locus of feelings. It can be thought of as the center of emotional intelligence, which is about your relationship to your feelings and your ability to respond to and manage them. The idea of the heart as the organ of both emotional and intuitive intelligence is not new. Ancient peoples believed that the heart was the true center of a human being, a spiritual center of the body. The Egyptians went to great lengths to preserve the heart with their highly developed embalming skills but threw away the brain. The Egyptians may have been limited in their understanding of biomechanics, but (like most indigenous cultures) they knew the heart is more than just a pump and considered it to be a spiritual center of the body. Since strong emotions obscure if not derail intuition, emotional intelligence is a foundational aspect of personal maturity for those cultivating intuitive intelligence (as we shall explore in chapter 6).

In traditional Ayurvedic medicine of India, the heart center is the location of one of the "chakras," or energy centers of the body. Appropriately, the heart center is the middle one of the seven chakras, the junction where love, courage, and wisdom meet. In French, the word for heart is *coeur*, the root of the word "courage" in English. It takes courage to love in the highest sense, where you actively care for the well-being of another whether it advantages you or not. It's a courage that propels us toward wisdom—beyond mere concern for self-interest or ego.

Striving to love someone unconditionally may feel like a big personal risk, but it will inspire you to learn and evolve, and expand your capacity for success and joy. To honor love is a way of cocreating a life with the help of Infinite Intelligence. Doing what you love or what you are good at (which will be something you probably enjoy) plays a critical role by supporting your fascinations and heartfelt desires. Inspiration and intuition acting in concert produce the deepest level of desire, which is the magnetic force behind the famous law of attraction, wherein the object of your attention is drawn to you. You still have to make good decisions, but the manifestation process starts with your fascination and focus.

Change Makes Success More Challenging

"No man ever steps in the same river twice," said the Greek philosopher Heraclitus. Change is constant, in other words. In fact, it is the only constant, because everything is always changing. Lately, on our increasingly crowded and chaotic planet, we've been seeing bigger changes more often and we are required to respond and adapt more quickly, which makes good decision-making more difficult. But resistance is futile. When we resist change, we just might ask ourselves: Do we really believe we can stop the river of life from flowing?

Opportunities arise, and along with them conflicting interests and tradeoffs. For instance, in my personal story, the option of building on a secure career came into conflict with an exciting vocational opportunity that didn't pay and, in fact, might never have given me a return on my investment other than the educational value of trying. I couldn't know.

Changes happen, often with an unpredictability that a controlling ego-self finds maddening. Anything is possible. You could be offered a higher-paying position, but in a field that you find less exciting. Or an employer might announce that keeping your job depends on relocating to a different city. You could be laid off from a job that you really like or offered a promotion to a position that you won't. Someone you love could announce that your relationship needs to change big-time, pronto.

Whatever the case, throughout our lives each of us has to deal with significant unexpected changes that demand a response and a decision. Under pressure, decision-making is downright stressful. We face turning points and dilemmas, and make strategic choices that substantially alter our lives, relationships, bank accounts, and futures. To achieve success and create meaning for ourselves, we need to be ready to pivot when major challenges and new opportunities arise.

How we make important decisions is more critical to our freedom, abundance, and joy than anything else we do. Well-made decisions lead to skillful actions executed at the right time, positioning us to take advantage of opportunities and creating new ones that align with our expanding sense of self. I developed the concept of "Visionary Decision Making" (VDM) to help others to better understand the long-term ramifications and the forward-thinking approach that strategic decisions require.

Making big decisions can be stressful, even debilitating. In their efforts to cope with the challenge of big decisions, people's responses can range between impulsiveness (getting it over with) to overanalytical procrastination (avoiding the stress of making a decision by putting it off until later). Past regrets, future fears, all-or-nothing thinking, focusing too much on the details, telling ourselves that we need to wait for more information—reactions like these stifle creative potential.

Fortunately, decision-making is a skill that we can learn to improve, even in a hectic, complex world where making the right moves at the right time has become increasingly challenging.

The Biggest Challenge to Success— Strategic Decision-Making

Jeff Bezos, founder of Amazon.com, gave a commencement talk at Princeton University a few years ago, in which he emphasized the central importance of decision-making: "I will hazard a prediction. When you are eighty years old, and in a quiet moment of reflection narrating for only yourself the most personal version of your life story, the telling that will be most compact and meaningful will be the series of choices you have made. In the end, we are our choices."[2]

It's a straightforward trajectory: Making good decisions now sets us up for even better ones in the future. Conversely, bad decisions only lead to more, in a downward spiral. When you make shortsighted choices, you jeopardize access to resources and find yourself increasingly constrained. Poor decision-making will ultimately hem you in until you feel trapped. If you make ill-considered choices long enough, you will lose your freedom—perhaps physically as well as psychologically. In contrast, if you consistently make choices skillfully, effective decision-making becomes ever easier and steadily supports learning and eventual success. To make better decisions more often and gain such an advantage, all you have to do is develop skills and practices that help you exercise your intuitive intelligence.

There are three levels of decision-making: mundane, tactical, and strategic. Most of the choices we make each day are mundane, or routine, and without much consequence. Tactical decisions have to do with choosing how we might implement a strategy. For instance, if we want a new direction in our relationships or careers (strategic), we will think of steps to take (tactical). It's the strategy-level decisions that can alter the theme of a person's life or business and determine potential. Because the most profound of these are rooted in our vision of who we are—as we shall examine more closely in the next chapter—I refer to them as "visionary" decisions. The primary focus of VDM are life's major turning points—those strategic choice-points that can influence and determine one's career, important relationships, personal growth, business dealings, or politics. Unlike our mundane or routine choices, major decisions of a personal, organizational, or societal nature require a deliberative process that is informed by logic but primarily driven by intuitive intelligence.

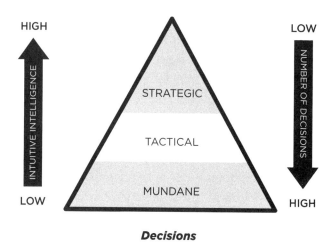

Decisions

These days we have instant access to virtually unlimited information and a rapidly evolving understanding of human psychology. With our amazing innate capacity to envision and intuit, plus the array of powerful resources at our disposal, one might assume that human beings are already excellent strategic decision-makers. After all, we are the only species we know of that is able to visualize possible outcomes from different possible choices. Unfortunately, most of us have lost the sensitivity we were born with and don't even know it, much less recognize the significance. Nevertheless, once we wake up to what we are missing, we can cultivate the ability to reconnect with our instincts, including that most subtle of all—intuition. Indeed, we must, if we want to make decisions that support our success and happiness.

A Modern Decision-Making Crisis

There is nothing more frightful than ignorance in action.

—J. W. von Goethe

The average person makes thousands of decisions, mostly mundane ones, every day. Driving a car, we choose to go this way or that. In the supermarket, we select a brand of toothpaste or, in a restaurant, appetizers from a menu. We decide which movie to watch or magazine to read. Most of these choices we make by habit or impulse. Unlike strategic choices, they are not stressful because not much is at stake.

Having too many choices, however, can tax us to such an extent that we lose the ability to see and think clearly. Alvin Toffler named the problem "overchoice" in his 1970 book *Future Shock*, written long before the rate of change had accelerated to anything near current levels. Toffler had the foresight to envision a world where too many choices, coupled with accelerated change, would cause life to become more stressful rather than liberating. Fifty years later, we are living in that world. The Chinese curse "May you live in interesting times" has come true . . . with a vengeance!

It's easy to make awful decisions: You might act prematurely or impulsively when under the influence of fear, anxiety, overeagerness, or fatigue. You might procrastinate, putting off the decision-making process to avoid stress but then making a hasty, ill-informed choice. You might overanalyze and miss your window of opportunity, or command someone else to take the risk and decide for you. You might decide that decision-making is just too much work or too fraught with hazard, so you let others do it for you, effectively remaining a child. Remember, being passive or delegating to avoid the stressful work of decision-making is a decision too—one that could boomerang with unintended and unwanted consequences.

Fear of failure adds extra stress to the equation. Suppose your choice turns out to be a mistake. Not only will you suffer the consequences, but you'll get the blame. If you leave the decision to someone else and things go wrong, you might be able blame them, but decisions made by others will never help you develop confidence in your intuitive intelligence.

A Problem of Too Much Information

Good decisions require intuitive insight for creative solutions, not just more information. But modern media deliver an overabundance of information. Our overworked imaginations fill in information gaps, and this fixation can drive us crazy. Theoretically, more data should augment understanding, increase options, and improve ability to make skillful choices. But, paradoxically, as Barry Schwartz points out in *The Paradox of Choice: Why More Is Less*, an abundance of choices greatly increases the challenge of making good ones. Besides, whether we have many or a few, choices are not always made from a clear list. Key decisions in important areas of life—such as relationships, career, and personal finance—are emotionally charged and defy logic.

These days our minds are bobbing in a vast sea of streaming information. Bombarded on all sides by conflicting messages through advertising, talk shows, reviews, magazines, newsletters, websites, email, text messages, and tweets, it is virtually impossible to logically sort through so much information in the hopes of finding something useful. Instead, excessive input causes cognitive overload and confusion, compromising our ability to think straight or be decisive.

So, how can we separate good information from bad? What information should we trust? Given today's accelerated rate of change, accessing the right information at the right time is a vital if more short-lived opportunity. And with so many conflicting messages, it's difficult to tell the reliable from the bogus. To make matters worse, information becomes obsolete more quickly, so even currently pertinent information has a shorter "shelf life." So an agile intuition is needed—if only to decide which information to trust, to sort the wheat from the massive preponderance of chaff out there.

Logic and intuition are both important, but, driven by intuitive intelligence, the VDM approach is more art than science. It's closer to painting or sculpting than figuring out a formula or reverse engineering. Some of our artful efforts are good, others less so. And like any work of art, strategic decision-making requires a certain amount of work—something many people would prefer to minimize or avoid altogether. Visionary decisions require a broader perspective based on higher levels of insight and wisdom, making the process both more rewarding and more challenging.

Another factor that can impact the quality of important decision-making is what the *New York Times* described as "decision fatigue"—the decline of attention span when people are called upon to make too many decisions in a limited amount of time. A new kind of stress occurs when the brain is not capable of sorting an overabundance of information. In addition, instantaneous communication technologies—cell phones, text messages, and email—add an exaggerated sense of urgency and the pressure to make decisions more quickly. Another person's expectation of rapid decision-making on our part can add to the pressure to execute a call to action without having done sufficient homework or due diligence.

Align with the Collective Good

Consideration of what is the greater good for the most people is an ethical standard for any wisely governed society. Improved decision-making needs to be a personal priority, but especially on a crowded planet, it is also critical for society at large. Our human tribe has incredible capacities for cooperation, communication, empathy, and love, but we are in desperate need of superior leadership, which relies above all on decision-making skill. It is becoming abundantly clear that the very survival of our planet depends on whether or not society's leaders will represent all the people and make long-term decisions for the collective good. And that those who don't will pay for their shortsightedness. We are all interconnected, and they will go down with the ship they have effectively sunk while trying to take advantage of others.

No matter what your position in society, the most important aspect of your job in this lifetime is to make critical decisions for yourself and those who depend on you for support or leadership. Who you support to represent you is one such decision too. Throughout history, societies have delegated the responsibility for sweeping decisions to sovereigns, presidents, experts, priests, and oracles. Decision-making is so important we richly compensate political leaders and CEOs for primarily doing that. Talented decision-makers command a high pay scale, and if they truly contribute to or protect the collective good, they may deserve it. A president's international diplomacy may affect the balance of world power; a CEO's strategic move may affect an entire market; a pension-fund manager who sells short might cause a ripple effect felt throughout the economy. Making these kinds of decisions—the crux of good government—deserves strong support, and sincere efforts by honest politicians should be expected, appreciated, and rewarded.

Big decisions have big consequences; such is the nature of global change and the connected world in which we live. Decisions made at a societal level are materially impacting life on this planet, some in ways that may be felt for centuries. Globalized problems like climate catastrophes and large disparities in wealth and resource distribution affect the lives of everyone. All of us—both the rich elite and common citizens—will be devastated together by out-of-control global problems. So, we all have a tremendous stake in how wisely our leaders deliberate the critical choices we face. Unfortunately, with all the propaganda and false advertising that goes into elections, there is no guarantee that our business leaders, elected politicians, or representatives will be visionary decision-makers. Or that they will represent our interests at all.

With the growing complexity of today's global problems—as populations grow and consume finite resources—we need enlightened decision-making more than we ever have in the history of humanity. The materialism of nineteenth- and twentieth-century capitalism was based on an illusion of unlimited frontiers and resources, but we urgently need to upgrade that belief system. To align with our own good, each of us needs to consider the common good in all our decision-making. All truly good decisions are good for us . . . and for everybody else as well. This belief is the essence of the "win-win" approach, as opposed to a "win-lose" approach where winning depends upon others losing out. As long as your decision-making does not get you what you want by exploiting others, it passes the litmus test.

President George W. Bush famously declared himself "the Decider." As executive director of our government, his humorous description was correct. His number-one responsibility was to make decisions for the millions of citizens of the country, affecting billions of lives around the planet. Likewise, every one of us is the "decider" in our personal realm. As an adult, your consciousness is the CEO of your life, whether or not you like having the responsibility for the outcomes you create through the choices you make.

Complexity Also Produces Opportunities

Life is more complicated and stressful than ever, but there is a bright side to the tidal wave of information that renders decision-making so much more challenging. This age is characterized by massive change that may cause stress but also provides new opportunities and openings for creativity and innovation.

Complexity can work to your advantage if you develop the intuition to identify underlying patterns and connect the dots. This is the key talent of product visionaries like Steve Jobs. For my part, I entered the complex and rapidly changing field of software at the right time and was intuitive enough to envision future possibilities of multimedia and the internet to become a successful entrepreneur in those realms.

Strategic decision-making always involves taking a chance on a major change or transformation. It is always something of a gamble, but that's just the nature of the beast. Every decision contains the risk of unintended consequences. Sometimes we can roughly calculate the odds of a desired outcome; often this is too difficult. As Eileen Shapiro, author of *Make Your Own Luck*, writes, "Humans are gambling animals. We all gamble, all the time. Every time we act, we invest time, or reputation, or effort, or money with no guarantee that the results that we seek, no matter how likely they may seem, will occur as we have planned—or as we will desire when the results occur."[3]

One could say that developing better intuition will improve your risk-taking odds across the board. While I can't guarantee specific results from adopting the philosophy and practicing the skills presented in this book, I can promise that your odds of succeeding at what you set out to do will increase dramatically. Will you lose some bets? Of course. Will there be setbacks? Of course, but even mistakes become less costly as decision-making becomes more conscious and actions well-timed.

The Visionary Decision Making Process

Good decisions require a responsible attitude; a specific, well-honed skillset; and coordination between logic and intuition. Making strategic decisions skillfully is the secret to success in every area of life. It's an art, and it requires more than logical analysis of pros and cons, combined with courage and positive thinking (although those are necessary ingredients). Farsighted decision-making also depends upon intuition, imagination, timing, receptivity, attitude, and commitment. Your perspective, belief system, and attitude will determine the quality of your decisions and, ultimately, the extent to which you fulfill your destiny. I call this level "Visionary Decision Making" because it is as strategic as a personal decision can get. Because it is based on self-knowledge, strong natural desires, and your unique vision for yourself, it is a way to consciously resolve major choice-points and dilemmas that come your way, and to make bold decisions that align with who you really are.

The VDM process uses the interplay of intuition and logic, imagination and introspection. To help you creatively make the changes that will manifest your highest ideals, VDM taps underused sources of information that have always been—and will always be—available to you.

It's tempting to believe that to get what you want, all you have to is form a mental picture of it in your head. Indeed, some bestselling books and DVDs on the "secrets" of material success offer some such simplistic formula, but manifestation is not as easy as strongly desiring something and obsessing on your fantasies about it. Although intuition is still not fully understood, and the results of VDM may seem somewhat miraculous, the skillful use of intuition is not magic. It is an extension of our own experience and instincts. We may not fully understand or be able to prove how intuition works, but like electricity we can still harness it and put it to good use.

VDM is based on a vision, but it goes beyond visualization, attraction, affirmations, and obsessing about what you want. It includes coming to a decision and committing to an action, making your best next move, and pulling it off at the right time. This is the only reliable path to achieving success in any area of life. By taking the trouble to awaken and engage that hard-to-get intuitive sense, you greatly improve the odds of achieving a positive outcome, regardless of what you focus on.

Being decisive is a hallmark of maturity, adulthood. The ability to make a decision is a skill itself, and making big decisions requires courage. Your decisions will define your character, allowing you to build trust and confidence, to establish a path toward accomplishing your goals.

In other words, Visionary Decision Making is the pathway to success and happiness.

2

Self-Discovery—Answering the "Who Am I?" Question

As far as we can discern, the sole purpose of human existence is to kindle a light in the darkness of mere being.

—**Carl Jung**

Respond to every call that excites your spirit.

—**Rumi**

You are born to certain parents at a certain time in a certain society. This sets the stage for the challenges and opportunities of a lifetime, and it means facing a set of circumstances: parents; siblings (or lack of); gender; nationality; race; socioeconomic class; certain talents, tendencies, and predispositions; and a body that looks and acts a certain way, among many other factors. Even so, your destiny is never predetermined. The unfolding of destiny results from the intersection between the hand you were dealt and the way you play your cards. The situation you were born into, no matter how unfortunate or limited it may have been, is not your fault, and you have freedom of choice in how you play the cards you were dealt. How skillfully you do this defines your character and makes all the difference. Your success and happiness depend on exercising your power to make wise decisions.

Through our choices and noble efforts, we can make the most of what we're given and surpass expectations.

The guiding light for skillful decision-making is self-knowledge. Making great decisions starts with learning who you are—a process of self-discovery that can and should last a lifetime. No matter your age, self-knowledge benefits from a process of introspection. Look closely at your personal history—including major lessons you've learned, the nature of your strongest interests, your unique mix of talents, and your set of values. Knowing these things will help you become clear about your life-purpose and your calling—what you are meant to do and contribute in this lifetime. Such clarity is not always easy, of course, due to a multitude of tasks and distractions and because our priorities shift as we grow, learn, and evolve.

Now, we should note the difference between a calling and a career. Most of us have both; sometimes they intersect, more often they do not. To me, your calling is the expression of the unique gifts you bring to the world. Your career is how you pay the rent and provide for life's necessities. Visionary Decision Making can apply to both.

In some cases (like my own), calling and career intersect, and a calling is expressed through the vehicle of an occupation or career. It's wonderful to make a living doing something you love, but don't feel bad if your career path is different than your calling. This is normal. As much as you might like to, if you haven't found a way to make a living expressing your soul, just remember that many aspects of running a business are not creative or fun. Your poetry or your art or your volunteer work are just as important and may well benefit future generations. While working at the patent office, Einstein did some of the most creative work of his life, producing no fewer than four groundbreaking articles in 1905 alone. The monumental poet T. S. Eliot was a banker for four decades. Phillip Glass created avant-garde operas and musical "happenings" while he worked as a cab driver and plumber.

As long as your job doesn't cause harm to anyone or the world—and if it contributes to the upkeep of yourself and possibly others as well—

it qualifies as what the Buddhists called "right livelihood." According to the ancient Buddhist definition, harmlessness was the only real criteria. The average person was not expected to express a sublimely creative life-purpose through work. Other than appreciating work for providing us with goods or services, your career does not have to be that part of the self that channels creative power and most inspires or enlivens your soul. Your creative life-purpose is your calling, pointing to the destiny that you are evolving toward. Becoming more conscious and coming to terms with this vision—including the challenge of it—is the ultimate victory of self-knowledge. Your life-purpose—what you are here to do—isn't what comes easiest. Its fulfillment will be a crowning achievement of the inner hero part of the self. The fire-breathing dragons in your unconscious need to be slain (or at the very least reconciled) along the way.

The Three Stages of Life

Life can be divided into three stages, and each offers certain decisions and a need to revamp priorities as we change and grow. Staying aware of your current priorities is always a vital piece of self-knowledge , which is important to review as you move through life, growing, learning, and evolving.

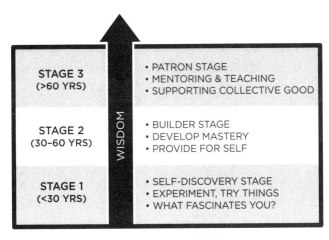

VDM Stages of Life

Stage One: Self-Discovery

Self-discovery continues throughout a life, but it is the primary and central function of an effective Stage One, which focuses on learning who you are, what you are good at, and what you love to do. Stage One learning is best accomplished by experimenting through trial and error, trying any number of different things. (Studies show that developing a range of interests may boost grades and predict future successes.) I'm defining Stage One as the first 29.5 years of life—the same amount of time as one orbit of the planet Saturn around the sun.

I call Stage One the student stage, because it is all about learning—learning who you are. Curiosity and a passion for learning come naturally (except in some children damaged by neglect or abuse, though nurturing can help cultivate it again). I myself was so eager to learn that one bright morning when I was four years old, I hopped onto the school bus with my five-year-old neighbor friend who was going off to kindergarten. (This was in a safer day and age, when children could walk to the school bus on their own.) When my mother discovered that I wasn't in the back-yard playing as usual, and was nowhere to be found, she reported me missing. The police went looking and they eventually located me—much to everyone's surprise—sitting on the classroom floor with the rest of the children in a kindergarten class, having a wide-eyed, interested time. So eager to be a part of the shared learning experience, I blended right in and the teacher hadn't noticed that I wasn't a member of the class!

The Saturn Cycle. In classical astrology, Saturn is the planet of structure and limits. It's the archetype for coming to terms with reality and being accountable for decisions you have made and the resulting karma. When Saturn completes its orbit and comes back to the position in the sky it held the moment you were born, after moving through all twelve signs, this is referred to as the "Saturn return." The first Saturn return, around age 29.5, is often accompanied by major changes and difficult growth, marking the transition from youth into adulthood. Saturn returns approximately every 29.5 years. In astrology, these returns mark beginnings and endings of major movement in life, so I have used them to demarcate three stages of life.

Although Stage One starts at birth, we generally are not empowered to make strategic decisions before age eighteen or so. From that point, in my view, the consistently most important decision that young adults (between eighteen and twenty-nine) need to make is what to try and learn about next. It is only natural to want to explore compelling interests, passions, and fascinations, and that is exactly what you should do in your twenties. As Jonathan Fields, founder of the Good Life Project, so aptly put it, "[The twenties are] best used to run a series of experiments designed to let you figure out the sweet spot between what lights you up, what you're good at and what the world will pay you for."[1] As long as your curiosity-driven pursuits cause no harm to yourself or others, Stage One is meant for honoring your inquisitive nature and giving yourself permission to explore and experiment.

Satisfying curiosity ought to be fun, but elders often cut it short by putting pressure on young adults to specialize and make premature commitments. College students generally feel excessive pressure to make long-term decisions, like committing to a career before they know who they are. It's not uncommon for students to believe there is something wrong with them if they can't confidently choose a major, let alone definitively pick a career. Some are further dispirited by comparisons between themselves and highly touted young media prodigies in entertainment, sports, or business. Without permission to try whatever they want, young people easily become self-critical and second-guess themselves, and their natural curiosity dampens as a result of tremendous (and misguided) social pressures.

It is an exceptional phenomenon when a gifted child gets started very young on what will become his or her career (Mozart, for instance). But even in modern societies where children have access to education, this is extremely rare. There are not many like the world-class violinist Itzhak Perlman, who smashed the toy violin he was given as a young boy because he felt he needed to play a real one (eventually, a Stradivarius, of course). Most of us are not such prodigies that we get in touch with a deep level of fascination so early in life—and if kids did anything like that these days, they'd probably be forced to take medications for acting out!

Child psychologists are starting to work with a wider age range, going up to twenty-five rather than stopping at eighteen. Considering that the neocortex doesn't stop physically growing until around age twenty-six, doesn't it make sense that young adults should be free to explore their natural interests without having to make long-term commitments? As long as it's not harmful, having permission to follow what motivates us allows character to develop in harmony with our natural interests. Being weighed down by the pressure to make huge decisions you are not psychologically or emotionally prepared for makes self-discovery difficult, if not impossible. Like when a nineteen-year-old takes on a huge amount of debt for the sake of getting an advanced degree and enters a profession that may turn out to be unsuited to their temperament. The crushing burden of servicing extreme indebtedness makes it much harder to find time and energy to discover new things, experiment with new interests, or have a healthy work-leisure balance. Such a financial burden impacts one's ability to relax, develop intuitive intelligence, and make good decisions. High levels of debt promise to negatively impact one's life for decades.

Even if we have been denied chances at home to be adventurous as children, we will have ample opportunities to make meaningful self-discoveries from age eighteen to thirty, when we have the freedom to make our own decisions. Experimenting is the order of the day in Stage One (although self-discovery can continue throughout our lives, especially when we are faced with changing circumstances and new opportunities).

Stage Two: Building and Providing

Stage Two, which begins around age thirty, is about "doing." It involves making a commitment to developing skills to express whatever fascination you are passionate about or have an aptitude for. This is when you develop and master the skills that will make you able to provide for yourself and others. In the process, you are building a life—a career or family (or both)—and gaining resources. Your priorities reorder away from exploration and discovery in favor of creating a stable platform for yourself and your family group or tribe. You accomplish things. You gain mastery at your craft or calling by being of service in your best way. You find personal fulfillment and joy in contributing energy and expertise toward building something for yourself and those you are connected to.

Productivity is a natural human desire and at the center of Stage Two. Only in modern—and some would say decadent—times have so many people come to self-identify first as consumers, rather than producers (an attitude severely exacerbated by the immature and careless attitude toward debt that is fostered at every level of our society). From the VDM point of view, consumerism is a psychological malaise that demotivates people from achieving goals that are worthy of them, accomplishing meaningful things, and making a difference in the world.

Stage Three: Giving Back

Stage Three, the sponsor or patron stage, starts around age fifty-nine (sometimes later in this age of extended active lifespans). It is characterized by a shift from "doing" to "being" and the natural inclination to give back by sharing your hard-earned wisdom to help others and future generations. This could take the form of writing a book, starting a business, volunteering, or passing on wisdom or skills as a teacher or mentor. In this stage, a builder-provider orientation evolves into a higher form of awareness through meditation and contemplation. A spiritual dimension of self comes to fruition that fosters calmness and groundedness—supportive values desperately needed in chaotic times. This awareness of life's spiritual dimension gives rise to compassion and generosity for the sake of the collective good and future. Serving as a wise elder, one might be drawn to mentoring receptive young people to help them clarify Stage One and Stage Two choices, and to reassure them that they are on their unique path. The generous exercise of providing guidance and support to those who would receive it can give you great joy in Stage Three.

Stage Three began for me after I sold my business. I set up a small educational nonprofit to give myself a new identity, built around my desire to give back. I called it the Divination Foundation, because I am an I Ching author who made his mark inventing divination software. Having since extended our research scope, we now sometimes refer to it as IntuitiveIntelligence.org. The ways I found to give back in Stage Three align with my personal aptitudes as a writer, teacher, speaker, and mentor. Yours can be anything. You might volunteer, campaign for a cause, write letters to the editor. You might put energy into art or a craft that allows you to express and share your spirit. Whatever it is, it becomes your priority as over time you devote more time and energy.

Calibrate Visionary Decision Making to your current stage of life. For instance, consider putting off making lifelong commitments in Stage One, until you know yourself. Although Stage One decisions can be strategically important, it is generally advisable to save long-term commitments for Stage Two, when you know and are ready to focus on what fascinates you. Give yourself time to be sufficiently engaged and inspired before trying to build a productive career, family, or intimate partnership. By its end, your Stage Two experience of doing will have given you a wealth of knowledge and resources, allowing you to graduate and start slowing down intentionally, in order to support the wisdom of being truly present, and generously loving of others, in Stage Three.

Stage One Fascinations Highlight Self-Discovery

The fascinations discovered in Stage One are especially important keys to self-knowledge. Beyond appealing to your curiosity, a fascination is a phenomenon that attracts and delights you. It is part of human nature. Babies are fascinated by all kinds of things because everything is utterly new. By the time you are a young adult, fewer things fascinate you, and the ones that inspire you most will be an outgrowth of your temperament and aptitudes. In the long run, your strongest interests have the potential to enchant you and lead you down a path toward fulfillment of your personal destiny. As the great mythologist Joseph Campbell wrote, "If you follow your bliss, you put yourself on a kind of track that has been there all the while, waiting for you, and the life that you ought to be living is the one you are living."[2]

The two fascinations that were the strongest for me both occurred when I was in college. As a teenager in the San Francisco Bay area, I came of age during a crazy, tumultuous time. Anti–Vietnam War protests caused riots at the University of California where the student body and teachers were on strike for nine consecutive quarters. A cultural revolution, called the "counterculture," was in full swing. Feeling flush with personal freedom for the first time in my own life, anything and everything seemed possible in a rapidly changing world.

One day on campus, I perked up in a conversation with an attractive girl who showed me a large book called the *Book of Changes* (*I Ching* or *Yijing* in Chinese), a modern translation of an ancient tome that she claimed could provide insights and timely advice about any dilemma or problem. I tried not to let my skepticism show. The company of this pleasant girl appealed to me, even if it involved playing some silly (or so I thought) fortune-telling game. When she asked me to write down a request for advice, I played along by scribbling a few words that didn't hold any real significance for me. While I was intrigued by the idea of an ancient book that was oracular, at the time I was just trying to humor her. She asked me to focus on my question (which I could not) and had me toss three Chinese coins six times. After she decoded my coin tosses into a six-line pattern, we looked up the pattern—aptly called a "hexagram."

Ironically, my first I Ching reading returned Hexagram 4, "Youthful Folly." This archetype refers to the lack of respect an immature student has for the teacher. This reading seemed to be a calling out of my flippant query, and it threw me. At the age of nineteen, I knew nothing of divination systems or Jungian psychology. I was expecting some kind of Magic Eight Ball that I could have a good laugh about. Instead, the I Ching dismissed my frivolous query and reflected my shallowness back to me with some sound advice about the need to straighten up. "Youthful Folly" was actually a pretty accurate description of my life at that time: cutting classes, smoking pot, chasing girls. The I Ching caught my attention by mirroring my attitude and energy. Now, more intrigued than ever, I asked my companion if I could try casting another reading.

Once again, I scribbled something that didn't have real import for me, but my intention was a bit more serious this time. I was testing the oracle, rather than just toying with it. Once again, the I Ching ignored my disingenuous query and came back with the text, "Questioning the sincerity of the seeker." Hmmm. When I had made fun of it, it made fun of me. Now, when I tested it, it tested me back! I intuitively began to understand that the meaning and value of an I Ching reading is not necessarily derived from predictions or specific answers, which I had assumed would be the case (as in fortune-telling), but from reading between the lines for greater insight. Thus began my fascination with—and reverence for—a powerful intuitive decision-making aid.

A few years later, I was awed by another fascination: the cutting-edge technology of computer software. In those days, few people even knew what software was. Apple didn't exist, and the first personal computer kits were a few years away. Programming courses at the university relied on feeding punch cards into huge computers. Web pages and public email would not arrive for another twenty-five years or so.

My good friend Jack was the principal programmer for a small non-profit computer center attached to the University of Oregon in Eugene.

He was in charge of the center's "minicomputer," a machine with gigantic magnetic tape drives and one tiny terminal. Despite its immense size, it was called "mini" because it merely filled a room, whereas IBM mainframes in those days took up entire floors. Minicomputers were the cutting-edge technology at the time, even though for $150,000 (in 1975 dollars), they had less computing power than an iPhone does today!

Jack and I would go to the computer center late at night to play *SpaceWar*, an early computer game developed for minicomputers by programmers at MIT. Playing one of the first computer games on a huge computer was my introduction to the phenomenon of software.

The interactivity of the experience fascinated me. I saw programming as a new form of creative artistry with potential to support educational and personal development, which were already strong interests of mine. I envisioned computers delivering sophisticated entertainment and educational content fifteen years before the first graphics-based computer (the Macintosh), and twenty years before CD-ROMs. I immediately felt a powerful desire to enter this nascent industry.

I had dropped out of college rather than go into debt, so I didn't have educational credentials. However, with Jack's help, I was able to get hired as office secretary at his computer center because of my typing speed. (The first primitive word-processing terminals were still many years off.) Taking a low-paying secretarial job in order to gain real-world experience in one of my fascinations turned out to be a visionary decision and proved to be a pivotal step toward my calling. For the second time in my life, I had stumbled upon a fascination that would become a personal game-changer.

As I took a serious interest in the intersection between the two technologies that fascinated me—one ancient, one new—I became aware of a significant historical connection between them. Gottfried Leibniz, who "discovered" binary mathematics in 1666, found confirmation for his theories in the I Ching. Leibniz was impressed by its representation of the universe, as combinations of dualistic polarities—yin and yang—that could flip from one state to the other. Heartened by his insight that the I Ching is based on a binary system, Leibniz refined his mathematical model: he transposed the Arabic ten-digit numeral system—one that Europe had not fully adopted until the tenth century—into a binary system of ones and zeros. Although there was little practical use for it at the time, modern information theory and the basis for how computers and software work were derived from Leibniz's formulations.

While still in Stage One, after I had spent fifteen years developing direct-marketing skills in the software industry, I had a vision of an intersection between my two primary fascinations—the I Ching and multimedia software—which led to the first I Ching software and, in effect, the invention of the divination software category. Even though making a business out of it did not seem to be a shrewd move, my impulse to go for it anyway and become an entrepreneur was supported by the I Ching, my intuition, and my enthusiasm for both of my strongest fascinations coming together. So, I took a leap of faith and went for it. I made the visionary decision to honor my passions and see where it might lead. I decided to surrender to my heart and its natural interests, despite all inherent risks. This was going against the advice of everyone I knew, but I honored my natural fascinations and took Joseph Campbell's advice to follow my bliss.

Self-Knowledge and Risk Tolerance

How you play your cards in life is related to how you strike a balance between freedom and security. You've got to have both, but knowing where you are on the spectrum is helpful for conscious risk-taking. My basic sense of security derived from a confidence that I was intelligent and resourceful and felt sure that I could always find a more conventional job in the growing software industry if I needed to. My freedom to take career and financial risks was emboldened by my enthusiasm to learn everything I could about the two things that fascinated me most.

When I founded an I Ching software company in 1988, I was the single father of a son, but I was able to tolerate a higher level of insecurity than the average single parent. My risk tolerance supported pursuing my dream of creative freedom—the idea that I could get our needs met and be creative at the same time. I was learning through experience that a scrappy resourcefulness that includes the ability to learn skills is the one sort of security that nobody can ever take from you.

Of course, human beings want both security and freedom, and everyone has to deal with tension between these conflicting needs. Since beginning Stage Three, for instance, I feel less desire to compete for rewards or status. My desire for freedom of thought and self-expression is as strong as ever, but my focus is more on cultivating wisdom, compassion, and loving relationships. These days I am inspired to do what I can to help humanity make paradigm shifts that produce a positive, healing difference in the world.

Where would you peg yourself on the security-freedom spectrum? No matter what level of risk you are ready to take—whether your path is to be an entrepreneur or an artist, or work within a corporation or nonprofit organization—in the final analysis you are always working for yourself. Even as a corporate employee, you have the freedom to quit or negotiate with your employer for better opportunities and more pay. In a free market–based society, all legal employment is based on consent. You are essentially working for yourself even if you are "renting" yourself out. It is your right to choose which livelihood path to take in your life. Accept this reality—and responsibility—right now. Living in a free society means that you are the executive decision-maker (CEO or whatever executive archetype you prefer) of your own life. This means that you are the decision-maker for yourself and others who may rely on you. You have influence in your sphere no matter how large or how small. You have personal power. If you think of yourself as a victim of circumstances, you are giving that power away.

So, make maintaining the awareness of your decision-making responsibility a top priority—that is, what you want to do the *most*, so you can make a commitment to mastering that. For VDM, self-discovery is coming to know what you love and getting clear about what you would like to do, to make the passage from Stage One (self-discovery) to Stage Two (contributing and accomplishing, building and providing). Your higher value desires are what carry the most meaning for you, which is the essence of personal wisdom and key to Visionary Decision Making.

Your Hierarchy of Values

It's easy to be confused about your real values when you focus on who you would like to be—or think you *should* be—rather than discovering who you naturally are. What we often come to expect from ourselves is adopted from socially defined and agreed-upon success and happiness metrics. Let go of the "shoulds"—that entire shadowy psychic realm of uninformed beliefs, societal expectations, and other people's unlived dreams projected onto you. Tag it as a black cloud of unknowing that is just passing through. It's not who you are and it's not yours, even if it is something you may have become accustomed to. It's a big mistake to blindly identify with inherited or adopted beliefs about what *should* be important. How can you know what is truly important for you?

One practical, and logically quantifiable, way to measure your real values is to analyze and quantify how you spend your time, energy, and money. John Demartini developed an approach that I have found helpful. The Demartini Value Determination Process[3] is a method to increase and maintain awareness of your "hierarchy of values"—the activities you value and how you prioritize your interests and desires.

Demartini uses the word "values" in a specific, practical, and relatively measurable way. In his system, values are not prioritized by how they theoretically align with your ideals, moral codes, or entrenched beliefs. Rather, you identify your real values by analyzing how much time, energy, money, and thought you actually invest in them. As Dr. Demartini points out, the answers to thirteen questions will reveal a few common threads.[4] Those are your real values.

1. How do you fill your space?
2. How do you spend your time?
3. How do you spend your energy?
4. How do you spend your money?
5. Where are you most organized?
6. Where are you most reliable?
7. What dominates your thoughts?
8. What do you visualize most?
9. What do you most often talk to yourself about?
10. What do you most often talk to others about?
11. What inspires you?
12. What goals stand out in your life and have stood the test of time?
13. What do you love to learn or read about most?

Keep your list of your life's real values on your computer or smartphone, or keep a small printed copy in your wallet or purse. Glance at it sometimes, to remind yourself of your top values and avoid getting sidetracked by competing temptations. Edit and refine your list as you evolve and become more and more clear about your personal, unique hierarchy of values.

Using Demartini's method is not complicated, but emotional factors and conflicts of interest can make it challenging to get priorities clear. For instance, you might spend more of your time working at your job than anything else. This would reveal being productive as one of your highest values. Even if you don't like your job, you obviously value being employed—enough to show up! The job provides something (a paycheck) you need and value highly as a means to an end. Taking care of your needs—and maybe others close to you—by making a steady living is a top priority for most adults.

Things can get complicated when major life passages reshuffle your top priorities. For example, a woman who has invested years of her time and energy being a great mother is likely to experience massive internal changes when her youngest child leaves home. She may start to think less about mothering and more about plans to take classes, start a business, play music, or return to painting.

The children who move out of the family home will also think and act differently. Instead of continuing to be dependent on their parents and preoccupied with the carefree fun of childhood, they will begin experimenting and developing skills they need to take care of themselves and make their own way in the world. If and when they have their own children, providing for them will become their high-priority value. Priorities, like fascinations, change as we proceed through the stages of life.

We Attract What We Focus On

Although the law of attraction concept has been around for over a hundred years, it has been reintroduced to the world in recent years though bestselling books and DVDs such as *The Secret*. The power of focus is as relevant as ever to modern decision-making and manifestation.

The law of attraction is based on the idea that what you expect is what you get. The mind exerts a magnetic attraction on whatever it focuses on, even subconsciously. Once a person gets fixated on something—whether it's a worry or a joy—the subconscious will do everything it can to find evidence to prove that idea or perspective is right, no matter how off base it may all be. I'm sure you've had an experience of vividly noticing something you don't like (my boss is so picky, my housemate is so messy, etc.), and then for days after you see what appears to be all kinds of evidence that your point of view was correct. For instance, you may start noticing every time your partner leaves a drinking glass lying around, but because you are focused on that and the law of attraction shows you what you are looking for, you completely overlook the fact that he picked up your dry cleaning or washed your car.

Like it or not, our thinking minds are like magnets. They are always attracting more of whatever they are thinking about. We strongly tend to see what we expect to see, and we also attract and receive what we expect to get, consciously or subconsciously. We attract what we want by focusing on it, and we attract what we don't want the same way. Even when you concentrate on things you don't want, the act of giving mind energy to negative outcomes draws them to you.

The game of golf elegantly illustrates this dynamic. Although swinging a golf club is an athletic skill, the game has a significant mental component. To make a good swing in golf, you need to be relaxed and focused at the same time, and either or both of these states can be impacted by the considerable time between shots, which gives the mind time to ruminate. Your thoughts and attitude and comfort level will have a major impact on your next swing and its outcome. To help achieve that synchronicity, so that you're relaxed and focused ("in the zone"), one of the first lessons taught in the inner game of golf is to focus exclusively on the target, and not pay any attention to any hazards (a sand trap or a pond, for instance). The best shots are inspired by a clear vision of where you want the ball to go—not where you don't want it to go or are afraid it *might* go. Focusing on avoiding hazards is the worst thing you can do in golf—and in life. Any golfer can tell you that dwelling on the ponds and sand traps will invariably skew a shot to fly right into them. In golf—as in life—what you focus on is what you attract and that's what you ultimately get.

Being aware of what you don't want can be helpful, but unless there is a real and present danger, it's always more skillful to focus instead on what you *do* want. Where we put our attention is an immediate and important decision that we make from moment to moment. How you formulate goals affects your ability to stay focused on them. Aside from writing them down, sharing them with a wise friend can help you achieve mental clarity and reduce tendencies toward fearful or negative thinking. You'll find that helpers and clarifying tools are everywhere when you follow your bliss.

The Creative Manifestation Treatment

I developed this special focusing technique, which I have now taught for thirty years, as a self-guided meditation to support clarity and amplify the law of attraction around what you seriously desire. (See a generic, customizable example of the full Creative Manifestation Treatment in appendix A, which you can adapt and read to yourself.)

The meditation's first two steps help you call forth the Creative Power archetype and get in alignment with your internal resources (as we shall further explore in chapter 7, "Invoking Archetypes"). In the third step, your "Declaration," you clarify and articulate your vision. Step 4 proactively calls up a feeling of gratitude, followed by step 5, which helps you release the tendency to try to control the form that your good will take. Provided you have articulated a clear declaration, step 6 is the most powerful of all. I call it "Emotional Magnetization," because this is where you begin to feel your vision as if it is already manifest and know that by doing so you are drawing the object of your desire toward you. Finally, the treatment segues into decision-making and action-taking steps. Customizing this guided meditation script for yourself and reading it every morning will take you beyond the law of attraction and help strengthen your focus and intention.

You Can't Have It All, Baby

There is an old saying, "You can have anything you want, but not everything you want." Choosing where to focus your time and energy is critical to achieving real success. The word "decide" comes from the Latin *cedere*, which means "to cut off." Stay aware of your hierarchy of values, so the most important activities get the attention they deserve in the face of so many competing distractions. Find your calling by following your interests and values, not by combing the classifieds to find a franchising opportunity or coming up with a business plan designed to make lots of money. Devotion to inspiration and the flow of creative power will help you discover your true livelihood, your path, and your personal destiny.

Once you are clear about what you want, making progress will depend on clear goals, making and keeping commitments, and making the right moves at the right time. This involves letting go of "lesser affections" that would compete for attention and distract you—things you may enjoy, but which are not skillful investments of time, energy, or resources. The sacrificing of lesser pleasures is essential to making progress toward a strategic vision around a "higher affection"—a heart-centered desire that reflects your deepest values. Knowing who you are and attending to your top priorities is central to making visionary decisions and creatively manifesting the results you want in any area of life.

3

Synchronicity—The Psychology of Perfect Timing

Synchronicity is the confirmation that all things are interconnected.

—**Meredith Miller**

I am open to the guidance of synchronicity, and do not let expectations hinder my path.

—**His Holiness, the Dalai Lama**

Western science has made a lot of progress investigating causal relationships in three-dimensional space. In high school science class, we learned the second law of thermodynamics: for every action there will be an equal and opposite reaction. The phenomenon is easily observed with billiard balls, or anywhere material things collide or bounce off each other. We instinctively understand that things are interconnected in the realm of matter, because we can generally perceive it. We're not quite so sure how things connect in the fourth dimension of time, however. But we sense that timing is important.

In fact, "timing is everything," the old saying goes. We consider ourselves lucky when events unfold the way we want, or when we are in the right place at the right time. Good timing seems so special that we marvel at it and attribute an almost magical power to those we see benefitting from it with any consistency. The experience of getting the timing just right is almost ecstatic, but it is also deeply meaningful.

If things are also connected in time, how does timing work? We can feel it, but the answer to this question cannot be explained by physical laws of causality like the second law of thermodynamics. Therefore, our sense of timing depends almost entirely upon intuition.

The idea that significant things happen randomly has always been difficult for humans to accept. We crave some explanation of why, when, and how things happen, even though we usually aren't able to understand the reasons until sometime after the fact, if ever. Meaning is hugely important to us, because human beings thrive on understanding not only *how* things happen, but *why*. We are wired that way. The human mind has an innate drive to find meaning and purpose. Our evolution toward happiness depends upon motivation and the will to thrive, based on the perception that a meaningful life remains worth the effort. We owe the search for meaning to ourselves.

In the West, ancient Greco-Roman cosmologies included many deities. In particular, the goddesses of Destiny (Roman) or the Fates (Greek) were believed to have powerful influence over the lives of mortals. It was considered divine intervention when good things happened; it meant you were favored by the gods. Compared to imagining a totally chaotic universe, these kinds of beliefs provided a sense of order and reassurance. Today, our traditional approach to the sacred—historically associated with deities and temples of worship, rituals, and holy days— has lost its meaning for us and has been misdirected into more secular forms of adoration such as the passionate pursuit of status, power, or romance. (Robert Johnson offers an interesting angle on this in his book *We: Understanding the Psychology of Romantic Love.* He makes the point that love of the divine has been replaced by a modern obsession with romantic love—placing unwieldy demands on intimate partnerships in the process.)

Rather than ascribing events to any sort of divine intervention, strictly rational types go to the opposite extreme. To the extent that they believe in a random universe ruled by chance, they assume an even weaker position relative to change. Being a helpless pawn in the cosmic casino is not a particularly empowering or reassuring point of view.

The religious traditions of the East, including Hinduism and Buddhism, take a spiritual but nontheistic approach to the question of why things happen. One of their principle tenets is the impersonal *Law of Karma*. Essentially, "What goes around comes around," or as the same idea is put in the Christian context, "As you sow, so shall you reap." From a karmic point of view, your intentions, attitude, and actions influence how the universe will respond to you and the returns you will get. According to such concepts of cosmic justice, we each ultimately get what we deserve, good and bad. The Greek Fates operated in a somewhat similar manner.

Our sense of meaning atrophies when the culture's belief systems become obsolete or start to break down because they make little sense anymore. Without a stable operating system of beliefs that continues to make sense and work well, people lack an important psychological support structure, and they struggle more to discern whether a certain course of action is in their best interests or not. This can lead to despair and impulsive decision-making. In social and political spheres, it lends itself to the rise of tyranny by dominant thought police, who represent the ruling class and forcefully appoint themselves to tell everyone else what things mean—in terms that are to their advantage and to others' detriment.

When we blindly believe what we are taught, we are limited because we do not gain the benefit of new discoveries. If we don't test and upgrade our beliefs (see chapter 11 for how to do this), we sacrifice the personal power we need to create a believable sense of meaning for ourselves, which will make it easier to accept and skillfully deal with major changes, no matter how challenging or disruptive they may be. When we find and embrace meaning in our lives, we feel a healthy sense of personal power.

The Visionary Decision Making paradigm is a boon for personal freedom. When we are equipped with self-knowledge, and are in tune with who we really are, we are much more than victims of fate or the pawns of other people's choices. We are free to cocreate our own destinies, even though this requires faith in ourselves, and committed personal effort.

The Synchronicity Principle

Even the most cynical people enjoy getting what they want, but it is the rare person who masters the art of consistently manifesting good fortune. With the right understanding and skills, you can learn how to significantly improve your odds by developing and using a better sense of timing. In this chapter, we explore Carl Jung's sophisticated psychology on timing, on how to be in sync with change. This was one of his greatest discoveries, one that provides a breakthrough for understanding the phenomenon of perfect timing, one that helps us to make sense of things and to grow, rather than shrink, ourselves.

Carl Jung's impact on the field of psychology was enormous. Among other things, he is famous for introducing the concept of extroverted and introverted personality types, which led to the development of the popular Myers-Briggs personality test. He was a forerunner in the art of dream analysis, which he enhanced with the "active imagination" exercise (a technique his friend, Albert Einstein, used to excel in the realm of physics). In addition to his empirical work as a clinical psychiatrist, Jung spent decades studying Eastern and Western philosophies, mythologies, and divination systems like the I Ching and tarot, as well as sociology, literature, and the arts. Jung's range of knowledge and intellectual fluency was broad and deep, and he made prodigious contributions to furthering a deeper understanding of these areas.

Jung provided elegant ways to understand the human mind, the meaning of an individual's life, and the way things happen. Foremost among these was his synchronicity principle, which shows how events have a relationship in time as well as in space. Synchronicity can be defined as the coincidence of two or more events that are not related in a linear way by cause and effect but, even though their connection may seem mysterious, we sense that it is meaningful. In the VDM paradigm, synchronicity reflects something about the present moment, offering a sign that something important is ready or trying to happen. As Jung put it, "Things arising in a particular moment of time all share the characteristics of that moment."[1]

Synchronicity is an intersection of an individual's conscious mind with a vastly larger collective reservoir of consciousness (which is unconscious as far as the individual is concerned) that surrounds it. David Richo, a Jungian psychotherapist, writes:

> Meaningfulness happens when an event or experience in conscious life puts us in contact with unconscious forces that lead us to a fulfillment of our destiny. Our destiny is anything that leads to birth, death, finding a life purpose, or awakening to spiritual consciousness. Coincidence is a bond between two hitherto unconnected realities. Synchronicity joins something going on outside us with something happening inside us.[2]

Intuition is an instinct that can bring conscious awareness to what was unconscious, in its ability to perceive coincidental connections as well as ferret out their meanings. As you start noticing synchronicities, you come to better understand what they mean for you. In their subtle way, synchronicities serve as gentle alarms that wake your intuitive intelligence, to better discern the meaning in your life and to help you individuate and become truly who you are.

The Interconnected World

Although Jung was the first scientist to focus on the phenomenon of timing and the meaningfulness of inscrutable coincidences, the idea behind his synchronicity principle had been known for centuries. What we call synchronicities were taken as "signs and omens" in older cultures (often noted in the Torah or Old Testament). Human beings in various cultures have long noted that events tend to cluster in time, evidenced by folk sayings like "Good things happen in threes." Long before the seventeenth century, when Newton enthroned causality—the notion that every effect has a definite traceable cause—as a central principle of physical science, many Eastern cultures took synchronicity seriously. Human actions were not viewed simply as an expression of one's will or any single cause, but as an element in the context of an exquisitely interconnected society and universe.

In Buddhist philosophy, the concept of "codependent origination" holds that no part of the universe has an independent existence separate from everything else. All the parts are interconnected and depend upon the whole for an identity. This awareness comes naturally to indigenous peoples, where no tribal elder would consider a significant undertaking without examining the congruence of that action with respect to the context of the whole community—including the timing. Jungian analyst and author Robert Hopcke observed this about indigenous spirituality: "To act, within this worldview, is a humble, careful process. This way of thinking, in which one's subjective experience of interconnection with the world is more important than individual mastery over the environment through cause and effect, is a mode of living which accommodates the reality of meaningful chance quite easily."[3]

We are now learning what the sages of old have always known—the value of recognizing significant portents and an ability to sense their long-term meaning, while garnering a better sense of short-term direction. Try to stay aware, so you notice how life is providing signals that point in the direction of your destiny, your heart's desires, and your unique calling. If we are to be cocreators of our own lives—manifesting a unique creative path of being and doing and giving back—paying attention and taking note of signposts is our job. Meaningful coincidences will expand your understanding of how the world is working on your behalf and help you to call up hidden talents. Don't just rationalize and explain away amazing coincidences that occur in your life. Learn to pay attention to the signs that are turning up for you. Look for possible meaning and you will often find it. It is the Jungian contention of this book that we dismiss messages from the universe that come to us as synchronistic coincidences. Jung observed and catalogued this in his own journals, as well as his therapy patients, and millions of us have discovered it in our lives, especially at turning points. Be a scientific observer. Experiment with your intuition (which we shall explore in detail in chapter 6). Give synchronicity a chance even if you can't explain it!

Parallels between Twentieth-Century Physics and Psychology

It seems a meaningful coincidence to me that Carl Jung noted the phenomenal new subatomic physics discoveries by his friends Albert Einstein and Wolfgang Pauli at the same time he was studying the mythology and cultures of the world and coming up with the synchronicity principle. For the sake of modern psychological understanding, that was perfect timing!

Jung's discovery of the psychological relationship between timing and meaning paralleled the new discoveries of the new physics in that both fields recognized the limits of causality in our understanding of the universe. Until the early twentieth century, the bedrock of scientific method since Newton had been an absolute faith in *causality*—the idea that every effect has a logical cause that eventually can be identified, traced, and understood. Once a fundamental belief of the scientific worldview, this ideological hegemony started to crack with Einstein's theory of relativity and new discoveries in quantum physics in the early twentieth century.

Quantum mechanics dealt with the existence of subatomic particles—or waves, depending upon how they were observed—that seemed to flicker in and out of existence and which could be observed to be in more than one place at the same time. To make things even more disorienting, Einstein's theory of relativity described a reality in which time moved faster or slower depending on velocity. This was all very challenging—

and still remains challenging—because humans derive comfort from the idea of cause and effect, a concept our senses can perceive to be the case in daily life.

Around the same time that his friends were shaking up physics with proofs of acausal behavior in the subatomic realm, during one of his phases of profound visionary insight, Jung came up with the synchronicity principle, which was just as counterintuitive and challenging to the psychological establishment as subatomic physics was to Newtonian physics. He started noticing acausal phenomena arising in the experiences and dreams of his patients—psychic material that was not related to the patients' real life experience—whereby he came to realize that synchronicity was a bona fide psychological phenomenon. Like the new physics, his psychology was iconoclastic, breaking free of the limitations of the cause-and-effect paradigm, which makes it impossible at this stage to prove. Now, this is not to say that Jung denied all cause-and-effect relationships in the psychological realm. Rather, he pointed out that there are categories of personal experience in which a dynamic of synchronicity transcends the normal cause-and-effect operations.

The radical discoveries in subatomic physics and psychology upset the highly mechanical model of the universe that had held sway since Newton's era. These radical theories, mathematically proven in physics, challenged a prevailing linear concept of time, fortified by the invention of mechanical clocks and subordination of human activities to them. Even now, scientific experimentation disregards the dimension of time. It is assumed that a controlled physics or chemistry experiment will turn out the same whether you do it Tuesday at noon or in the middle of Saturday night. That is because, in most scientific experiments outside of biology, timing is never factored in as a part of the equation.

Einstein was Jung's occasional dinner guest in the 1920s. According to Jung's letters, Einstein supported Jung's formulation of synchronicity, noting how it might be considered as a theory of relativity applied to the dimension of time. Jung wrote, "It was Einstein who first started me off thinking about a possible relativity of time as well as space, and their psychic conditionality. More than thirty years later this stimulus led to my relation with the physicist Professor W. Pauli and to my thesis of psychological synchronicity."[4]

From the traditional scientific point of view, the synchronicity principle was absurd, a form of magical thinking. But it became more palatable when considered alongside the radical new discoveries of subatomic physics. Jung's theory of synchronicity got further support from Werner Heisenberg's proof of the uncertainty principle in 1927. Heisenberg posited that the position and velocity of a subatomic particle could not be simultaneously measured, because, at the subatomic level, the act of perceiving or measuring affects and changes that which is being perceived. In other words, an exact objective measurement of anything—including physical reality—is impossible.

For those who perceive synchronicity, it's not a big stretch to appreciate how everything that happens in a given situation at a given time participates with, and affects, everything else in that situation—including the consciousness of the perceiver. In fact, this is a good way to define the synchronicity principle.

I once had the honor to videotape the late Terence McKenna for my multimedia Oracle of Changes CD-ROM back in the nineties—one of the most brilliant people I have ever interviewed. McKenna was an amazing impromptu genius, whose brainy raps are featured in many YouTube videos to this day. (I used to quip that Terence had "the widest bandwidth between brain and mouth" of anyone I'd ever met.) McKenna, an American philosopher, ethnobotanist, lecturer, and author, spoke and wrote about a variety of subjects, including plant-based entheogens, shamanism, metaphysics, alchemy, language, culture, technology, and the origins of human consciousness. Our shared interests in technology and the I Ching brought us together. He had formulated a concept about the nature of time based on fractal patterns he discovered in the arrangement of the hexagrams of the I Ching, which he dubbed "novelty theory."

In the interview, McKenna explained the essential difference between Western science and the traditional Chinese approach. Western science, he pointed out, had successfully focused on asking what things are made of and how they work, which led to outstanding breakthroughs and inventions. In contrast, Chinese civilization had also made formidable scientific advances, but the wisdom of this much older civilization focused on answering a different question: How do things go together in time? To the highly civilized Chinese, this was important for all kinds of reasons. Good timing was essential for emperors and kings to keep order in the kingdom, conduct meaningful rituals, and know when to launch political moves, campaigns, and major enterprises. Even now, timing is a critical factor in extremely important areas of life where logic is of limited help, such as relationships, negotiations, and interventions, as well as scheduling campaigns, social rituals, marriages, and other important events.

Synchronicity as Perfect Timing

When it comes to innovation, it's easy to see how synchronizing two or more disciplines or technologies can intersect to make something different manifest in a novel way. According to a timing all its own, some sort of Infinite Intelligence (which Jung the psychologist called the "collective unconscious") seems to dynamically generate synchronicities, like a metaphysical lightning storm. If we are on the lookout for them, amazing coincidences will occasionally flash into our consciousness along with symbols that we intuitively know are too relevant to be totally accidental or meaningless.

Synchronicities happen constantly, even if the majority seem too mundane to warrant special attention. In the sense that in every moment, a multifaceted convergence of factors is coming together in time, synchronicity is the very definition of the universe's perfect timing. According to a synchronistic viewpoint, everything happens in its own good time, even if it may not seem like it from your ego's point of view. Ultimately, synchronicity means that there are no accidents, not even down to the tiniest detail. Everything happens for a reason and is unfolding perfectly according to a pattern, a plan, or laws, even if the plan is inscrutable to human logic and the laws are still to be understood in human terms. It only makes sense that nature's intelligence would operate according to a creative pattern that is beyond the human mind's ability to measure, or even detect. After all, nature encompasses all interconnected reality, and the human mind is a microscope. As we shall see in the next chapter, nature's Infinite Intelligence is a fertile resource from which new ideas and events arise like bubbles from a seething cauldron of creative potential.

Because they are acausal by definition (that is, outside the bounds of cause and effect) synchronicities are not amenable to measurement and scientific proof—any more than we can get a fix on a subatomic particle or wave. On the other hand, the belief that everything happens for a reason—that there is a divine order beyond sensory appearances—can never be disproved and is psychologically useful (as we shall see in chapter 11). From a practical point of view—and in alignment with this book's theme—accepting the inscrutability of life's evolutionary dynamic, while availing ourselves of whatever meaning is currently discernable by our limited minds, will help us to make better and better decisions.

Let us humbly accept that it's not our place to ever fully understand the reasons things unfold the way they do. Maybe we'll get it in a few months, or a few years, or maybe not in this lifetime. Our primary task in the here-and-now is to take note of a synchronicity, act as if there is a good reason (even if we don't know what it is), and try to glean a sense of direction so that we can better answer the immediate and more useful question of what is our best next move. In the VDM approach, we use a belief in synchronicity as an operating assumption, choosing to accept the mystical patterns of destiny and learn how to let ourselves find support and guidance in the meaningful signals that come our way.

This useful attitude reminds me of "pronoia," a word coined to describe a state of mind that is the opposite of paranoia. Whereas a person suffering from paranoia feels that people or entities are conspiring against them, a person experiencing pronoia feels that the world around them conspires to do them good, harboring a kind of suspicion that the universe is conspiring on their behalf. As Pollyannaish as this idea seems on the surface, it represents an attitude that works entirely better as an operating assumption in terms of getting what we positively desire, rather than fearing the consequences of not getting it.

Even in the case of genuinely disappointing experiences, we can benefit from the synchronistic point of view. It can be calming and healing to assume that cosmic timing is at work and that an intelligent force is clearing the way for something better to come. It may be humbling to accept that we are not capable of fully understanding the big picture, but it is true. Nevertheless, we can still take advantage of meaningful signs and omens—some of which appear in the form of synchronicities and dream symbols—which can be very helpful during transitional periods of dramatic change.

The Dreamlike Aspect of Synchronicity

The synchronicity principle suggests that there are no accidents, and that synchronicity is actually the way of things and operating all the time. In this paradigm, events unfold according to some higher order, even if it is beyond our ability to understand the cosmic blueprint. Viewing the world through synchronistic eyes allows you to perceive the underlying web of connectedness that weaves itself through nature and human lives. This is not about wishful thinking or even imaginative interpretation, but analogous to being inside of a dream while being aware that it is a dream. According to lucid dreaming experts, the awareness that we are dreaming allows us to digest the dream world and its lessons.

As lucid dreamers know, changing perspective within a dream doesn't cause it to become a dream. It was always a dream; we just hadn't recognized it as such. In a similar way, when we realize that we live in a synchronistic universe, by becoming aware of meaning in coincidences and other signals, the universe reveals its synchronistic structure more vividly.

In his clinical practice, Jung asked his patients to record their dreams and daily experiences to become aware of strange symbols, archetypes, and any special coincidences. Under the old paradigm, these would have probably been overlooked, dismissed as mere chance or, worse, as mental garbage. As Jung developed a point of view that was more attuned to synchronicity, he began to perceive meaningful coincidences more often, which in turn stimulated more new insights. All of this happened quite naturally.

The more you are on the lookout for synchronicities, the more you will start to notice them. Synchronicities, like the symbolic representations in your dreams, are not really separate from you, the perceiver. The events may seem external, but the meaning and ultimate impact is internal and intimate, and needs the awareness and attention of you, the perceiver. Once you become lucid in this waking dream of normal life and become more highly aware of the fact that you are living in a synchronistic universe, your life will clearly reflect the rich fabric of that reality back to you. Recognizing the synchronistic matrix that provides a substratum for your experiences will empower you to be a creative, cooperative, and active partner in your own awakening and process of personal development.

Jung's exploration of the phenomenon of meaningful coincidence was one of his great contributions to our self-understanding. It helps us see human life as an interconnected web of subjective and objective experiences with synchronicity providing a link between the two. In one of his letters to Jung, the physicist Wolfgang Pauli referred to the synchronicity principle as Jung's "spiritual testament."[5] Although he was not a religious person, in synchronicity, Jung acknowledged creative power at work in human nature.

Tracking and Cultivating Synchronicities

Becoming more keenly aware of synchronicities as they happen is a huge advantage for any decision-maker. Learning to notice and leverage synchronicities supports a holistic and creative perspective—where timing is not only considered but recognized as a vital factor, if not the most vital factor, for successful manifestation. Great timing depends on respecting the dimension of time to become more sensitive to special intersections, and then scheduling any tactical or strategic moves you may want to make. This will help you make better plans, clarify situations, and realize when a new direction needs to be taken.

The synchronistic "aha!" experience conveys useful timing information beyond the limits of normal linear thinking. Since it's easy to overlook synchronicities when we are in a hurry, we need to slow down to consider possible meaning. Keeping a synchronicity journal is a useful experiment that can help you better notice signs and omens that the universe serves up for you. Some people prefer a traditional notebook. A notes app on your smartphone, tablet, or computer also works great. Make a habit of recording all your meaningful coincidences—as well as nightly dreams, uncanny feelings, chance encounters, hunches, and good ideas—as they occur, whether or not you understand what they mean. You can sort them out later when you have time to reflect.

Increasing awareness alone is a major benefit of keeping such a journal, as it attunes you to the rhythms of life, which will help you catch synchronicities and mysteries hiding in plain sight. As you become more familiar with these signs, you will notice them more quickly, and physical senses—a "gut feeling" or a "feeling in your bones"—will become sharper and more refined as you hone your intuition and make it more intelligent.

Recording and deciphering synchronicities will change your perspective and lead to new insights, new relationships, and new opportunities. This is the expansive way that creative power spirals upward. The deeper meaning of your ideas, the real significance of the people you meet, and exciting potentialities will become clearer as time goes on. I suggest going back and looking them over once a week or so, adding reflections and insights as you attain a deeper understanding of meaningful patterns over time. This will help you to expand your consciousness beyond the preoccupations of your ego.

Even just slightly increasing your awareness of synchronicity works on your behalf like compound interest, building on itself to make your life more abundant and meaningful, full of generosity and wisdom. Synchronicity may reveal the universe's perfect timing, but human beings will never be able to fully comprehend it. Nor will we ever achieve perfection in our decision-making or timing. Nevertheless, even a slight improvement in our ability to notice and leverage synchronicities will produce better decisions and timing, along with the subsequent advantages and opportunities. In part II, we explore more practices you can employ for greater synchronicity. In the meantime, let's take a look at other resources uncovered by Jung's research that are available to help us on our journey to success, greater meaning, and loving fulfillment.

4

The Infinite Intelligence of Nature and Spirit

Within all energy is an intelligence that is infinite, eternal and purposeful. This Infinite Intelligence, which we sometimes refer to as God, or simply love, is the source of all creative expression and the essential Power in the Universe.

—**Arnold Patent**

In the early twentieth century, Napoleon Hill, famous motivational teacher and author of one of the most famous self-help best sellers of all time, *Think and Grow Rich*, interviewed five hundred of the most successful people in America. He concluded that, without exception, their monumental success depended upon an ability to access a level of intelligence that transcended personal consciousness. He referred to a universal resource, which he said those successful leaders had learned to tap, called "Infinite Intelligence."[1]

In the nineteenth century, American philosopher Ralph Waldo Emerson penned an essay entitled "The Over-Soul." Now considered one of his greatest works, it's about how all of our creative potential comes from connecting to a larger field of consciousness, which envelops us even when we are not aware of its presence. Emerson was among many philosophers who tried to identify this power. He called it "universal mind" or "superconscious mind."

Carl Jung's research confirmed the realizations of Hill and Emerson, but he characterized the vast reservoir of creative potentials as the "collective unconscious." Its contents are unavailable to us until we become conscious of parts of it, but it is a vast extension of the unconscious mind that goes beyond the personal mind. The collective unconscious is a vast mindfield that contains creative powers that we can access, channel, and even start to consciously direct.

The collective unconscious is our shared reservoir of patterns, symbols, creative ideas, and energetic dynamisms that can intersect with and operate through what Sigmund Freud labelled the personal unconscious mind. Freud thought of the personal unconscious as an internal psychological vault stuffed with repressed thoughts and feelings, but Jung was the first psychologist to explore an unconscious connection to a nonpersonal repository of mythologies and archetypal themes that affect everyone. Highly creative individuals throughout history have understood this and pinpointed the unconscious as the source of creative breakthroughs that lead to personal transformations, as well as great inventions in art, science, and business. To quote George Tyrrell, modernist theologian and scholar,

> It is a highly significant, though generally neglected fact that those creations of the human mind which have borne preeminently the stamp of originality and greatness, have not come from within the region of consciousness. They have come from beyond consciousness, knocking at its door for admittance: they have flowed into it . . . often with a burst of overwhelming power.[2]

Unlike psychological complexes and phobias, which are reactions to personal experience and conditioning, the contents of the collective unconscious, according to Jung, have their origin in a shared cultural heredity that influences and maps the evolution of our culture and species. Explaining the magnitude and significance of the collective unconscious, Jung wrote:

> The collective unconscious is ... the mighty deposit of ancestral experience accumulated over millions of years. . . . Because the collective unconscious is, in the last analysis, a deposit of world-processes embedded in the structure of the brain and in the sympathetic nervous system, it constitutes in its totality a sort of timeless and eternal world-image which counterbalances our conscious, momentary picture of the world.[3]

It is "collective" because it belongs to everyone, and operates through us to different degrees depending upon our awareness. It stimulates the personal unconscious—for instance, by means of dreams and synchronicities—whether we are consciously aware of the unconscious connections or not. As Jung put it, "I have chosen the term 'collective' because this part of the unconscious is not personal but universal; in contrast to the personal psyche, it has contents and modes of behavior that are more or less the same everywhere and in all individuals."[4]

As evidence for the collective unconscious, Jung noted that major elements of his therapy patients' dreams did not refer to their own actual experiences or relationships. In fact, much of the material that appeared in dreams was strange to patients and had no connection to their personal experience. "It is a fatal mistake to regard the human psyche as a purely personal affair and to explain it exclusively from a personal point of view," he wrote.[5] Even when they could not personally relate to the content of their own dreams, patients could still discover meaning in them—sometimes even transformational meaning. For Jung, this pointed to a broad, impersonal dimension of mind that operates both within and beyond the scope of an individual's life.

Freud had treated the unconscious as a kind of personal toxic waste dump, but for Jung it was more of a creative gold mine. By pointing out a wider collective aspect of the unconscious, Jung provided a psychological explanation of previously unexplainable factors like creativity, intuition, and consciousness itself. Jung saw enormous power and potential in the collective unconscious: "[The collective unconscious] is of absolutely revolutionary significance in that it could radically alter our view of the world. Even if no more than the perceptions taking place in such a second psychic system were carried over into ego-consciousness, we should have the possibility of enormously extending the bounds of our mental horizon."[6]

Jung's revelation of the collective unconscious as the psychic inheritance of all humankind transformed our understanding of self and its relationship to the world—a realm beyond our egocentric bundle of personal wishes, fears, hopes, and ambitions. More than just investigating ways to cure mental illness, his scientific curiosity explored humanity's psychological (and spiritual) potential—with huge ramifications for creativity and leadership—informed and supported by the historic continuity of muses, heroic characters, and other archetypes.

A Powerful Resource for Expanding Horizons

The term "Infinite Intelligence" appeals to me as a moniker for the collective unconscious, because I am focusing on it as an unlimited resource of inspiration, energy, new ideas, and synchronistic signals that inform creative decision-making and good timing. From a practical point of view, it doesn't matter whether you think of connecting with this cosmic intelligence as psychological self-actualization or spiritual practice. Either approach supports the expansion of consciousness—in contrast to a reliance on current beliefs.

Intentionally accessing this resource of great ideas and creative inspiration is what differentiates Visionary Decision Making from the more common reactive decision-making that is characterized by small-minded goals, self-limiting beliefs, and personal defensiveness.

Infinite Intelligence can be thought of as an extension of personal consciousness, analogous to an online "cloud" containing vast amounts of information in a sort of cosmic server. As you will learn in the next chapter, you can use your intuitive sense to make a "wireless connection" and tap into this cloud to download information in the form of impressions, flashes of insight, and inspirations. Although it is always available to you to inform or stimulate your imagination, the information in this collective reservoir is not owned or controlled by you, any individual, or a government agency.

Infinite Intelligence has three characteristics that support the VDM process: it is the origin of all great ideas, it is the source of personal and creative power, and it is the energy field generating synchronicities and meaningful connections. It is the intuitive decision-maker's largest and most supportive asset, and it's always there for you. All you have to do is make the connection and tap into it.

The Source of Great Ideas and Inspirations

When we arrive at new ideas, we love to think that they originated with us. We "thought them up," we say; we own them. But what we consider to be our thoughts only seem like ours, because we identified with them, invested time and energy, and became attached to them. When they arise we can almost automatically identify with them. Thus, they feel like they're ours, like we came up with them. But we didn't. They came to us but they don't belong to us. With this recognition comes greater freedom to choose whether we should invest in them and act on them.

Anyone who learns meditation soon realizes that the thoughts that pop onto our field of attention do not originate with us, if only because they usually pop up uninvited. If they seem familiar, it is because we made a nest for them in the past, by dwelling on them. Meditation, which is generally practiced as a way to transcend the personal mind in favor of a more open and receptive consciousness, teaches us to let go of thoughts as they arise and merely note their passing. Even so, thoughts will continue to arise in the mind's field of attention, of their own accord. Even though a meditator is choosing not to actively engage with or think about them, they still come—out of habit or streaming from the collective unconscious. From the point of view of the letting-go exercise that typically characterizes meditation, thoughts are a nuisance, static on the line as it were. From a VDM point of view, however, thoughts in the form of creative insights have value, even if they occur when you are meditating (perhaps *especially* when you are meditating . . . we will look at how to take advantage of this in chapter 6).

Everyone knows that Thomas Edison invented the light bulb, but so did at least twenty-three other inventors. Two of them even sued over the patent rights, since their prototypes were so similar. This is an extremely common experience. In fact, a study in 1960 led sociology professor Robert Merton to declare, "The pattern of independent multiple discoveries in science is in principle the dominant pattern, rather than a subsidiary one."[7]

While such concurrent insights may seem disconnected and merely coincidental, the concept of the collective unconscious provides an explanation—that we are all plugged into the same reservoir of creative power. The difference in terms of creative power depends on how well developed is one's intuitive intelligence and how well an individual can tune their intuitive antenna (which we will explore in chapter 6). A good idea is one whose time has come. It is an evolved thought form picked up by individuals with a receptive and activated intuitive sense. Great ideas, emanating from Infinite Intelligence, may occur to us as dreams, as good advice from advisors, in meditation, or as an authentic divination experience like the I Ching.

The fact that we are the recipients—and not really the inventors—of great ideas is elegantly expressed by Bob Proctor, author of *You Were Born Rich*, who wrote, "I am grateful for the idea that has used me."[8] It's as if every idea, from the light bulb to the Slinky, already circulated within the universe, along with an astounding number of other new ones. Finding your "muse," or guiding creative spirit, is part of becoming a visionary decision-maker. Everyone is creative in his or her own way—it's just a matter of tapping into your personal talents and connecting with Infinite

Intelligence. The German polymath Goethe said he wrote his famous novel *The Sorrows of Young Werther* "almost unconsciously, like a somnambulist," and that he was amazed when he realized what he had done.

The Collective Unconscious Contains Powerful Archetypes

Infinite Intelligence—Jung's collective unconscious—is an unlimited source of creativity that is always available. It is a wellspring of energy and psychic power that you can access via your intuition and from which you can receive ideas and inspirations. It is also the province of archetypes, which are symbols, instinctual patterns of behavior, and powerful personality dynamics that we can call upon, because they also reside within us. These "figures and movements," as Jung put it, are universal human models of personality or patterns of behavior.

Archetypes have been expressed in the hopes, dreams, fears, and desires of humanity across cultures and throughout time, in the form of myths, deities, heroes, and demons. One way to think of an archetype is as a generic version of a personality type, which can inform or reinforce aspects of an individual personality. For example, the "mother figure" archetype is psychologically active in individuals who may not be mothers but who otherwise manifest ways of nurturing.

The concept of archetypes has been around since Plato and the Greeks and the more ancient cultures of India and China before that. Carl Jung brought renewed interest to the subject when he introduced it as an important element of psychology in 1919. For our purposes, invoking archetypes, particularly archetypes as they relate to creativity and power, helps you trust your intuition and turn on your personal power, both vital to superior decision-making.

With the support of many archetypes—each powerful in a different way—you can facilitate significant changes in your career, relationships, and your entire life. After you learn how to invoke the power of various archetypes that are particularly useful for VDM, some will seem more natural to you than others based on your personality traits. In fact, archetypes operating in and through your unconscious have helped to shape your personality and character. (We learn how to invoke powerful archetypes in chapter 7.)

When you know how to tap into the power of Infinite Intelligence, it becomes your power on loan to channel through your attitude, thoughts, and actions. Throughout the ages, people have relied on rulers, priests, gurus, and other middlemen to mediate with archetypal gods on their behalf. Now everyone can access the knowledge needed to go there directly. Always remember that creative energy is flowing through and around you. In order to leverage it, all you need to do is consciously connect to the deeper reservoir, which has been hidden in the collective unconscious. Your physical self and your breathing provide excellent touchstones to help you maintain a more conscious connection with nature and spirit. Infinite Intelligence will provide support, safety, and security once you learn to be receptive and open to the inspirations and ideas that are picked up by your intuitive sense.

Our Relationship to Infinite Intelligence

Our quest for the intuitive intelligence to make visionary decisions challenges us to extend the bounds of our mental horizons and reach for creative powers that would be individually beyond any one of us. We are each part of the "world mind," according to Jung, so the creative powers of Infinite Intelligence are always present and available for our conscious connection. And it's not that hard to connect—just having the intention, paying attention, and maintaining awareness of the connection makes up 80 percent of the required effort. This spiritual and creative dimension is always at our beck and call, but actually connecting to Infinite Intelligence is up to us. In addition to simply paying attention, we have to bring intention, commitment, and skillful practices to the equation.

Mindfulness is a primary skill that allows us to pay attention to Infinite Intelligence, which we will learn how to exercise in chapter 6.

Without mindfulness, we may miss creative solutions, as well as subtle timing signals that pop up in the form of synchronicities, hunches, etc. Obviously, this is a different orientation to Infinite Intelligence than monotheistic religions proffer. Rather than imagining an omniscient god that watches over us and pays attention to us as if we are childlike subjects of a king begging for favors, VDM's psychological and spiritual development point of view would have us tap into the creative powers of Infinite Intelligence and cooperate with them.

Making life-changing decisions is more work than just beseeching God (or consulting higher power via a divination system like the I Ching) for direction, to give you what you need, or to tell you what to do. You are required to exercise free will and cooperate as a cocreator, as a partner in the unfolding pattern of your life and destiny, as an intuitive channel of Infinite Intelligence. Use your head, heart, and intuition. Be willing to do the work of paying attention, making and taking responsibility for your decisions, and undertaking the risks that bold decisions entail. Once you develop a habit of tapping Infinite Intelligence to inform your important decision-making, your attitude and your future will automatically begin to improve.

The Divine

Even though Jung—in the service of psychology as a science—was careful to use secular terminology when referring to the collective unconscious, many observers like myself consider it to also be a spiritual resource. After all, it is a realm populated by archetypes including divine beings, though it's fine to personalize the divine in your own mind, if that's what you prefer. Just remember that your decisions affect the unfolding of your destiny more than anything you can imagine the Fates or God might have in store for you.

During the year I lived in India, I observed that everyone had complete freedom to relate to his or her own preferred representation of the divine without apology or explanation. In the open-minded Hindu culture, it was easy and natural to have conversations about God or the spiritual dimension of life with just about anyone—even a stranger on a bus—without a hint of conflict. Some Hindus have affection for Krishna while others favor Shiva, Vishnu, or Ganesh; some even prefer Jesus as their favorite deity.

Classical Buddhists, in contrast, perceive the divine in an impersonal way—as a resource of creative power that they can tap anytime, a concept that seems similar to the collective unconscious. Taoists also conceive of divine power as an impersonal repository, rather than a patriarchal Creator-God who controls or judges his creation. Like Buddhists, the Taoists related to the divine as an impersonal resource that is always on tap. They refer to it as "nature."

Each individual is entitled to his or her unique conception of the ineffable divine. When I was a struggling bootstrap entrepreneur and people would ask me if I had investors (which in the normal sense I did not), I would reflect on Infinite Intelligence and smile, thinking, "My backer has infinite resources."

Ultimately, it is not important how you choose to conceive of or visualize the realm of Infinite Intelligence; just remember that it's a supportive resource that is always there for you. Through it, our intuitive sense has access to unlimited information at any moment. Tuning in to this dimension of higher consciousness will enable you to take advantage of ideas, recognize good timing, and make more enlightened decisions.

Part II

The Visionary Decision Making Process

5

Your Strategic Vision: Answering the "What" Question

You've got to think about big things while you're doing small things, so that all the small things go in the right direction.

—**Alvin Toffler**

As the name implies, Visionary Decision Making depends upon having a vision. The VDM skillset comes into play once you are clear about a strategic goal—something that will inspire you to make a bold or life-changing move when the timing is right. Certainly, depending on what's at stake, few personal decisions are of a strategic nature. Those that are potential life-changers may coincide with major passages or transitions in life, but exceptional opportunities for change arise only occasionally. They are impossible to precisely predict, but having a clear vision will help these big decisions take form and move you in your desired direction.

You may wonder, what is the difference between a vision and a daydream about something you desire? The VDM visioning process is similar to daydreaming, but enhanced with intention and the discipline of brainstorming. Visions concern big goals that are related to who you are inside, and feel worth the effort of manifesting.

A vision becomes "strategic" when it represents a long-term desire that is important to you at a given stage of life. A strategic vision that inspires you will lead to setting goals. To be motivating, long-term goals need to be clearly declared, then visualized and felt. Logic plays a part too, helping us get the clarity we need, as we shall see later in this chapter.

To lead to success, your strategic vision and the goals that you commit to will require making some big decisions along the way. Such visionary and transformative decisions are rooted in the depths of your being and are an active expression of who you have discovered yourself to be. In time, they are life changing. The focus can be in any area of your life: finding a partner, experiencing a higher level of health, adopting a cause, or shifting to a more fulfilling career. It might involve something that you are inspired to achieve even if it requires hard work—for instance, learning something new or breaking unproductive coping habits. It could be the result of a recurring dream that aligns with strong interests or talents.

If you notice a desire within yourself or that the same opportunities keep arising for you, or if conditions in an area of life become chronically unpleasant, these patterns are trying to tell you that it is time to make a profound change. A compelling vision isn't so much about the form or the details of what you want as much as it is about the level of personal meaning that making the shift would hold for you. Don't get hung up on the details. Just declare your "good"—your positive vision—in terms of what it means and how it will make you feel. Let form follow the essence of your desire and the particulars will take care of themselves.

In my own entrepreneurial hero's journey, as told in the introduction, the strategic visioning was in the area of vocation: my dream of being able to make a living doing something creative and meaningful to me. After fifteen years of cultivating business and marketing skills at "day jobs" that paid the rent, a personal vision was ready to come forward and be realized. In my case, this was to take the form of developing a new kind of software that leveraged ancient wisdom to help people improve their intuitive intelligence. Developing the intersection between two personal fascinations—the I Ching and multimedia software—was profoundly meaningful to me, and I went for it one step at a time, not having any idea where it would all lead.

Once you know who you are—your most important values, and what inspires you—the central driving questions of Visionary Decision Making are the "what" questions, as in: "What is my good?" "What does my heart desire?" "What would it look like and feel like?" Or, as in a game of chess, "What is the best next move to make?"

Games like chess and Go are excellent ways to exercise strategic thinking. Success in games of strategy relies on thinking ahead and making the best moves you can to put yourself at an advantage. It also requires adapting and responding to shifts in position by the other players or other challenging circumstances. The depth of your calculations depends on the strength of your logic in analyzing possible moves, along with your intuition in anticipating what other players or influential forces might do.

Frame a Clear Picture of Your Heart's Desire

The first step in formulating a strategic vision is to declare the good that your heart desires as if it already exists or is already in process. Bring the picture to your mind even if it's difficult for parts of you to accept that it is truly possible, even if it is something you can hardly imagine because of self-limiting beliefs. Essentially, you make an agreement with yourself that facilitates the manifestation of an inspiration that is in alignment with who you are. The declaration step—the third step of the Creative Manifestation Treatment (see appendix A)—provides focus and structure for your creative vision. In this step, you identify what your heart desires—whether that be the resolution of a personally meaningful challenge or dilemma, or a wide-eyed opportunity that inspires you—and frame it as a specific objective that you can focus on and channel energy toward.

Brainstorm how to formulate your declaration step until you can write it down with a level of clarity that lets you see it in your mind's eye. Does it resonate with who you are? Does it turn you on? Whatever the vision, write it down and play with it, revise the wording until it makes sense to you. Declare your intention clearly and powerfully in just one or two sentences.

Such clarification through the declaration step is empowering in itself. Making a clear and strong declaration can be a challenge because of limiting beliefs—especially not believing in yourself and your capabilities—but this is a challenge you can overcome, and the process will make you stronger and more confident. If you become aware that you're making a mountain out of a molehill—overthinking or "sweating the small stuff"— you can let it go and redirect your energy in a more constructive direction.

Work at it. Take your time with the declaration step. Brainstorm with yourself. Play with diagrams and flow charts. Play with ideas and words. Whatever it takes, it's critically important to clearly define your vision before you consider what decisions you need to make or dilemma you need to resolve to support its unfolding. To arrive at a clear declaration, commit yourself to staying open-minded and keeping a creative frame of mind around what's possible. Rather than approaching your desire as merely a problem to be solved, reframe it as a learning opportunity to be seized, and a mystery to be experienced.

It helps to be in an environment that supports clarity and peace of mind, as both your inner mindset and outer setting are important. You can't make an effective choice or decision of any importance if you are distracted. Conflicts of interest, wanting too many things at once, and random distractions drain attention and potency. For example, you can hardly help but be disturbed if you are in a traffic jam behind a truck with a broken exhaust system spewing toxins. When faced with a visionary decision, you need to be in a place where you can be in that special zone where you can be both relaxed and focused.

Comfortably settling within yourself and your environment supports confidence that there will be signs. Tap into the belief that you will be provided with the clues and information that will help you attain your objective. Believe that you will come to understand what a given dilemma or fork in the road means for you, and that you will eventually know the best course of action. Don't expect a miraculous windfall to deliver your goal into your lap. Prepare to notice clues in the form of meaningful coincidences by maintaining your conscious intention to perceive signals that can help guide you one step at a time.

The Power of Logic

The Visionary Decision Making process is primarily driven by intuition, but the use of logic for focusing plays a critical role too. Some of my worst decisions were purely emotional, knee-jerk reactions to jarring events that did not allow logic enough space and time to weigh in. Though relying on logic all by itself is not sufficient for the most important decisions, logical analysis does help you distill the best choices from an array of options.

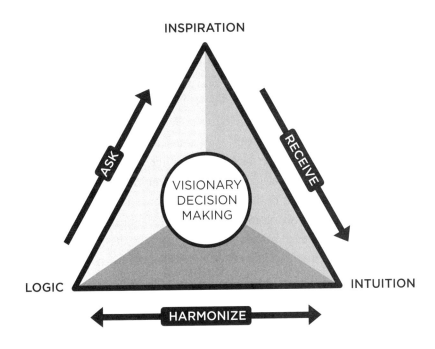

A wise mentor once counseled me against black-and-white thinking by reminding me that *there are always more than two solutions to any problem.* This is an excellent adage to remember because we tend to think in all-or-nothing terms. Do your best to recognize *all* the viable options and apply a dose of logic as an antidote to getting carried away by strong emotions. That is logic's job and its rightful role. Wishful thinkers abandon logic at their own risk!

Of Two Minds

Humans have the largest neocortex-to-brain ratio of any mammal and this has supported the evolution of our capacity for reason and language, which are generally associated with the left hemisphere of the neocortex. Roger Sperry, a neurobiologist who pioneered split-brain studies (and won a Nobel Prize for it), demonstrated that the two hemispheres—which physically appear almost identical—are "two separate realms of conscious awareness; two sensing, perceiving, thinking, and remembering systems."[1] In more recent studies, what is becoming increasingly evident is that even the most specialized tasks activate areas across the brain. Research on brain functions is still evolving, but for our purposes here, we will refer to the left brain and right brain in the colloquial way.

Logical problem solving is considered a function of the left frontal lobe of the neocortex, loosely referred to as the "left brain." New discoveries in brain imaging have shown that the conscious, rational functions of thinking, planning, writing, and so forth are not entirely, but largely, based in the left frontal lobe. The other half—the right hemisphere of the neocortex—seems to be the locus of older, more instinctive forms of intelligence, including emotional and intuitive intelligence. It's almost as if we have two independent brains, each with its own memory and units of storage. These two halves of the neocortex can be at odds—and often are—or they can work it out like different political parties in a functioning government.

Those who are right-brained tend toward qualitative, big-picture thinking. They are the intuitive and creative freethinkers, who experience the world in descriptive, subjective terms (we will be delving into right-brained thinking in the next chapter). Left-brained thinkers tend toward a quantitative and analytical approach: they pay attention to details and are ruled by logic. Logic is a process of analyzing and taking things apart to figure out what they're made of or how they work. This kind of "reverse engineering" can play a useful role in creativity. Once you take something apart and figure out how it works, it's possible to reassemble the pieces in a new configuration to serve a different purpose. This brand of thinking has played a huge role in the development of human culture in the past five thousand years, especially since the Renaissance and the birth of the scientific method. Countless modern innovations have been the result of a scientific approach (often spiced by intuition). Human engineering, which has changed everything from farming to transportation to medical cures, has enhanced the survival of our species, even as the overuse or misuse of technology has also created serious hazards that threaten our ongoing existence.

As the hemisphere that governs language processing, the left brain stores information in the form of words, thoughts, ideas, and plans. For the purposes of strategic decision-making, logic provides a useful filter that helps distill options through comparative evaluation and a process of elimination. It helps us to differentiate between a more farsighted decision and an impulsive or emotional one. In an information-saturated world where we have so many choices, an educated logical ability to compare and sort is essential.

Facts versus Biases

Facts provide a basis for logical deduction. Facts are determined by observation and measurement, which is why fields like science, engineering, and law are characterized by strict adherence to logic. Emotions and relationship dynamics, on the other hand, cannot be measured or quantified, which is why it's impossible to be totally scientific when it comes to decisions about politics, love affairs, or timing. All kinds of important areas in life cannot be empirically measured, which does not mean that they are not important. (This reminds me of the adage: "Absence of measurable evidence is not evidence of absence.")

There is a strong tendency to define our reality by choosing to ignore facts that don't fit the way we'd like to see things, and exaggerating observations that affirm our biases or a desired point of view. In its most innocent form, this is referred to as "confirmation bias," which simply means we believe what we want to believe. This is a universal phenomenon, and often negatively inclined under the influence of conspiracy theories and fearmongering. Psychologist Dan Staso was quoted saying:

> Negative beliefs cause us to filter out information long before it reaches our conscious mind. This system of false beliefs filters in information that is consistent with our long-held assumptions and filters out information that contradicts those beliefs. The results include failure to see or create opportunities, reluctance to utilize resources that are easily available or to assert oneself in situations that could lead to new possibilities, failure to believe others when they offer support, and refusal to accept help from those who could make a difference.[2]

In some cases, confirmation bias can lead to risky and dangerous delusions. One example is human-made climate change, which is killing life on the planet and causing sea levels to rise. There is overwhelming evidence that our dramatic climate disruptions are due to human causes. Peer-reviewed climate scientists almost unanimously agree that the drastic changes in weather, rising sea levels, and melting snowpacks are the result of air pollution from massive increases in the burning of coal and oil since the smokestacks of the industrial revolution in the nineteenth century. However, a handful of scientists take a contrary position, based on fake research funded by energy companies who want to deny the harmful potential of their products for the sake of profits. The unwanted mountain of scientific evidence is totally ignored while self-serving investigations proceed along "logical" lines to generate the desired conclusion.

It can be difficult to know if something is fact or merely strong opinion—especially in a networked age where people (and rogue governments) have the capacity to loudly and anonymously broadcast opinions and represent them as facts, without being accountable for evidence or sources. Reality-based logic is a powerful decision-making aid, but we need to bear in mind how thin the line between facts and opinions can be . . . and how challenging it is, given our biases, to know the difference.

To become visionary decision-makers, we must be ready and willing to question everything—using our intuitive intelligence, including that baked-in form known as "common sense." We often formulate opinions based on our perceptions of possible facts, and we often need to accept expert evidence that is beyond our ability to figure out for ourselves. If we use our intuition and would prefer that our beliefs be based on reality rather than comfort, convenience, or fantasies, this is not a problem. But in a world rife with cultural regression into political and religious fundamentalism, we have to be especially careful before pledging allegiance to any opinion from professional rabble-rousers, political or religious. When people become unquestioningly devoted to a belief system, they propagate the self-serving beliefs of their leaders and make terrible decisions—often by doing what they are told by despots who tell them not to trust their own senses or believe any information not fed or censored by them.

Chaos Theory Reveals a Higher Order of Logic

In the 1960s, meteorologist Edward Lorenz developed a new field of scientific study known as "chaos theory" to help account for nonlinear patterns in weather prediction. In its broadest sense, chaos theory demonstrates that apparent disorder is largely a matter of perspective. If we step back far enough—or step up close enough—unseen patterns emerge. Since it was formulated, chaos theory has had applications in physics, engineering, economics, biology, philosophy, and meteorology. It is a good example of the dynamic of a decision-making process that allows for meaning among events that on the surface only seem to be happening randomly.

Chaos theory is an example of a change in perspective that takes us beyond the black-and-white thinking that has been epidemic in human society. True, many areas of education—arithmetic, for example—do have specific right and wrong answers. In the entirely logical domain of mathematics, linear thinking works just fine. Chaos theory is a much more nuanced and inclusive way of looking at reality and how things work—whether it's the motion of clouds and galaxies or the trajectory of a baseball (or, perhaps, even the dynamics of an intimate relationship).

Assuming a new point of view requires intuitive big-picture pattern recognition. Just as we discern the subtle patterns in clouds, tree roots, or shorelines, we intuitively understand that our lives and our minds are also patterns of nature. This insight provides a new level of confidence in our ability to use intuitive intelligence to make sense of larger patterns, including the shape and trajectory of our own lives.

The Logic of the Greater Good

We have all heard English poet John Donne's expression "No man is an island." On our crowded planet, we are more interconnected than ever before, but mostly we're not feeling it. Human beings generally operate egocentrically, as if there were enough space on earth to wall themselves off with their families in their own gated communities. Such a self-centered definition of "independence" is, at this point, a throwback. It represents a lower rung on the ladder of humanity's cultural evolution. In the United States at the time of this writing, a fierce strain of this kind of narcissistic hyper-independence is stronger than ever.

In the eighteenth century, when economics was just becoming a formal discipline, philosopher Adam Smith proposed that the "wealth of nations" increases when individual citizens further their self-interest.

Smith coined the metaphor of an "invisible hand": an unconscious positive effect on the macro level that results when each person acts for his or her own personal benefit. According to the thesis, if you do what's best for yourself, and I do what's best for myself—and each person acts rationally in his or her own best interests—the results will be positive for society as a whole.

There are several problems with this, beginning with the fact that, as we have seen, people are generally not rational decision-makers. Furthermore, it is often the case that the interests of one individual conflict with those of another. According to the pure self-interest ethic, this creates an economic "survival of the fittest" situation. The markets will determine the individual winners and the losers, but society as a whole will benefit and the wealth of nations will increase. All of this is fine, theoretically, especially when frontiers full of natural resources seem to be infinite. Indeed, it seemed that way when Adam Smith formulated his theory. But now we know that our collective resources are indeed limited.

At the same time, as we face a shrinking pool of resources, we are all more interconnected than most people realize. Modern physics demonstrates this with the "butterfly effect," coined by Edward Lorenz, which stipulates that a tiny action in one place (such as the flap of a butterfly's wings in Brazil) can be part of the cause of a larger effect in a different place (like a tornado in Texas). The point is, whether beneficial or damaging, every action affects the global system as a whole. If you understand our common interconnection, you realize that a capitalist fantasy of unregulated self-interest is a dangerous idea masquerading as fair and altruistic. There is such a thing as getting too good a deal, and when you do, it will come back to bite you. A primary task for logic is the process of eliminating options that violate your ethical or spiritual standards.

Tragedy of the Commons

A zero-sum, win-lose mentality never yields long-term positive results in interactions between individuals, businesses, or nations. The reason for this was elegantly explained by Garrett Hardin, an ecologist and professor at the University of California at Santa Barbara, in a 1968 article titled "The Tragedy of the Commons," published in the journal *Science*.

His basic concept is simple: using a limited but shared resource selfishly will hurt everyone—*including oneself.* In his example, Hardin describes a village of herdsmen whose sheep share a common pasture for grazing. Each herdsman will realize a short-term advantage when unilaterally acquiring and adding animals to his herd, despite the impacts on the shared resource. Eventually the long-term overexploitation by such self-interested individuals leads to the deterioration and destruction of the entire pasture and all the animals, causing huge losses for everyone, including the self-centered exploiters. This is a great way of explaining how it is that win-lose strategies always produce lose-lose outcomes.

The tragedy of the commons shows that when it comes to common resources, we are interdependent, whether we like it or not. On a crowded planet with billions of human beings making increasing demands on limited resources, we can no longer afford to make decisions based solely on individual short-term benefits. Our long-term interests are inextricably bound with the common good. We ultimately do not benefit as individuals if we disregard the interests of others—all others, not just family and friends. This is not naive altruism. Considering what we know now, it's pragmatism; it's been scientifically demonstrated and it is logical common sense.

Consideration of the collective good, including our personal good, is an important filter for a visionary decision-maker. This principle is elegantly expressed by the Sanskrit word *ahimsa*, a three-thousand-year-old term that translates as "harmlessness." *Ahimsa* describes choices and actions that treat the collective good with consideration rather than indifference or carelessness. It's an idea reflected in the core teachings of all the great religions, from the Golden Rule of Christianity and Islam to the karmic law of cause and effect taught by Hinduism and Buddhism. Whatever you call it, it's in your best interests to cultivate an ethic of harmlessness.

A growing awareness of our interconnectedness is why, even in intellectually rigorous settings such as the Harvard Business School, more attention is being paid to teaching the ethical aspects of decision-making. Does the choice you're considering support you in becoming your best self and also have a positive effect on others? Is there anyone who could be harmed by you acting on behalf of your personal interests or furthering your competitive advantage?

A logical filter for the highest-quality decision-making sounds something like this: If something that I want would bring any kind of harm to anyone else (beyond a simple competitive disadvantage within the rules of a playful game), I will choose to disregard it as a viable option for me. It's that simple. But when self-interest is involved, simple is not always the same as easy.

Using Logic in Visionary Decision Making

As discussed, VDM requires a well-balanced, holistic, and focused approach that incorporates logical thinking. By itself, logic is usually not enough to resolve human dilemmas—especially in categories like relationships, negotiations, or matters of timing—but it adds value. Let's review important ways that logic supports the process of manifesting a personal vision and the strategic decision-making that will be required along the way:

- **Testing and reaffirming highest priorities.** Getting clear about your hierarchy of values—your priorities—is essential. How are they ordered right now? And what desires and tendencies might be distracting you from pursuing what is more highly important? Demartini's Hierarchy of Values technique (described in chapter 2) is an excellent way to logically analyze how you spend your energy and what you spend the most time thinking about. However you get there, refine what matters to you from a practical perspective. Whatever is most important gets the highest priority, but priorities do shift during different stages of a person's life.

- **Sacrificing a lesser value for a greater value.** Although it's not a popular concept, sacrifice, or renunciation, often needs to play a part in your prioritization. When you are aware of all your choices, you also become more aware of the fact that you will have to give up something, that you may be called upon to sacrifice a lesser good for the greater. This lesser good may still be attractive—very appealing in its way—but when you focus on what you need most, the "shiny objects" and addictive compensations lose their luster and power over you. Giving up something lesser makes room for something better. Back in the 1970s, there was an advertising slogan aimed at women: "You can have it all, baby!" A bold promise, but not even close to being true. You may be able to have *anything* you want, but not *everything* you want. You have to give up something.

- **Letting strong emotions calm down.** Common advice for being intuitive has been to trust your feelings, but this is somewhat misleading. Don't expect to be objective when you're angry, frightened, or emotionally overwrought. Even an over-the-top joyful feeling can render it impossible to be objective. Bear in mind this counterintuitive rule: No matter how it feels—good or bad—*the stronger the feeling, the less you can trust it* as a guide for a decision or action! Do not let how strongly you desire or fear a thing influence important decision-making. The strength of an emotion may indicate that something important to you is in play but it is not an indicator of intuition. Quite the contrary. Intuitive impressions usually present themselves with a quieter signal, with more subtlety. Again, the strength of your emotions is not a trustworthy basis for making decisions or significant choices. Things are never as good or as bad as they seem. Always put off important decision-making until an emotional state has calmed down.

- **Enlarging the scope of your options.** Sometimes it looks like there are no good options. Often it seems that there are only two choices; this is black-and-white thinking, a widespread habit that adversely affects decision-making for most people and keeps them stuck in an unhealthy "fight or flight" pattern. Once again, as my mentor would tell me, there are always more than two solutions to any problem. I find it a useful reminder whenever I feel pulled by opposing choices. Consider a wider field of possibilities and find a third alternative, even if it is simply to let things pass and do nothing for the time being.

- **Sorting out superior options.** Sorting the relative value of your best options weeds out the less appealing ones until you reduce the set to the two or three best options. For this purpose, many people use a logical pros-and-cons process made famous by American philosopher Benjamin Franklin, based on the idea that the benefits and disadvantages be weighed against one another. So, a certain item in the pros column can cancel an item in the cons column when they are of equal weight. Similarly, two small pro items might cancel a single large con.

For some choices, considering pros and cons will work well enough if you're dealing with abstract or non-emotional decisions. However, Franklin's system has a serious psychological shortcoming, known in psychological circles as "loss aversion." Fear of losing generally feels stronger than the allure of potential gain, because fear is more urgently motivating than optimism or faith (for good reason, since the fight-or-flight reaction evolved in response to fear to keep our ancestors safe from the dangers of the jungle). In other words, the impact of cons—negative possibilities that we fear could happen—has a stronger influence on us than the allure of positive potentials. The solution to this problem? Eliminate the cons!

For Better Logic Try the Weighted-Pros Technique

To balance out the emotional impact of loss aversion, I use a variation on Ben Franklin's pros-and-cons technique that I call "weighted pros." It's a practical approach, useful in every major decision-making situation. When faced with a strategic decision, create a simple table with your three or four best options across the top. Take some time to visualize each choice and its worst possible outcome. If any are potentially injurious or fatal, do not include them no matter how fantastic the upside might seem. Our Visionary Decision Making approach is not generally oriented toward high-stakes gambles, all-or-nothing plays. You don't want to risk bankruptcy by taking on an unmanageable amount of overhead, liability, or financial responsibility. You might get lucky, but the odds are against you and, depending on how young and brazen and fearless you are, you might go crazy worrying about it. If it's potentially dangerous to your physical or mental or emotional health, strike it immediately!

OK, let's look at an example of the weighted-pros technique. Let's say your decision has to do with finding the right place to live. You might boil it down to three options like this:

rent downtown condo
buy house in suburbs
house-sit for friends

Instead of listing pros and cons below each of your options, list only its advantages. I've found two benefits for only listing positives and not tallying the negatives. First, the con of one choice is usually an inversion of one of the pros of another choice. For instance, in the example above, a con of renting is lack of ownership, whereas ownership is a pro of buying a house. The pro of renting in this case might be freedom from responsibility for property maintenance, taxes, and so forth, which would be an item to list under the rent option.

On an emotional level, the pro of one choice can seem more compelling when viewed as the con of another. Because ours is a nervous species wired to be wary of attack, it is just easier for the human mind to focus on what it doesn't want rather than what it does want. But making a concerted effort to counteract that tendency and take the fear element out of the calculations will get you better results. After you have listed all the pros (and only the pros) for all your viable options, give each of the positive factors a weighted value on a scale of 1 to 10 (10 being the highest positive value, meaning it's the most important), and then add up the total values for each column. Consider the option that offers your highest value as your best logical choice.

The weighted-pros technique is a simple but excellent way to use logic to narrow down the options in any situation, and a good place to begin strategic decision-making. You may encounter times where nothing more than this level of logical sorting will be needed to make the best decision, but probably not when it comes to potentially life-changing strategic decisions.

Limitations of Logic for Decision-Making

The economist Herbert Simon won a Nobel Prize for his work on decision-making and problem solving. His work showed how, in complex situations, facts and information pile up so quickly that a decision-making process relying on logic alone becomes unreliable and virtually impossible. To counter this, Simon studied intuition development as a form of pattern recognition that develops over years of experience in a wide variety of circumstances. Intuition—a process that operates outside the bounds of pure logic—proved to be an important tool for arriving at the optimal decision. All told, Simon's work on "bounded rationality" is a powerful endorsement of intuitive decision-making, while recognizing the important role of rational analysis.

As we have seen, a logic-based approach is the classical model of decision-making and works well with measurable phenomena, but it cannot take on the subjective realms of morality, society, love affairs, office politics, creativity, or spiritual considerations. Often, choices we are called upon to make cannot be logically defined, partly because there are too many variables. And, by its nature, logic finds it absolutely impossible to resolve anything paradoxical or mysterious.

Worse, even the information we currently accept as true has a shorter timeframe of relevance. Rapid change makes the best current information (including our beliefs and assumptions) obsolete more quickly than ever. Certainly, having good information to weigh and analyze is a vital component of great decision-making. However, in a world where there is too much information—and no easy way to prove which bits are reliable or true—intuitive intelligence is required if only to decide which information we should trust.

The analytical process is only as good as the available information. As Gary Klein, a business authority on decision-making and author of *Sources of Power: How People Make Decisions*, puts it so well, "Analysis has a proper role as a supporting tool for making intuitive decisions. When time and the necessary information are available, analysis can help uncover cues and patterns. It can sometimes help evaluate a decision. But it cannot replace the intuition that is at the center of the decision-making process."[3]

Another possible problem is that many logical decision-makers tend to put off making important decisions to await more information, or simply procrastinate. Unfortunately, many an info-gathering delay has resulted in a missed window of opportunity. Gerd Gigerenzer, a German psychologist who has studied rationality in decision-making, said, "The trick is not to amass information, but to discard it: to know intuitively what one doesn't need to know."[4] The trick is to use logic to clearly define your strategic vision and goals that flow from it, then opening yourself to intuitive insights once you have done so.

It is understandable that humanity has revered reason for the last several centuries, but as my personal story and this book attest, we are foolish if we ignore the wisdom of intuitive intelligence. When it comes to strategic decisions of utmost personal or organizational importance, using logic is important, but depending on logic alone for strategic decision-making will not produce radically great results. As Blaise Pascal wrote, "Reason's last step is recognizing that an infinity of things surpass it."[5] After you have skillfully applied the filters of logic, it's time to open yourself to the parts of your mind that go beyond the reach of logical analysis—your intuitive intelligence.

6

Intuitive Intelligence

The mind can only proceed so far upon what it knows and can prove. There comes a point when the mind takes a leap—call it intuition or what you will—and comes out upon a higher plane of knowledge, but can never prove how it got there.

—**Albert Einstein**

I often tell my friends: When you don't know what to do, do nothing. Get quiet so you can hear the still, small voice—your inner GPS guiding you to true North.

—**Oprah Winfrey**

Using logic—and its noble offspring, science—humanity has invented sophisticated technologies that come in handy in myriad ways and help us solve formidable problems. But as mentioned, we are still not so adept at dealing with major areas of life that are not well managed by a strictly logical approach, such as relationships, politics, negotiations, the timing of strategic moves, and mystical experiences, to mention an important few.

This book is about establishing a fruitful relationship with a form of higher intelligence that is not strictly logical, that is way beyond rational, so that we can find solutions outside the boundaries of what we know now, to deal with the kinds of problems that science and logic can't handle. Knowing how to make the right moves at the right time requires a feeling-based skill that bypasses the strictures of logical analysis. We can refer to this innate human capacity as intuitive intelligence.

As we saw in the previous chapter, logic does play an important role in strategic decision-making—which argues for being educated in thinking critically—but that is the easier part of Visionary Decision Making. Logical processes help you to define what you want and what is good for you. But to make the visionary decisions—as well as execute them with good timing—we need to go outside the rationality box to access a bigger mind: the collective unconscious that we all share and the Infinite Intelligence that it contains. Thankfully, we have all been given Einstein's "sacred gift" of the intuitive mind, with which we can access these mysterious realms. We just need to learn to trust our intuitive sense and tune in to it. Cultivating intuitive intelligence and mastering the art of putting it to good use are at the heart of the Visionary Decision Making approach. In this chapter, we will explore some techniques for opening up to and developing your intuitive intelligence birthright.

Intuition is commonly defined as the ability to acquire knowledge without inference or the use of reason. It is a holistic and nonverbal instinct that takes in the big picture and receives impressive information directly, sensing patterns without regulation by, or interference from, the analytical mind. The analytical mind is superb at taking things apart and putting them back together again as best it can. A holistic approach to perception, however, hinges on understanding that the totality of a system is more than the sum of its parts and—for managing the big picture—much more important.

Unfortunately, the reception of information by the intuitive sense cannot be switched on or willed into action like logical thinking can be. It's more feminine than that. Its operation depends on being open and receptive to a spontaneous flow of impressions, insights, ideas, unusual occurrences, coincidences, hunches, and inspirations that arise in your personal mindscape. Such noticing just can't be forced—the mental circuits have to let go of rumination to free up the mind so that it may be "allowed." It requires setting thinking aside in favor of a holistic ability to take in entire patterns, where all the dots and interconnections are not visible, when the situation is not outlined enough to be traced or logically analyzed.

> Carl Jung was the first psychologist to deeply investigate intuition and its psychic potentials. In *Psychological Types*, published in 1923, Jung described intuition as a perception of realities which are not known to the conscious mind, and which comes to us through the unconscious.[1] Intuition is not merely a perception, he said, but a creative process that has the capacity to inspire. Jung noted that the mind requires intuition to function at maximum performance and that our dreams, so rich in symbolic value, cannot be interpreted without the intuitive intelligence. Besides dreams, a historical example of intuition connecting the dots—quite literally, in this case—is the perception of the star constellations of the zodiac, giving form to ancient archetypes that not only guide navigation but offer mirrors to the human condition through mythologies and stories—which were also exhaustively studied by Jung.

As a faculty, intuition is a subtle instinct compared to the five physical senses, although it can piggyback on the others—perhaps in the form of a sensation, an emotional feeling, an image or picture, a dreamy vision, or a quiet voice. It pays to set aside some "me time"—twenty to thirty minutes or more. Make it a fun thing to do, like daydreaming. Just make an effort to hear this quiet voice or close your eyes and allow a picture or vision to come to mind. In our rushed society, we rarely accommodate our need to let go of thinking, of left-brain processing therapists often refer to as "rumination." We are dealing with so many thoughts and feelings, plans and projects at a time that we are typically in a hurry and easily overwhelmed. Our nerves get jangled and we tend to compulsively clutch at what we want or need when we get the chance. In a rush, we try to make things happen and get other people to change in a hurry. This syndrome is called "hurry sickness."

The urge to relieve ourselves of the anxiety of modern speeded-up living makes us constantly rush things, leading in turn to fitful sleep and a lot of bad decisions. Once we have learned how to create the space—and patience—to receive information, and we can relax enough to tune in to its subtle frequency, intuition will enlighten us a bit, give us more freedom of choice, and save us much wasted time overall. It may support a timely impulse to make a move in a specific direction, to retreat, or sometimes to do nothing at all and let circumstances change on their own. As we shall explore in chapter 8, divination systems like the *I Ching*, or *Book of Changes*, are excellent intuition-support tools, because they provide a ritual that helps us step back for perspective on the bigger picture. From that vantage point we can see more than two solutions to any dilemma and we can see more good options than black-and-white thinking allows.

An intuitive perception is a sort of mystical experience that can take shape as a thought or a vision, or be physically felt "in your gut." You might say, "I had a hunch," "It just felt right," or "In a flash it became clear to me." Accurate intuitive insights often occur quickly, as in a strongly felt first impression—the central point of Malcolm Gladwell's book *Blink*—but strategic decisions are of a much grander vision and require more processing than just trusting and going along with a first impression.

Intuitive intelligence helps us read between the lines of dreams, sessions of active imagination, or an I Ching reading to ferret out the meaning and personal relevance of symbols and archetypes that show up. Intuitive perceptions are like sparks that bridge the gap between the receptivity of a stable, grounded mind (Earth) and the spontaneous lightning of creative power (Heaven). When information is taken in via intuition, it can produce the "aha" moment that presents a new idea, point of view, or sense of direction. To further understand the role of intuition, let's consider the complex interplay between the different parts of the human brain.

The Triune Brain

Human beings have what neuroscientists refer to as a "triune brain," which can be divided into three major parts: the reptilian brain or brain stem (responsible for basic survival instincts), the mammalian or limbic brain (which controls emotions), and a large neocortex with left and right hemispheres. As Dr. Caron Goode notes, "The neocortex is the thinking brain, choosing information we should listen to and act on from the reservoir of our memory."[2] In addition to pulling from its own memory storage, where items as stored as words and ideas, the left brain can also take in the nonverbal impressions that make it across the corpus collosum, the tissue that connects the left brain from the right brain, whence impressions have been perceived via our feelings and senses, including our intuitive sense, and are stored there in a very different way.

Einstein's quote at the beginning of this chapter asserts that the rational mind ought to support the intuitive mind, which is notable because of his background as a physicist. He also said:

> Intuition makes us look at unrelated facts and then think about them until they can all be brought under one law. To look for related facts means holding onto what one has instead of searching for new facts. Intuition is the father of new knowledge, while empiricism is nothing but an accumulation of old knowledge. Intuition, not intellect, is the "open sesame" of yourself.[3]

I recommend *The Right Brain and the Limbic Unconscious: Emotion, Forgotten Memories, Self-Deception, Bad
Relationships* by R. Joseph for further reading on the connection between intuition and both the right hemisphere
of the neocortex and the limbic brain.[4]

Dr. Roger Sperry's Nobel Prize–winning split-brain research "gave a physical basis to the ability to work with images, intuition, and holistic thinking in the right brain hemisphere."[5] Further research proved that people whose right hemisphere has been seriously damaged lack the sensitivity to feel energies, instincts, and nuances innate to normal humans and mammals.[6] We are wired for intuitive intelligence.

Intuitive receptivity is challenging, in part, because of the structure of the brain itself. Psychiatrists and authors Thomas Lewis and Fari Amini describe it: "The swirling interactions of humanity's three brains [are] like the shuttling of cups in a shell game. . . . Because people are most aware of the verbal, rational part of their brains, they assume that every part of their mind should be amenable to the pressure of argument and will. Not so. Words, good ideas, and logic mean nothing to at least two brains out of three."[7] To complicate matters further, it seems that memories are stored separately in the left and right hemispheres in different formats.

For intuitive reception, the personal unconscious (right brain) first makes its "wireless" connection to receive impressions, via the intuitive sense, from the collective unconscious. The holistic, nonverbal right brain is perceiving bits of a larger pattern, which can include synchronicities, archetypes, hunches, and flashes of insight. These are stored in the right brain's nonverbal memory as images, impressions, or emotional feeling states. The left brain's separate memory, on the other hand, stores things in the form of linear, logical parcels of thoughts, words, and ideas.

The conscious mind—the inner executive in charge of our strategic decision-making—depends on awareness of intuitive information received by the right brain after it has traversed that dense highway of fibers called the corpus callosum. To be useful, the left brain needs to translate those impressions into ideas and words it can make sense of. This is left-brain translation work. Without it, the conscious mind can't take advantage of intuitive impressions and images for decision-making, planning, innovation, or mystical experiences.

As stated, to become useful in any practical or creative way, intuitive impressions stored in the right brain need to be brought to consciousness so they can be deciphered by the left brain. In this effort, the left brain strives to make sense of these often strange impressions, rather than disregard or censor them according to the biases and outdated beliefs in its own stored memories. The task is to convert the intuitively received impressions, feelings, and images into thoughts and ideas that can be used for deliberate decision-making or creative pursuits. Translating intuitive information is where some knowledge of archetypes, dream images, and the I Ching can help out. As a bonus, once the left brain learns to make sense of intuition's perceptions, noticeable hunches start to increase and also prove more reliable.

For visionary success, logical analysis should *follow* intuitive and sensory perception, rather than govern or direct it. We make the most far-reaching discoveries and decisions when we allow creative synapses to fire—*before* logical processing becomes too involved. Scientific visionaries like Einstein and Jung and neurobiologists like Roger Perry understood this, though Western science as a whole has glorified logic at the expense of anything that does not conform to measurement and analysis. While logic performs an important filtering function in the Visionary Decision Making process by helping us to sort out options, breakthrough decisions are almost always driven by intuitive feelings or sensations rather than logic or emotional reaction. In fact, an overreliance on logical analysis will derail the intuitive mind's ability to receive signals and its ability to contribute its valuable sense of important patterns. Reductionistic science may take the position that something is not meaningful or real unless you can measure it, but this is quite a restrictive approach to reality. The extreme and highly limiting scientific attitude that "absence of evidence is evidence of absence" is a highly limiting operating assumption, and unscientific insofar as true science must remain open to new possibilities and new evidence about what it does not yet know or understand.

Modern education has tended to propagate a staunch bias toward logic, despite numerous studies that show that successful leaders and inventors have relied heavily on intuitive intelligence. A report by Applied Predictive Technologies found that 73 percent of respondents trust their own intuition for decision-making. Even among executive decision-makers who described themselves as "data-driven," more than two-thirds (68 percent) said they trusted their intuition in the decision-making process.[8]

Unfortunately, we can't deploy intuition at will; we can't force it to kick in and work on demand. Since it operates outside the realm of cause and effect, it is impossible to come up with a logical or linear formula to force intuition's activation. Like relaxation or meditation, it requires a "letting go" dynamic that depends on context and cannot be forced. That's why I like to visualize our intuitive sense as a small, highly specialized antenna.

For thousands of years intuition has been called the sixth sense. Our minds receive massive inputs of streaming information from the first five senses, which can be construed as giant antennae bringing massive amounts of information into the brain and mind. The visual antenna is by far the largest, taking in the most information for visual processing, which has been shown to have the most neurons in the brain (30 percent). Sights, sounds, feelings, smells, and tastes are all data streams that vibrate at different bandwidths and frequencies. Our intuitive sensory organ receives its own rarified kind of information—by way of a much more faint, high-frequency signal.

Our "sixth sense" is like a small antenna calibrated to a quiet signal, like a cat's sensitive whiskers, which tingle as they pick up subtle frequencies that tell them something is in the air or about to happen. The more experienced you become at tuning this right-brain antenna, the better you will get at receiving clear information and the more trustworthy it will prove to be. With practice, and the greater sense of confidence that results, your insights will become more and more accurate and timely. Because of the wide-lens nature of intuitive perceiving, just tuning in to this sensitive antenna, just using this sense at all, expands the mind.

In terms of making the best decisions in life and being as creative as you can be, it pays to be as open-minded as possible. In this regard, our motivations strengthen when we regularly remind ourselves of the benefits of cultivating intuitive intelligence.

Benefits of Intuitive Intelligence

Good intuition helps in every area of life, but its genius is especially apparent in the areas that involve creativity, empathy, spirituality, strategic decision-making, and timing.

Creativity

Those who work in the creative arts and can give their fantasies and imagination free rein test out as highly intuitive people. Carla Woolf, an author and expert on intuitive intelligence development in young children, explains on the Creativity Post website, "Intuition and creativity are fundamentally interdependent and interchangeable"—so true at any age! Artistic expression represents the intersection of intuitive intelligence, with techniques that are learned and mastered. One function of intuition is finding the patterns within, or making sense of, symbolic content—some of which can come via our dreams—and then portraying those patterns so they can be appreciated by others.

Creativity manifested for me through my foray into multimedia software after fifteen years of daydreaming about its potential for facilitating meaningful interactive experiences. In what was at the time a nonexistent niche, I was a product visionary—someone who imagined a new intersection between design and function in the form of a product or service that people didn't yet know they would like. As Akio Morita, cofounder of Sony, once put it, even though they had a huge budget for all the marketing research in the world, none of it could have predicted how well something radically new like the Sony Walkman would do. Probably the most famous product visionary of all time, Steve Jobs, also eschewed marketing research in favor of intuition, going on to produce so many things that people could not know they would like before they experienced them. In my case, this involved authentic do-it-yourself I Ching and Tarot card readings, astrology reports, and so forth—types of products that had never existed before.

A famous example of creative expression coming through a dream is the Beatles' song "Yesterday," the melody of which came to Paul McCartney in his sleep. Dreams and fantasy have also played a role in phenomenal scientific discoveries and technological innovations. For instance, the familiar double-helix structure of the DNA molecule was revealed to Nobel Prize winner James Watson in a dream featuring spiral staircases. Dr. Caron Goode also notes that "Brain mapping using EEG topography found that creativity and intuition are associated with theta waves usually linked with daydreaming or fantasizing . . . intuitive ability is finally recognized as the fuel behind innovation, creative thinking, inspiration and psychic experiences."[9]

Empathy

Empathy is a form of intuitive intelligence that allows you to perceive subtle feelings and pick up on what is going on within the mind and heart of another human being—even when that other person may not be aware of it. You can say that empathy is the ability to understand another's feelings from the inside out. Two-way empathy is an important expression of intuition, because it supports intimacy.

"Limbic resonance" is a term used to describe people who are so close that they subconsciously influence each other's nervous system and brain chemistry. Ideally, limbic resonance starts in a baby's relationship with its mother. The authors of *A General Theory of Love* give another example of limbic resonating: "women who spend time together frequently find their menstrual cycles coming into spontaneous alignment. This harmonious, hormonal communion demonstrates a bodily connection that is limbic in nature, because close friends who have feelings for each other achieve synchrony more readily than those who merely room together."[10] People who are able to resonate limbically are naturally more empathic; basically, they have an ability to feel each other's feelings and read each other's minds.

Empathy and compassion inspire us to provide emotional and physical support to each other. This aspect of intuitive intelligence is innate to all humans, but needs to be encouraged in an increasingly anxious, crowded, and competitive world. We are social animals, meant to depend upon each other, with a profound need for secure connection. Political and religious ideologies that seek to divide and control people need to be outgrown, like the narcissistic stage of life we all go through as infants.

Spirituality

Every human being is endowed with a mystical capacity, even if the vast majority of us are hardly aware of it. Intuition is vital to experience the spiritual dimension, which is about our relationship to God, Spirit, the Universe, or whatever we choose to call what philosopher Alan Watts referred to as the "Ultimate Ground of Being." Philosophically, intuition lets us form a picture of the broadest patterns, and nothing requires greater broad-mindedness than the complexities of an infinite universe. Once we know and accept our humble position—and our relative lack of power—in the cosmic scheme of things, we can better appreciate the synchronistic aspects of how our lives unfold. On a personal level, spiritual awareness can provide a psychological sense of freedom from existential suffering; knowing we are meant to be part of something so beautiful and grand infuses us with calm and clarity, and inspires profound feelings of gratitude.

Decision-Making

The complexity of our problems and the scope of our creative potential exceed logic's processing capability, which is why intuitive intelligence is essential for Visionary Decision Making and why VDM is important for the wise stewardship of one's life and place in the world. Maintaining a high level of receptivity to intuitive intelligence requires being clear about and committed to what is meaningful. Insights and inspiration—the happy fruits of an active intuition—provide direction and awareness of new opportunities. Intuition used for decision-making is similar to the interpersonal limbic resonance noted above. In this case, however, you can think of it as limbic resonance with Infinite Intelligence where insights and inspirations are free to come to you in a way that you can intuitively sense.

Superior Timing

Timing is the secret sauce of successful strategic decision-making. Arriving at a conclusion and committing to it is hard enough. But your odds of producing a successful outcome depend greatly on whether you have good timing in executing your decision. Deciding what should be your best move may be largely intuitive, aided by logic, but deciding when to make that move is almost entirely intuitive. (Chapter 9 explores the sublime skill of great timing and how to know when to execute important decisions.)

Obstacles to Intuitive Receptivity

There are plenty of ways to benefit from intuitive intelligence, but it needs some freedom to operate. Intuition cannot be forced; activating it is a lot about letting go. A large part of intuitive awakening involves identifying, then letting go of, obstacles and destructive tendencies that block the delicate antenna's ability to receive and store impressions that can be useful to the conscious mind.

Static on the Line

The five senses channel so much sensory information that it consumes our attention. Obsessive rumination or sensory distractions overwhelm intuition's receptive capacity. Indian yogis for thousands of years have humorously referred to the noise of the chattering mind as the "monkey mind," when subtle intuitive signals are drowned out by all that's going on inside. Receiving signals from the reservoir of Infinite Intelligence is like downloading information via a wireless network. To do this, you need a clear connection—one that does not have much static interference competing for the mental bandwidth.

Addictions

Emotion-backed desires of the ego to avoid possible failure or embarrassment can give rise to compulsive habits or addictions, which create blind spots and place exhausting demands on consciousness. Desires that are preferences that lead to creative decisions are helpful, as we have seen. Addiction is a desire that has become a craving, an emotional attachment to a wished-for result that is so strong it takes over, ultimately becoming a cause of hardship or suffering. Trying to satisfy the seemingly insatiable appetites of ego—which may be trying to compensate for deep needs for love that were not met in early childhood—always keeps us from being able to make a clear intuitive connection.

With an addictive level of emotional attachment, even getting and possessing the object of desire produces some suffering—if only in the fear of losing it or running out or never having enough to feel secure. An addict has an impossible time tapping into intuition in the face of obsessions, which results in a downward spiral of bad decisions leading to fewer good choices until a person is desperate and trapped and makes the very worst decisions of all.

Trauma

Physical or emotional trauma throws the intuitive antenna all out of whack. Whether it's a result of a personal or family tragedy, a health crisis, or some other event that turns your world upside down, trauma blocks intuitive sensitivity. Trauma can be emotionally overwhelming for a protracted period of post-traumatic stress depending upon the severity of the event and personality factors. Intuitive intelligence that you might otherwise have had access to isn't readily available until you have processed the trauma. Until you are free from its impact, it is never advisable to make a strategic decision during or following a traumatic event. If you are suffering from any kind of trauma or PTSD, put off making strategic decisions until you recover a level of emotional and psychological balance.

Emotional Blocks

When emotional expression shuts down, it's generally because painful, unresolved feelings are lurking in the shadows, ready to be restimulated or "triggered." Until we bring stuck feelings into the light of consciousness—until we face the inner demons on our particular "hero's journey"—sensitive emotional vulnerabilities can be a regular ongoing cause of unease and apprehension, severely blunting intuitive sensitivity.

The biggest blocks to intuition's clear reception are caused by interference in the form of strongly felt emotions like worry, anxiety, anger, depression, greed, and fear. When your mind reacts to and ruminates on compelling or obsessive thoughts or feelings, awareness constricts and you are less able to notice synchronicities and hunches, let alone send them to the left side of the brain for processing.

At the bottom of most emotional reactivity is the core emotion of fear. If we peel fear back, we will touch on many fears: fear of vulnerability, fear of being abandoned, fear of losing agency and being controlled, fear of getting hurt in some way, and, ultimately, fear of dying. It's not fun to feel these fears, but the hero's journey calls on us to rise up and slay our dragons. The only other choice is to hide and wither. When we are brave enough to become more open and vulnerable, our intuition and ability to visualize creative pathways becomes stronger too.

Anything that reduces fear clears the way for intuitive insights. I compare being in a fear-based state to tuning in to a wireless signal from inside a steel bunker. The signal can't get through. Unfortunately, in a fearful state, we lose the benefit of intuition when we need it most.

Sometimes we carry fearful beliefs we were taught or otherwise accepted when we were young. Perhaps our caretakers were well-intentioned and just wanted to scare us away from making mistakes or committing wrongful acts. The unfortunate side effect of security-oriented beliefs is that they teach us to avoid taking risks instead of trusting intuition, which blocks our ability to tap our full potential. Such beliefs give rise to emotional reactions that may feel similar to an abdominal sensation of intuition (like when we literally have a "gut feeling"). It's common to mistake a strong feeling of anxiety as an indicator of what is the right or wrong way to go, when there may be a third, or even a fourth, option we haven't considered yet—so we must be especially mindful of what is driving our emotions (aka emotional intelligence).

In a society that glorifies rationality—while paradoxically also consecrating the irrationality of blind faith—a person who trusts intuition and the grace of synchronicity is all the more brave and daring. Every great discovery and bold move is accompanied by some risk and fear. If not physical fear, it can be fear of ridicule, fear of loss, fear of judgment, fear of embarrassment. I can't tell you how many times my anxiety levels were through the roof over some daring move I felt compelled to make when I literally could not afford to fail. As we have seen, in my case these moves included starting an unproven business model without capital or investors, betting the farm on Karma Coins, entering into a massive supplier contract with AOL, and a few other major risks. As entrepreneur Rick Beneteau put it, "Not a single person has ever accomplished anything of significance without first feeling scared to death!"[11] I can attest to this. Creating a new improved vision and sense of purpose for yourself—and then making visionary decisions—is not for the faint of heart!

In her book *Feel the Fear . . . and Do It Anyway*, Susan Jeffers— an author I interviewed for my *Pathways* radio show/podcast (weekly show currently offered via iTunes and other podcast servers)—shared a technique for peeling back and getting to the bottom of fears. When faced with a debilitating fear, Ms. Jeffers counsels us to ask a series of "What if?" questions. "What if it [this thing I am fearing] were to happen . . . then what? What is the worst thing that could happen as a result of this fear coming true?"[12] After you answer that question, you repeat the process. For example, "If that happened, what is the worst thing that might happen as a result of that?" and so on. If you take this series of what-ifs as far as you can, you eventually get down to the bottom line of all fears: the fear that you won't be able to handle it, that you won't be able to manage or cope, or that you could fall apart and die.

Once you acknowledge that primordial fear of collapse and death, the next step is to recall your personal history. Even though you've been afraid many times in your life—perhaps sometimes scared out of your wits—the good news is that you have invariably managed to somehow resolve the predicament and come out intact, if not unscathed. Putting things in perspective like this makes it easier to appreciate that if you consciously cultivate the self-confidence to believe that you can handle whatever comes up, you *will* be able to handle it—because you always *have*! Your life history is proof that you are more resourceful and resilient than you may generally give yourself credit for. Sages have taught us that life never offers us a problem we can't handle. No matter what comes up, if you are reading this book, it is almost a sure thing that your personal history has proven you can—and will—handle it. Peeling back your fears like this is an excellent way to keep your intuitive antenna from being totally blocked by fearful thinking.

When we succeed at accepting and letting go of fears, instead of focusing on what we don't want, we create a fresh opening for intuitive receptivity. We download impressions and receive inspirations, accept them gratefully, play with them, and, when we feel the timing is right, act on them. Positive changes may have been ready to happen for a long time, but fear was shutting down the reception of intuitive signals that could help us realize better, more creative opportunities. Anything we do to let go of fear will enhance our creative and intuitive intelligence, bringing us the freedom to choose and manifest whatever we desire.

Let the Heart Check the Gut

Fear and other strong emotions can be visualized as thick concrete bunkers encasing our little intuitive antenna, effectively blocking out all of its reception. Add this to the din of sensory distractions and the constant chattering of the mind, and it's a minor miracle that our sensitive intuition antenna ever picks up anything! When it does, the transmission of the signal can be so quiet and subtle that it is hard to tell that the intuition is operating. Intuitive reception can be a formidable challenge for your brain, but there is another center of bodily intelligence that can help.

The brain has long been considered the seat of intelligence, but science has recently discovered that millions of nerve cells are located in the human gastrointestinal system—almost as many as in the brain.[13] This essentially means that your gut has the ability to process information about what's going on and generate responses independent of the brain, like when survival requires an immediate reaction to danger.

The same gut feelings support intuitive decision-making—if you pay attention. "Go with your gut," as the saying goes. Author Malcolm Gladwell pointed out in *Blink* that our initial intuitive instincts often prove to be remarkably accurate.[14] It's the thinking mind that complicates things, causing us to dismiss what our feeling sense is trying to tell us. "I should have listened to my gut" is a common lament.

Since intuition often arrives in the form of a bodily feeling, it is important to differentiate the gut feeling of intuitive signals from the stronger physical sensations produced by emotional reactions. One way is to check with your heart: Is the feeling connected to something or someone that you care about? You will feel a positive, heartfelt component to intuitive signals, while an emotional reaction to fear will be more head-oriented (as in catastrophic thinking).

For millennia, indigenous cultures have believed that the mind and intuitive sense are located in the heart rather than the head. As we all know, in our romantic culture love has long been associated with the heart, which feels to us like the center for the experience of inspiration and attractions that can evolve into passion. Authentic heartfelt passion provides the launching power to propel you through a visionary decision and creative breakthroughs. If a desire is not coming from or through the heart, you can be fairly certain that it is ego-inspired rather than destiny-driven. The ego, that part of ourselves that governs self-image, operates in the past (on memories and residual feelings, including fears and regrets) or the future (goals, desires, and fantasies). The minute we pay attention to the present moment—the only moment there ever really is—the ego-self essentially dissolves. This mental state of pure being is called mindfulness, and it's a primary tool for the development of intuitive intelligence.

The Central Role of Mindfulness

To gain access to your innate intuitive intelligence and make truly visionary decisions, it is necessary to clear your mind, ground your energy, and pay attention to what comes up for you. Since the intuitive side of the brain needs space and quiet to receive hunches and signals via the intuitive antenna, the practice of mindfulness is an excellent way to consistently create these conditions. Letting go of thinking both pacifies the mind and frees it up to download creative ideas and inspirations. Tune your intuitive sense with any deliberate exercise that facilitates the wider awareness.

Mindfulness is the art of paying attention to whatever is on your mind and in your field of perception—including sensations, thoughts, feelings, intuitive impressions, and greater awareness of meaningful events and synchronicities. It is the moment of pure awareness before the ego-mind steps in to make interpretations and judgments. In daily life, mindfulness allows you to penetrate or absorb the truth of the moment so you have more freedom to make a conscious decision on how to respond before reactive, judgmental, or emotional responses take over. As a practice, it serves as an internal intervention against knee-jerk reactions, allowing you access to a wider array of options.

Mindfulness of the body is a traditional technique used in meditation practice. A person may experience intuition as either mental or emotional, but what happens in the mind and heart cannot be separated from how we experience the physical self. In practicing mindfulness of the body, you enhance receptivity to intuition and synchronicity by focusing on an aspect of the physical self—your breathing, body posture, sensation of muscles relaxing or tightening, and so on.

Take a minute and try it. Just pay close attention to the feelings in your body right now. If sitting, the feeling of your weight against the chair, the feeling of your skin against your clothing, the subtle sensation of your nostril hairs when breathing through your nose. During the day, practicing mindfulness may also be used to note subtle physical responses to information, people, and events that come your way. To feel the clues coming via physical sensations, like gut feelings, it's important to keep your body balanced and mind healthy and relaxed through nutrition, exercise, yoga, and meditation or prayer.

Progressive Relaxation Technique: Stress, whether emotional or physical, is always an obstacle to mindfulness. And relaxation is an important aid to achieving a receptive mindset. One of the most widely used techniques was developed more than fifty years ago by the physiologist Dr. Edmund Jacobson. Progressive relaxation exercises can be done anytime and anywhere, even sitting at a desk or in a cramped airplane seat. The technique works best when you're seated or lying down, but it can even be done while standing.

First, tighten the muscles in the calf of your right leg. Hold the tension for five to ten seconds, and then let the

muscles relax. Repeat the process with the muscles in the lower part of your left leg. Then move up your body, continuing the same contraction and release, isolating other muscle groups. When you release the tension in a particular muscle group, the muscle relaxes beyond its pre-tensed state. By tensing and relaxing all your major muscle groups, you'll feel a stabilizing, grounding sensation throughout your whole body and clarity in your mind.[15]

Paying Attention to What's Weird

Mindfulness essentially means paying attention to what's happening right now—both within our minds and all around us. It can pay extra dividends for intuitive development to pay special attention to unusual occurrences. The lovely city I have made home for decades—Portland, Oregon—is known as a hub for creative arts and enterprises. We even have a bumper sticker here, borrowed from our unofficial sister city Austin, Texas, and made somewhat famous by the TV series *Portlandia*: "Keep Portland Weird." It's an invitation to be more creative, to think outside the box, to respect a diversity of ideas, people, and new approaches to living. Portland culture cultivates an open-minded attitude toward the unusual, supporting people to think differently and embrace new possibilities. All of this supports the development of intuitive receptivity.

We all have theories based on our experiences, which contribute to our personal belief system and current opinions. Even though what we don't know far exceeds what we do, we evaluate through the lens of what we think we know—that is, our current beliefs. It's easy to casually dismiss unusual happenings that don't conform to the norm of our personal or societal expectations. But making a practice of noticing what seems different or strange supports the development of intuitive intelligence. Strange and unexpected occurrences are worth a second look.

As discussed, amazing coincidences, or synchronicities, can provide clear signals, and divination systems like the I Ching can make instructive synchronicities happen (as we shall see in chapter 8). But plenty of odd or mysterious things can cause us to pause, wonder, and, ultimately, "think different" (as Apple once famously put it). We just have to give our minds a chance to expand beyond black-and-white thinking in order to embrace the paradoxical and mysterious nature of life to see if we can read between the lines.

Life is not a problem to be solved, but a mystery to be experienced and a paradox to be managed. Don't expect it to ever make complete sense. A paradox is a contradictory proposition that does not make common sense—and will probably never make sense—as long as we cling to black-and-white thinking. When a former counselor used to remind me that there were always more than two solutions to any dilemma or problem, he was alluding to paradoxical possibilities that could transcend or resolve the apparent conflict between starkly conflicting options. To think paradoxically is to think outside the box, as the saying goes, setting aside logical analysis to open yourself to new possibilities and ideas emanating from the unconscious mind—especially including the collective unconscious reservoir of Infinite Intelligence—even if these extraordinary impressions, wild ideas, or strange feelings challenge common sense.

Great insights and hunches often start with a gut feeling. Francis Cholle, the brilliant French innovation expert, points out that new ideas are not found in the conscious mind. He advises clients who want to become more creative to stop thinking and start feeling. Of course, our most noticeable feelings in general are our strong emotional reactions to fears or cravings, which is why trusting your feelings is not always a good idea. If you allow your mind to embrace the paradoxical, which may seem weird, you will sometimes experience a subtler feeling prompted by intuition, making a higher sense of those things that just don't make sense from a conventional point of view. If you allow for it, you can find golden nuggets of meaning in the paradoxical.

The Creative Power of Play

Play offers more benefits than just pleasure: it's an enjoyable form of mindfulness in action. Generally, when we play, we are immersed in the flow of the present. This is what makes things fun. Play comes naturally to children, though adult interference or neglect often inhibit natural impulses with the burden of too much responsibility, like caring for younger siblings, or by a controlling parent who subtly or overtly discourages "wasting time." As fellow trauma survivor and personal growth coach Meredith Miller points out, "We are taught from a very young age to take life so damn seriously that most of us, by the time we are adults, end up missing the beauty, the wonder, the passion, and the play."[16]

Play is a healthy learning experience in itself and a beautiful expression of joy. It also opens us up to intuitive movements of mind and body. Play disrupts logic, allowing us to let go of thinking, creating an opening for insights and inspirations. As Cholle put it:

> Breakthroughs—even the most intellectual and sophisticated ones—can manifest only at times when we disengage from what we know and from what we understand logically. . . . [Play] dis-

connects us from reason and logic and opens us up to new and different thoughts we wouldn't otherwise have access to.[17] Intuitive intelligence activates the profound, yet often intangible, interactions between instinct and play.[18]

Intuitive intelligence, therefore, is something that we begin to access early in life, through play. Unfortunately, we are trained to leave play behind and stop nurturing intuitive intelligence too soon, in pursuit of rationality and logic instead. When intuitive development becomes diminished, we stop perceiving a large part of the world and we are less able to trust our feelings when making decisions. But we can recover, which is what this book is all about. Life can become more interesting and satisfying—and fun—in the process!

Play opens the mind and heart to receiving messages, to being receptive to new concepts, and to instinctively deciding what information is unimportant and can thus be discarded. Studies on the effects of play in childhood show how integral it is to developing the areas of the brain related to intelligence, adaptability, empathy, socialization, and creativity. Research has also shown that adults tend to solve problems best while in a relaxed, playful mood. So why stop playing?

Free-form play is purely instinctual, where you just feel what move to make. It involves instincts and intuition more than reason. By taking you out of your head, it is creative risk-taking in action. But even structured games like chess engage your intuition, if only to "read" your opponent and intuitively anticipate their responses to moves you could make.

Even in the world of thought, you can play with ideas and fantasies. Techniques like brainstorming, lateral thinking, and drawing mind-mapping diagrams on a whiteboard can induce the mind-freeing benefits of play. Daydreaming and freewriting or drawing can have the same effect. Don't overthink or overcomplicate play—let the pleasure and creative joy be enough!

Life takes on a more playful aspect when you are fully present. And you are fully engaged in the present moment when you play.

Remembering how to play and not feeling guilty about it is a key aid in cultivating intuitive intelligence. Incorporate a spirit of playfulness into daily life. Let the intuitive channels open. Intuitive sense has a chance whenever your rational, self-editing mind gets out of the way, so spending some time every day with playful activities will pay off exponentially over time, benefitting your relationships, health, career success, finances, and overall happiness.

Meditation—Mindfulness on Steroids

Because it involves the systematic use and cultivation of mindfulness, meditation benefits intuitive intelligence more than any other practice. Known for centuries in India as raja-yoga, or "royal yoga," meditation is actually part of every religious tradition—in the West as well as the East. Traditionally only practiced by monks and nuns, meditation has now gone mainstream, and its benefits are readily available for anyone who learns how. A regular meditation habit allows you to let go of unhelpful ruminations and become more open to life's signals and synchronicities, which increases intuitive sensitivity. It just takes a little determination to get the hang of it (a meditation retreat is an excellent way to break through). As those who have tried it can attest, meditation is not as hard as you might think.

The current widespread interest in meditation arose out of the popularization of Eastern practices like yoga. It was once difficult for Westerners to learn meditation without going to Asian countries, or at least adopting their cultural trappings, rituals, and, all too often, some religious dogma. These days, it is easy for anyone to learn to meditate without joining a religious group or adopting any particular beliefs. Buddhist meditation techniques are simple and great, because the path of Buddhism is largely meditation practice itself. Another interesting form of meditation is Tai Chi, which is like a cross between meditation and moving yoga. Buddhism and Taoism, paths sometimes referred to as religions, are exceptional, as they do not revolve around beliefs at all—

only practice. In any case, the practice of developing intuitive intelligence through mindfulness transcends all religions and ideologies. No beliefs are required, just a willingness to try the practice and see what happens.

No matter what you believe, connecting with spirit through meditation will bring a stronger sense of meaning to your life. The systematic practice of mindfulness of the body, breathing or focusing on an object, quiets the chattering mind, ignores distractions, and creates space for intuition to operate freely. It turns down the volume of the five physical senses so that you can fine-tune your inner "wireless connection" and find a clear channel in a wild and wooly sea of noise. What your intuition senses does not originate in your mind; insights are the natural result of conscious connection with Infinite Intelligence.

The Go Master's Secret Weapon: The board game Go is the national game of Japan, although it originated in China around the time of the I Ching, more than 2,500 years ago. According to legend, an ancient Chinese emperor commanded that a sage develop a game to improve the intelligence of his son, the prince. Like chess, Go is a board game for two players that uses black and white stones (yin

and yang). It is a marvelous training to learn how to balance forming good boundaries with the freedom of making expansive new connections—a good description of intuitive intelligence in action.

Master champions of Go are revered in Japan as national heroes. One of the most famous Go masters was known for using meditation as part of his strategy. Paradoxically, his meditation focus was to let go of caring about winning. And, of course, he usually won! He became famous and made a fortune, but he remained unattached to any of it. Despite his glory and fame, he remained a modest man whose example influenced the multitudes who followed him—and all because of his secret weapon: meditation.

How I Learned to Meditate

As mentioned, a meditation retreat is the best way to learn and break in a meditation practice. I had my first such experience near the end of Stage One. When I was twenty-nine years old, I took a sabbatical from my fledgling software career to embark on a worldwide pilgrimage. One of my destinations was India, where I wanted to delve into meditation and yoga and see if I could meet an "enlightened being." (I thought my odds would be better there.) Although I was attracted to visiting the homeland of the yogic arts, India was a vast, overpopulated country where I didn't know a soul. I thought it might be a good idea to learn how to meditate before I left home, so I enrolled in a ten-day meditation retreat at Ananda Village in northern California. There, a chance meeting and an unexpected proposition changed the course of my life. It was the end of a talk by Mataji Indra Devi, a well-known 83-year-old yoga teacher who was visiting the community from India. Until that day, I personally had never heard of her.

After an inspiring talk about the relationship between love and nonattachment (a theme I was destined to hear many more times), the four-feet-eleven, eighty-three-year-old yoga pioneer demonstrated some yoga poses, including standing on her head—an impressive feat at any age! At the end of her talk and demonstration, Mataji announced that she was looking for a strong person to help take her elderly naturopath husband, who had suffered a stroke in California and was now in a wheelchair, back to India. She would pay all expenses and provide the caretaker with a place to live and be of service at her compound in southern India. Any volunteers?

There I was, passport in hand, having disposed of my worldly possessions and ready to take a year to cap off my Stage One period of self-discovery. Along with visiting my new friend Nigel in New Zealand, going to India to study with masters of yoga and meditation had been at the top of my travel wish list for a long time. It was perfect synchronicity to meet Mataji at exactly the right place at the right time. My hand went up, but so did those of six other students. Impressed by the synchronicity of her announcement coupled with my total readiness to go, I had no doubt that I was destined to go to India and work for Mataji.

After a series of hits and misses trying to get a meeting with her, that is exactly what happened. But rather than employing me as her husband's caretaker, she came up with a new idea—to have me ghostwrite her autobiography. When I called her and she surprised me with this change of plans, I noted that it was another amazing coincidence. I told her I was an aspiring writer and a fast typist. She hadn't known this when she made me the offer, but ever comfortable with the workings of destiny, this wise woman replied, "Good!" as if she had all along.

After living in India, studying yoga with Mataji and other masters for eleven months, and visiting the ashrams and monasteries of several prominent gurus that she knew, I was bounced out of India for overstaying my visa. I jumped over to Sri Lanka, a nearby island nation, intending to get a new visa to return to India as soon as I could. Sri Lanka is a Buddhist country; I took my first meditation retreat there, offered by a German Buddhist nun named Ayya Khema at a beautiful hilltop meditation center. It was ten days in silence—quite a challenge for anyone, but especially for an extrovert like me.

And it was difficult. It involved six or seven hours of sitting meditation daily, plus a session or two of walking meditation and simple meals—all in complete silence with no distractions or trace of socializing, even during mealtime. Although there were students from all over the world, and English was not Ayya's first language, Ayya gave a little "dharma talk" in English each evening. In addition, each student had a daily consultation with Ayya, which was the only time we were allowed to speak.

True to Germanic stereotype, Ayya Khema had a serious personality. She understood that self-discipline and determined effort is what it takes to break through stubborn unconscious mental habits. Her retreat format was so strict that past students had come to lovingly refer to her as "Attila the nun!" By the third day of what felt like a severe "mental fasting" regimen, I was having a difficult time, feeling discouraged and getting down on myself for so frequently drifting off into daydream land. On the fourth day, during my interview with Ayya, I complained about my tendency to lose concentration and drift off. She simply asked me what I did when I realized that I had been daydreaming. I replied that I got angry with myself and, in my frustration, would berate myself.

Now, Ayya had taught us how to use a "noting" technique to help with letting go of thinking during meditation, whereby you label thoughts and feelings as they come up, using categorical tags like "thinking," "feeling," or "hearing." We avoided getting too specific with labels because that tends to bring up images and more thoughts, in a vicious cycle. For instance, "hearing" is a more practical label to use than "dog barking," because it's easier to let go if you don't create more thoughts and images about whatever is impinging on your senses. Just let it go, like a cloud passing in the sky.

Regarding my anger toward myself, Ayya suggested that I pay mindful attention when it happened and likewise give it a label, to make it easier to let go of. After toying with labels like "self-criticism," I decided to go with "self-hatred." This was powerful for me, because I had been plagued with criticism my whole life and had even been taught it was a positive thing. Self-hatred certainly seemed like a strong enough label to be an effective deterrent, a real encouragement to let go of that kind of thinking. I had to accept it before I could let it go, and accepting my self-loathing was not an easy pill to swallow. But I could hardly avoid it when it was insisting on disrupting my earnest efforts to let go of thinking!

On the fifth or sixth day of the retreat I broke through and experienced the graceful joy of meditation through just being, accepting whatever arose without getting hooked by, or dwelling on, related thoughts or feelings. It was the blissful feeling of my ego dissolving. During such moments of ecstasy, I imagined this was what it would feel like to be in the transporter of the Starship Enterprise. After this breakthrough experience, like riding a bicycle, it became relatively easy for me to quickly reach a balanced state of steady mindfulness. I am nothing but grateful for how this skill has served me well in countless situations ever since.

In one of our daily sessions, Ayya asked me what I had been doing during the year I had spent in India before coming to Sri Lanka. I shared that I had been ghostwriting a book for Mataji Indra Devi in India—whom Ayya knew personally—and she revealed that she also could use help putting a book together. She offered me an all-expenses-paid volunteer position as her assistant on her upcoming world tour, in which my primary job would be to help her compile her best talks in good English.

So I did. And while we traveled through Australia, New Zealand, and Europe and I worked on the book, she also trained me how to teach the simple Buddhist form of meditation, known as Vipassana, or "insight meditation." She even let me lead some of the groups and give the "dharma talk" on some aspects of Buddhist theory. This led to a new vocation for me. After I returned home from what turned out to be a two-year pilgrimage, I taught insight meditation classes for the City of Portland and became the meditation minister for a major New Thought church for a few years.

One of the textbooks I used in my meditation courses was *The Three-Minute Meditator* by David Harp. In this book, Harp explains how the essence of meditation is letting go of thinking about distracting thoughts and feelings that arise, while paying attention to and noting whatever arises in your conscious awareness. He emphasizes that this technique can be done anytime, anywhere, even in line at a grocery store or bank.[19]

So, in addition to setting aside a period for daily meditation practice, also look for ways to practice mindfulness throughout a busy day—if only for a few minutes at a time—by noticing thoughts or feelings as they arise and letting go of your attachments and reactions.

To anyone who says they don't have time to meditate, Donald Altman, a psychotherapist and author of *The Joy Compass* and *One-Minute Mindfulness*, points out that many people actually spend hours at a time in a sort of meditation—online. Engaging in ego-stimulating tasks—like surfing social networks, internet shopping, downloading videos, or following celebrities—are what he cites as examples of online "meditation." Taking responsibility for where you put your attention, and mindfully choosing activities that support clarity and relaxation instead of worry and anxiety, will make you less stressed, happier, and, incidentally, more in tune with intuition.

Meditation provides a clear channel for impressions from the unconscious. It hones concentration and insight, which, interestingly, are respectively analogous to hunter and gatherer energies. The yang, or hunter, side of meditation focuses on the object of concentration (mantra, breath, picture, candle flame, music, and so forth) in order to pointedly focus the mind. The yin, or gatherer, aspect is openness and receptivity to insights that arise via meditation after the mind has calmed down.

Concentration: The Left Brain's Role in Meditation

Formal meditation techniques facilitate a state of mental stillness by means of focused concentration. The exercise of paying attention to just one thing settles the mind, allowing the emotional brain to rest a bit (and the intuitive channel to open). A specific object of concentration helps the meditator focus, quieting random noise and internal dialogue. For this purpose, objects of concentration that have proven beneficial include breath, physical sensations, an external object such as a candle or mandala, repetition of a mantra, or just immersion in a feeling of joy, love, or compassion. Sometimes guided scripts, which can be read or listened to, help the mind let go of busyness to enter a more receptive state. I find the breath to be an excellent object of concentration because it is always with me, and because focusing on the sensation of breathing is ideal for discreetly practicing mindfulness in public.

I once heard the Indian meditation master Sai Baba use an interesting analogy to clarify the concentration object's function in meditation. He said to imagine stepping on a bed of thorns, symbolizing all the thoughts that tend to stick in your mind, and then to pull one out and use it to dig out the others. This is how using a thought, feeling, or sensation as your object of concentration (like a mantra or the breath) lets you more easily let go of the rest: you let go of thinking about all the other thoughts by focusing on that one. When you have let go of thinking about everything but the one single thorn, you can let go of that too and just notice whatever arises from that point on without attaching to any of it. This puts you into a blissful state of openness that the modern mystic Krishnamurti referred to as choiceless awareness.

When I was a meditation teacher, some students complained that they just couldn't meditate because they couldn't stop thoughts. This is a common misunderstanding about the aim of meditation: not to block thoughts but to learn how to observe without dwelling on them or even identifying with them as "my thoughts." By merely observing thoughts and feelings and letting them pass you by without thinking about them, you can avoid getting caught up in the spiral of thinking, then seeing images in your mind's eye that prompt an emotional reaction, which in turn leads to more thoughts—in an endless (and exhausting) cycle.

Letting go is the simplest thing in the world, but easy to forget. Letting go may be mechanically easy, but our attachments and aversions make it difficult. As I once heard an Indian poet eloquently express the paradox on Delhi TV, "It's simple to be happy, but it's difficult to be simple."

Although it has many benefits, meditation is not about achieving anything. Rather than a striving for perfection, it is a process of elimination, a sort of mental fasting. Like dietary fasting, it is a challenge. The mind has a habit of immediately "taking a bite" of whatever thoughts happen to show up. We often still refer to them as "my thoughts," although we didn't welcome or desire them. Human beings tend to identify with thoughts. Investing our attention in them is a compulsive mental habit most of the time. The thoughts that *seem* like they belong to you appear that way because you have identified with them in the past. You have made a nest for them. Each of us has thinking patterns we must be willing to break if we want to go beyond our comfort zone to do anything important or bold. We need to learn to pay attention and let mindfulness intervene to break up the way we reflexively identify with habits of thought.

Try this short exercise: Close your eyes for a few moments and release whatever thoughts come. Notice them, but just let them float by like passing clouds. Do this for a minute or two and you will find unwanted thoughts keep popping up. Soon, if you sit still long enough without getting hooked into thinking, you will start to experience a quieter, more spacious aspect of the mind that is like a clear sky. In the meantime, thoughts come and go, seemingly on their own. Since you didn't invite them or even want them, what makes the thoughts that arise yours any more than the clouds passing in the sky? Practice the natural mindfulness of our hunter-gatherer ancestors, to gain freedom from giving attention to recurring thoughts and worries that do you no good.

A Beginning Meditation

Here's an easy way to begin a meditation practice: Find a spot where you can be alone and undisturbed for fifteen or twenty minutes. Sit comfortably in a chair or on a cushion on the floor, close your eyes, and concentrate on your breath. Bring your attention to the sensation of inhaling and exhaling—not with any special kind of breathing, deep or otherwise. Quietly watch the rise and fall of the breath, noting the subtle physical sensation of air coming in and out of the nostrils. Or note the rise and fall of the abdomen with each breath.

Sit still long enough to allow the chattering of your mind to simmer down, which can take up to fifteen minutes. Use an object of concentration, like the breath or the hum of a fan, and continue until your mind gradually grows still.

I compare this slow settling down of the mind to how boiling water eventually settles after you take the pan off the burner. The flames represent the desires and attachments that stir up the mind. Even when you turn off the flames of desire, the boiling water will continue to churn before it cools to a more tranquil state. This takes ten or fifteen minutes at first. This process can be frustrating to a novice, who may wonder if their mind is ever going to settle. But after a bit of regular patient practice, you will find that you can slip into a meditative state more and more quickly.

When first starting a meditation session, I suggest using a timer and committing yourself to sitting still—and only that—for twenty minutes. Forget about achieving results (though you will soon enough). Psychologically, letting go of attachment to outcomes reduces a tendency to put pressure on yourself to do it right or to wonder if you are being successful at meditating. If you commit to just sitting still and stick to taking a daily "time out," you will start meditating—if only because as long as you are just sitting, there is nothing better to do! With practice, it becomes second nature to meditate wherever you are.

Let breath be your anchor. Your breath is an excellent object of concentrated awareness because it is always happening for you—when you are standing in line, when you are riding an elevator, and during in-between times throughout the day. And it's discreet in that it is not obvious that you are meditating.

While it is skillful to develop a regular sitting practice, you benefit from each and every possible instance of mindfulness throughout the day. Ayya Khema used to say that every single moment of mindfulness is mentally purifying. The technique is simple: let go of rapidly changing thoughts and feelings by concentrating on your breath (or mantra or other object), while being open to and mindful of whatever thoughts and feelings might arise in your field of consciousness.

The Letting-Go Mantra

As an alternative to mindfulness of breathing or the body, a mantra is a word or phrase that can be used as an object for concentration. In the ancient yoga tradition, a teacher or guru would assign a student a phrase in Sanskrit—the ancient language of India—to repeat as a mantra. By repeating a phrase over and over, the mind becomes "one-pointed"—concentrated on the mantra to the exclusion of other passing thoughts. The human brain can only focus on one thing at a time. You can't simultaneously write a poem and do a math problem. Nor can you remember your high school reunion and look forward to your son's college graduation in the same moment. Likewise, when you're focused on a mantra, the static in your mind has no choice but to simmer down because of your attention to one object.

When I taught meditation, I invented a mantra that I shared with my students. I found this phrase particularly useful for clearing the mind and increasing mindfulness throughout the day (which I later discovered made me better at noticing synchronicities). My little mantra consisted of only two words: *Letting Go.*

Try it right now. Just close your eyes and take a full breath, thinking the word *Letting* as you inhale and the word *Go* as you exhale. Repeat. When you reflect on the meaning of these two words, this mantra is reminding you to do what meditation is all about—the letting go of attachment to thoughts and feelings. You can use my letting-go mantra anywhere and at any time. (I do this one often every day.) It helps instill inner peace and serves as a conscious reminder that, rather than achieving anything, letting go is the key to having a clear and open mind. In addition, getting free of "busy mind" creates an opening for intuitive insights to alight like butterflies settling onto a sunflower.

The Let-Go License Plate: In 2016, when I leased a new hybrid car, the dealer offered to get me vanity plates. I said, "Okay, but only if I can have the same ones I had in 1979 on my hippie van"—a license plate I'd never been able to get again after selling everything and going to India. It was just two words: "Let Go."

The dealer got on the computer to look up availability and informed me that it was still not available, which I told him had been the case for the past thirty-five years. So, I asked him to just have the DMV send me whatever they would. I wanted those plates, but I let it go. Six weeks later, my new plates came in the mail from the state of Oregon. To my surprise, the large blue letters that matched the color of my new car read "LET GO." I could hardly believe it. I had let go of those plates and they came to me. What a beautiful reminder of the power of letting go! Ironically, now I have to deal with attachment, because I swear I will never let go of those plates again!

Harvesting Intuitive Insights during Meditation

Meditation aims to let go for the sake of cultivating transcendent consciousness. But, as we have seen, another major benefit is increased intuitive sensitivity. Vipassana, or "insight meditation," traditionally takes advantage of this fact to further insight into profound characteristics of existence (like impermanence, constant change, no lasting satisfactions, etc.).

Considering the value of creative insights that could arise during a meditation session, it can be useful to interrupt your concentration efforts long enough for the left brain to record them. Rather than placing all the emphasis on just releasing thoughts—especially if you are facing a major decision—it is fine to note whatever pops up during your sitting with a pen and paper or a recording device. Then, after making a note of it, return to your meditation.

Although unconventional, there is creative value in adapting your meditation practice like this if you are on the lookout for signs and omens. In this way, mindfulness develops your ability to hear the voice of intuition connecting you with Creative Power.

Intuitive Intelligence Tilts the Odds in Your Favor

Developing intuitive intelligence by paying attention to synchronicities and other unusual occurrences will improve your odds of manifesting anything that you can envision. Every individual is unique, so find your own way of cultivating intuitive mindfulness, something that feels natural to you. And then make it a habit.

Skillful decision-making is a litmus test for intuitive intelligence. The more you exercise intuitive intelligence and learn to trust it, the more reliable your higher instincts become. On the other hand, the less it is exercised, the less trust you will place in your intuition, and the more likely you'll end up letting others make important decisions for you. To make matters worse in the long run, by not trusting your intuition, you will miss more opportunities to develop it.

Intuitive intelligence is a skill that needs to be practiced, like dancing. At first you feel awkward and occasionally trip over your own feet. But through practice, you'll find your sense of rhythm, until you're in sync with a power much greater than anything you've ever known. Though it is not an exact science, cultivating intuitive mindfulness tilts the odds in your favor and gives you an advantage on every playing field in your life.

Improve Intuitive Skill by Taking Risks

Intuitive skill improves by trial and error. Actively test intuitive hunches by taking little risks. Make a game out of it—like gambling for insights.

Follow up your hunches by asking tough questions, interviewing others, and testing your perceptions. Was it truly intuition in action? How well can you differentiate between a gut feeling, a wonderfully imaginative idea, or ego-driven wishful thinking? You may be surprised at how many good hunches a controlling ego routinely overlooks or discredits!

For instance, if your intuition tells you this is a good time to make an important phone call, you don't have to think twice. Go with your hunch and just do it. By starting out with small risks, you can discover how good your sense of timing can be. You can learn how to let go of interference and blockage, and gain confidence in your ability to draw on intuitive intelligence when you need it most. Start with small bets, but do start taking risks.

The more you come to trust your intuition by awakening it through mindfulness practice, the more perceptive and aware you become over time. You will start noticing all kinds of guideposts and signs, including unexpected synchronicities, on a regular basis. Your intuitive antenna will vibrate and start to hum. Synchronicities—which have been happening the whole time—will become apparent more easily and often. Awareness of synchronicity will inform you and improve your decision-making—almost like a guardian angel. You will handle obstacles more easily, make fewer mistakes, and bounce back more quickly when you do. You will maintain a higher awareness of Infinite Intelligence and the creative powers available to you. Achieving goals will happen more easily and your confidence will progressively increase. It's gratifying how much more smooth life can become as you develop intuitive mindfulness, but this receptivity is just the first half of realizing intuitive intelligence.

The other half has to do with making sense of intuitive impressions. In the next few chapters, we will explore archetypes, dreams, and divination systems like the I Ching. Each can help the left brain translate and make sense of intuitive information received by the right brain so that our conscious mind can put it to good use.

7

Invoking Archetypes

Just as everybody possesses instincts, so he also possesses a stock of archetypal images. . . . In each of these images there is a little piece of human psychology and human fate, a remnant of the joys and sorrows that have been repeated countless times in our ancestral history.

—**Carl Jung**

In the previous chapter we considered ways to call forth our intuitive intelligence. Now we investigate how intuitive impressions can be interpreted and empowered by the conscious mind using psychological structures called archetypes. The archetype's role as a psychic structure emanating from our collective unconscious was one of Carl Jung's most groundbreaking contributions to psychology. According to Jung, an archetype is a pattern of thought or image that's collectively inherited, unconscious, and universally available to us via the unconscious mind.

For Jung, archetypes serve as a kind of psychic blueprint for how humans perceive, interpret, and respond to situations and experiences. Using archetypes, humanity has told and retold stories of our tragedies and triumphs, our fragilities and strengths, and how our soul evolves through the education of life.

Although each of us has a unique story, the overarching theme of archetypal stories is what Joseph Campbell called the "hero's journey." In Campbell's magnum opus *The Hero with a Thousand Faces* (1949), he discusses his theory of the journey of the archetypal hero found in mythologies from around the world.

Archetypal Psychology

From a psychological point of view, archetypes are innate to each of us but also universal—providing patterns, forms, or images, core ideas that pervade human experience and offer psychological power we can deliberately tap for strength and wisdom. They can be called up by a guided meditation or written treatment (see the template for a manifestation meditation in appendix A). They symbolize basic human motivations, values, and personality traits central to guiding the psyche. These inherited patterns may take the form of a familiar character, an image, a story, or even a feeling state. Archetypes, Jung wrote, are "a living system of reactions and aptitudes that determine the individual's life in invisible ways."[1]

Archetypes show up in religion, linguistics, rituals, art, myths, and legends. On a personal level, you can find them in your dreams, fantasies, and demeanor. They influence everything you feel, think, and do. They influence the people around you. You can think of them as preexisting patterns, a shared heritage of all mankind, which influence most kinds of human behavior, if on an unconscious level. Because they are "downloaded" from our collective consciousness (as Jung called it), archetypes are universal.

In *Man and His Symbols*, Jung explains that archetypes "are pieces of life itself—images that are integrally connected to the living individual by the bridge of the emotions."[2] Using what we have learned from archetypal psychology, we can map these emotions—from the most courageous energies of humankind to the darkest and most frightful. Many archetypes can be recognized by images and emotions with primitive origins, whose roots are wired deeply in the unconscious mind.

Often coming through dreams or fantasies, archetypes are picked up by the more instinctual and holistic right brain, as aspects of the unconscious attract our attention or prompt our impulses. The intuitive antenna that tunes the right brain in to the reservoir of archetypes—Jung's collective unconscious—helps us connect with archetypal energies, powers, themes, and patterns of behavior. Archetypes lend form to images and impressions taken in by the right brain, and ultimately help the conscious left brain to interpret and make sense of them.

Jung referenced three different kinds of archetypes: the four main aspects of the psyche, anthropomorphic or "personified" archetypes, and what he called "transformational archetypes." Personified archetypes are the ones that take a human form such as the Damsel in Distress, the Child, the Martyr, and so on. Transformational archetypes are life experiences and processes such as falling in love, growing old, having a religious experience, or losing a friend to betrayal.

According to Jung's approach, the four primary archetypes of the human psyche are the Personal Self (commonly known as Ego), the Shadow (the "dark" side of that ego containing disowned parts of one's larger Self, or soul), the Anima (the feminine aspects of a man's psyche and the masculine aspect of a woman's psyche), and the Persona (the appearance we present to the world—the mask, our ego presentation, our personality).

It's useful to think about archetypes as subpersonalities that we can call up from within our subconscious mind to protect and inspire us on our path to psychological individuation and personal fulfillment. Every archetype, both light and dark, serves a purpose on life's journey. Archetypal psychology, as it has evolved since Jung, is not interested in the integration of the multiple psychic persons to a unified Self. The profound Jungian analyst, James Hillman, who founded a movement toward archetypal psychology, suggested that forcing our subconscious selves into an abstract unity does not work and is often devaluing. He theorized that each archetype has its due and deserves respect in its own right. In other words, to tend to the soul, varieties of archetypes—such as the many that appear in traditional mythologies—must be acknowledged and nurtured.

Exploring the relationship between myth and his archetypal psychology, Hillman wrote:

> The [power] of myth, its reality, resides precisely in its power to seize and influence our psychic life. The Greeks knew this so well, and so they had no depth psychology and psychopathology such as we have. They had myths. And we have no myths as such—instead, depth psychology and psychopathology. Therefore . . . psychology shows myths in modern dress and myths show our depth psychology in ancient dress.[3]

Since they reside within the collective unconscious but operate through us individually, becoming more mindful of archetypes will expand your self-knowledge and guide your behaviors—including more skillful decision-making in the search for meaning.

As you watch film and television, pay attention to how significantly the role of archetypal characters embodies nearly all of storytelling. Archetypes may appear as mythological characters, but remember that such projections are colorful approximations. The cultural trappings that archetypes assume vary, but Jung discovered that the fundamental identities of archetypes remain intact throughout time and across cultures. Vividly featured in ancient myths, they are also on display in the popular culture of contemporary film and music. Marilyn Monroe can be thought of as the Siren or Goddess of Love and James Dean or Marlon Brando as the Rebel. The Wise Old Man is clearly embodied by Gandalf in *The Lord of The Rings*, as well as Obi-Wan Kenobi in the *Star Wars* films.

The Hero is a prime example of a universal archetype that has prominently appeared throughout human history. (Even at age five, my grandson related to the hero archetype in the form of Spiderman and other comic book superheroes.) The narrative patterns of the archetypal hero in ancient epic stories, religious writings, poems like Homer's *Odyssey*, and the myth of King Arthur, as well as modern storytelling, informed renowned mythologist Joseph Campbell's concept of the Hero's journey.[4] The Hero's journey reveals a roadmap of sorts for our personal struggle to individuate, and the process of an entire culture developing a collective identity. In fact, it is a central archetype for the courageous activity of strategic decision-making. In a sense, this book is about manifesting your inner Hero through bold decisions.

Archetypes in Dreams

Dreaming is a form of communication between the 'Self' archetype and the collective unconscious, where archetypes can operate as symbols within the dream, helping to facilitate some sort of interaction or dialogue. According to Jung, the symbols and images that appear in dreams represent factors related to the process of expressing and fully developing the Self. To become whole and able to fulfill our life's purpose, we can learn from archetypal symbols in our field of conscious awareness, including dreams that we remember and record. Dream interpretation, therefore, can be helpful in our development as visionaries.

Archetypal symbols and themes have appeared in the dreams of people of cultures around the world and throughout history. It is especially important to take note and analyze the occurrence of an archetypal dream—or "big dream," a term that Jung started using after visiting the Elongi tribe of East Africa. He learned that they distinguished between "little dreams" that carry personal meaning and "big dreams" that come from the collective memory and contain symbols that are common to all humans. Big dreams are often emotionally vibrant, occurring during times of great change or crisis, and contain messages from archetypal figures. For example, the Wise Old Man may show up as a teacher, father, or other authority figure offering guidance and wisdom. The Great Mother could appear as your mother, an old woman, a queen, or a goddess. An archetype can manifest in your dreams to provide nurturing support and positive reinforcement, but it could also appear as a dangerous and domineering figure, such as an ogre, a dragon or a trickster.

In modern times, many scientists have revealed that their most momentous discoveries came to them in dreams. We must never dismiss dreams as a resource for information and inspiration. At the very least, paying attention to them will put you in touch with subtle currents flowing inside your psyche and help you to accelerate the healing of inner conflicts or to detect aspects of your inner self that were previously unacknowledged.

Dreams can be understood in karmic terms, like in the movie *Groundhog Day*, where we keep having versions of the same dream (or life pattern) until we make some changes. If we ignore the offered guidance, there can be consequences. In this sense, archetypal dream interpretation is a powerful decision-making aid once you learn how to make use of the wisdom available to you.

Jung was a master of dream interpretation, a skill he developed beyond his peers. Freud recognized the significance of dreams, but he viewed dreams primarily as expressing repressed and disguised (naughty) desires. For Jung, dreams were more than a symptom of neurotic struggles. Part of his genius was showing how dreams, which indeed reflect the personal unconscious of unresolved conflicts, can also be "big dreams" acting as messengers from the collective unconscious.

Jung felt that our dreams were meant to be understood, shared, and lived. For him, the real purpose of dreams was as a catalyst for change and a guidepost to personal evolution. He taught that we should learn and manifest the lessons of our dreams in how we approach life. As Jung put it, "The dream provides the answer through the symbol, which one must understand."[5] Besides recording his own dreams, Jung taught his five children to keep dream books and to engage through them in a dialogue with the unconscious. (He also made visual images of his dreams, now beautifully collected in the *The Red Book*.)

Nowadays plenty of books, dictionaries, and websites help with dream interpretation, but symbols that appear in dreams are mostly subjective. They reflect the dreamer's personal experiences, conditioning, and memories. The context in which these images appear, which are as important as the image itself, may lend to a specific personal connotation and meaning.

Jung thought that dream guides were not very trustworthy because they assumed that the same symbol would always mean the same thing in any dream for any person. He had observed that the exact same thing dreamed by two different dreamers could easily mean two *totally different* things. Being carried away by water, for example by a flowing river, could mean freedom to one person and danger to another, depending on the context of the dream as well as the unconscious thoughts that lie behind the dream's content.

In light of this highly personal aspect, Jung believed everyone had the power within to unlock the meaning of their own unique dreams. He even advised activating your intuition before consulting an outside source. In a letter, he describes his dream perception process, which included asking some questions:

"Who or what has come alive in [the dream]? Who or what has entered my psychic life and created disturbances and wants to be heard?" To this you should add: "Let it speak!" Then switch off your noisy consciousness and listen quietly inwards and look at the images that appear before your inner eye, or hearken to the words which the muscles of your speech apparatus are trying to form. Write down what then comes without criticism. Images should be drawn or painted assiduously no matter whether you can do it or not. . . . Meditate on them afterwards and every day go on developing what is unsatisfactory about them. The important thing is to let the unconscious take the lead.[6]

There is more than one way to keep track of dreams. Jung kept a notebook at his bedside, as many people do. Upon waking, he would write down what he could remember of his dreams. If Jung could have recorded his dreams using a voice recorder—as I prefer to do—he probably would have embraced the newer technology. (It is so much easier, and you don't have to turn on the light or find the pen.) Once you've recorded your dreams, start trying to interpret what they mean. Avoid self-censoring or second-guessing your impressions. Let your mind generate free associations based on images you recall from the dream and record them.

Even if you're seeking insight into an important choice, don't narrow your dream interpretation to that specific issue—at least not at first. Be open-minded and receptive. Answers and insights may emerge in a different order than you were looking for. Record them as quickly as you can, without dwelling on what you put down. First impressions are most useful!

Since dreams are not to be taken literally, you may want to consult a dream dictionary to tease out some of the meaning, then reconstruct what you remember of the dream into a narrative story or letter to yourself. By the way, the familiar people and objects that appear in your dream do not represent the same people or objects in your waking reality. Every person who appears in a dream represents *an archetype* that is reflecting back a part of you that is psychologically active. (Explore Jung's methodologies of dream interpretation in *Dream Analysis: Notes of the Seminar Given in 1928–30.*)

Invoking an Archetype

You know how differently you can feel just by changing the way you dress? An archetype can be compared to a costume you put on to embody the energy of the Sage or Elder, the Sovereign or Warrior, the Trickster, Maiden, Eternal Child, God, Goddess, Demon, or Angel. Many people find personalized projections easier to relate to and through them are more easily able to commune with the mystical and unknowable.

Archetypes are not always anthropomorphic, however; some are templates for situations and experiences, such as growing and evolving, an epiphany or flash of enlightenment, loss of innocence, being stuck in an unresolvable conflict, or achieving ecstatic union with Divine

Mystery. Dreams can be thought of as synchronistic occurrences themselves, bringing "situational" archetypes to our attention.

Archetypes reside in the collective unconscious, that reservoir of Infinite Intelligence to which we all have access. These power resources are not off in the distance on a foggy mountaintop. When called upon, they immediately come alive within you, in your heart and soul. These are recognizable energies that you can learn to channel, to resolve dilemmas or make creative decisions.

When you call up an archetype, you are drawing from a realm of awesome power, so don't get carried away. Like the two wires that run power to an electrical appliance, the ability to safely channel this powerful current requires care. You are allowing a bit of some powerful current to flow through you, rather than generating an energy from within yourself. The danger is that people can get so caught up running archetypal energy that they forget who they are, overidentify with the archetype, or start to believe they are personally all-powerful. When the ego gets overinflated, we start to run into trouble; we are in danger of burning out or going crazy.

We must find the right relationship to our archetypal energy without being overtaken by it. Believing that you *are* a god or goddess is a grandiose delusion. Becoming possessed by an archetype to that extent is overwhelming and self-destructive and, in extreme cases, can feed a narcissistic personality disorder or overempower other shadowy subpersonalities. The Goddess or Sovereign gets greedy and becomes the Tyrant. The Warrior turns into a Pillager. The Lover transforms into an Addict. The Magician becomes the evil Sorcerer, and so forth.

We certainly do not want to reenact the folly of young Icarus of Greek myth who, against the advice of his father, soared too close to the sun, melting his wax wings and crashing into the sea. You won't be consumed by archetypal power if you use it carefully. And once you learn how to channel archetypes, these powerful resources can help you make more effective and timely decisions and produce significant positive changes in your career and life.

Archetypes That Support Visionary Decision Making

Many archetypes play a role in decision-making, including the Mentor, the Trickster, and even the Lover (especially when someone is inspired to do what they love). Archetypes central to VDM are the Muse, the Sovereign, and the Magician. The Warrior is another crucial archetype that one must activate when it becomes necessary to defend boundaries.

Both the Hunter and the Gatherer are dynamic, active archetypes that are also relevant to Visionary Decision Making. To the Greeks (and Romans), Demeter (or Ceres) was the goddess of the harvest, the ultimate gatherer, and Artemis (or Diana) was the goddess of the hunt. The Hunter is more outgoing and the Gatherer more receiving, but they are two sides of the same harvesting coin. They both play an active and important role in the VDM process.

The Hunter archetype connects us with the energy of vigilance, exploration, and focused attention. It helps you set your sights on what you want the most. All forms of vigilance are associated with the Hunter because she (or he) is sensitively attuned to noticing clues and signals. In the VDM process, this especially includes being on the lookout for signals and synchronicities.

Invoking the Gatherer results in a greater receptivity to the bounty of Infinite Intelligence, which can manifest in the form of good ideas, inspirations, and intuitive sensations. It is a receptive dynamic, an active and deliberate openness. You are opening to the bounty of the universe—to what will specifically nourish you and your group or tribe. The Hunter and Gatherer archetypes reinforce one another toward the attainment of their overarching objective, which is the realization of abundance for personal and collective well-being.

To understand the Hunter and Gatherer energy dynamic, I return to my cousin Lennie, who embodies both. Though he never kills for sport, Lennie often wins the annual award for most successful deer hunter in the county; he is also an exceptional fisherman and gardener. Operating from the solar-assisted house he built for himself in the woods, Lennie has carved out a highly self-sufficient life through a combination of hunting and gathering, of initiated action and receptivity to opportunity.

The Hunter and Gatherer archetypes correspond to the Taoist principles of yin and yang—two complementary energies that mix in physical reality and also in thought, emotion, and consciousness. Yang is associated with left-brained functions. Exploration and analysis are the yang elements of the Hunter archetype. The active probing and scanning function of the intuitive antenna is a yang function—as in probing the creative aspect of Infinite Intelligence, collecting information, and analyzing what it means. Yin, on the other hand, is open and receptive. Yin reflects what we sometimes refer to as right-brain energy. Yin creates the inner conditions that attract and pick up on insights. The law of attraction, which we looked at earlier, is about leveraging your receptive yin power.

Another powerful archetype is the Muse, a psychological agent of fascination that can help us channel the power of attraction and magnetize a creative direction. In Greek mythology, the Muses were minor goddesses who personified knowledge and inspiration. Invoking the Muse stimulates intuition and creativity, but writers, artists, and musicians aren't the only ones who can benefit from the Muse's help. Channeling her can help anyone tap into Infinite Intelligence to activate the expression of his or her talents while illuminating truths with sustained energy.

Visionary Decision Making leverages the four foundational archetypes presented in James Hillman's book *King, Warrior, Magician, Lover*. Each of these plays a central role in the VDM process.

The Lover increases passion for your highest vocational or personal priority, facilitating a fulfilling outcome for any inspiration, dream, or aspiration. The Lover archetype inspired the meme, "Do what you love and the money will follow." Focused love becomes passion, which affixes your attention and energy to your goal. Devotion—whether to a cause or creative invention or path in life—is the booster rocket that gets you into orbit where you can navigate life almost effortlessly through one adjustment at a time. The shadow side of the Lover archetype is the Addict or Addicted Lover, whose depth of passion becomes insatiable, and the persistent desire and need for personal fulfillment becomes destructive to himself and others around him.

Invoking the Magician energizes creativity and inventiveness. The Magician archetype enhances your ability to see new combinations and connections and helps with innovative solutions. It can effortlessly bridge the inner world of mind and spirit to the outer world of creation and physical manifestation. The Magician views all problems as learning adventures, sees through appearances, and gets right to the heart of things. This archetype ultimately creates a more abundant playing field. In my experience, Magician energy supported me in the invention of multimedia versions of divination systems to aid intuitive decision-making. It served me so well that I made a giant replica of The Magus tarot card, which I keep in my office to remind me of my connection to it. The shadow side of the Magician is black magic—the use of creative power to manipulate or cast a spell to control, take advantage, deceive, distract, or even harm others.

Invoking the Warrior archetype isn't necessarily about being aggressive, though assertiveness may be called for under certain circumstances. The Warrior's primary job is to defend the boundaries and protect the tender unfolding of new directions and what we value most (including children, as in the "mama bear" phenomenon). Internally, the Warrior might guard against distractions and temptations that diminish our ability to pay attention to what's truly important. Addictive temptations or "shiny objects" that distract our attention are deliberately ignored until they fade out of mind. The shadow side of the Warrior archetype is the Masochist, a violent or abusive personality. In extreme cases, when the Warrior becomes a person's permanent state, the Sadist takes control of the psyche and the person becomes detached, cruel, and sometimes sociopathic.

The Sovereign (King, Queen, or CEO) makes decisions and sees that they are carried out for the welfare of the realm—the common good of a community or enterprise. The realm may be a corporate body with employees and customers, or it may be an extended family. The Sovereign's role is to exercise authority and allocate resources to take care of his or her people—not to be served by them (although that happens reciprocally). This executive function is at the very center of Visionary Decision Making. The shadow side of the Sovereign is a self-serving tyrant or power monger whose narcissism posits unattainably high standards for himself and those around him and who then seeks to blame others and win, overpower, or even destroy others for the sake of his ego.

The mature Sovereign is present in the histories and mythology of the world's religions. The Buddha was a prince and heir to a kingdom, with a beautiful wife and extreme comforts—all of which he left behind to dedicate himself to solving the problem of human suffering for all of us. According to biblical myth, King Solomon was invited by God to choose any power he wanted. He could have become an embodiment of the Magician, Warrior, Lover (according to the Bible, he already had seven hundred wives and three hundred concubines), or some other archetype with magical powers. Instead, he chose the Wise Ruler, or Elder, and became renowned for his decision-making.

Consciously connecting with the Sovereign archetype helped me better run my company—a small "kingdom" that included thirty employees and millions of subscribed members. I made a conscious effort daily to identify with the Sovereign and the Magician archetypes. Every morning I would recite an invocation similar to this: "Today I call upon the Powers that be to help me do a good job taking care of my people." Among others, I was invoking the Sovereign archetype to support, direct, and empower my job of taking care of business and "my people"—my employees, customers, and family—throughout the busy day.

Prayer as Invocation

If prayer was something you were taught as a child, you were being taught to invoke an archetype. Praying to an all-knowing, all-powerful God is the most common form of invoking an archetype in the West. You can envision Infinite Power as a single unitary deity—for example, God—or you can see it in terms of an impersonal universal law like the Buddhists. It can be a matter of belief for you, but in terms of your creativity and decision-making process, it doesn't matter either way. You might petition an almighty sovereign who grants favors, a forgiving Parent, Mother Earth, an all-knowing wise oracle, or simply Nature itself. In the Catholic church, they pray to archetypal saints, such as St. Anthony, who knows how to find things that are lost; St. Jude, who helps you find your way when you are lost; and St. Lawrence, the patron saint of cooking (martyred by being roasted on a spit).

The shortcoming of the way most of us were taught to pray as children is that it takes the form of petition—a passive plea for rescue. It is good to be humble, but petitioning prayer can blur the line between humility and low self-esteem.

Other forms of prayer, however, engage and cocreate with Creative Power (an impersonal way to conceive of the divine), which is psychologically different than begging a Creator to do something for you. In this more empowering form of prayer, you are channeling archetypal energies to assist or support you, not do for you. You invoke divine energy to bolster your confidence—your faith in yourself—to rise to an occasion, for blessings upon your endeavors, and to inspire you to do your best.

Throughout history, significant rites like births, weddings, and funerals have always begun with an invocative prayer. In the ancient world, aid was requested from the god or goddess whose help was considered relevant and beneficial. Thus, *The Iliad*, the Greek epic composed three thousand years ago, begins, "Sing, O goddess, of the anger of Achilles . . ." The poet is calling upon the goddess of poetry to aid in the recitation of the poem, but psychologically speaking, he is asking the goddess to sing *through* him. The poet essentially views himself as a channel for the divine archetype of poetry. In ancient times, events like wars, sports, marriages, and banquets all began with an invocative prayer to a god or goddess, and called forth an infusion of empowering archetypal energies.

Like the word "God," prayer is a word that can be compelling or offputting depending on your orientation to traditional religion. As noted, there is a major difference between the praying we were probably taught and invocative prayer that is part of the Visionary Decision Making approach. The primary function of invocative prayer is to implore creative and supportive archetypes that you invite to flow through you. It's an expression of intention and a feeling of gratitude-in-advance as you welcome good results that you and the creative powers are helping to cocreate.

Invocative prayer is the conscious summoning of archetypal energies. Unlike traditional religious prayers, invocative prayer is not a matter of asking for something from the higher power. And it is not bargaining. ("I'll be good if you help me one more time.") It's simply calling upon the kind of energy needed for a specific purpose or a decision. Courage, wisdom, creativity, resilience, and intuition—whatever energies are needed to make visionary decisions.

When going through major transitions, it's helpful to practice an invocative prayer ritual daily—not so different from the habit of morning and evening prayers or meditation. Returning to a ritual that frames every day will help you to stay more connected to Infinite Intelligence during the day and through dreams at night. After you wake up in the morning, you welcome a greater awareness of synchronicities throughout the coming day. Depending upon what you intend to create, build, or preserve that day, you also summon and activate other powers. At night, your affirmative prayer calls forth the healing and enlightening power of dreams.

One invocation to go through your day more open to insights is the Synchronicity Prayer: "May I notice and attend to synchronicities that arise during this day. If I don't understand their meaning, I trust that will be revealed in due course. In the meantime, I am grateful to notice the signals."

No matter how you word your prayers (I recommend composing your own), it helps to create a routine like this:

- Sit and breathe with a fairly straight back. If you need to lean against a cushion, wall, or back of a chair, that is fine. The mind tends to be sharper when we sit or stand in a balanced position rather than slumping or reclining. Take three deep breaths to let go of tension in your body. If you are not going to disturb anybody by doing so, try making an audible "ah" or "om" sound with each exhale.

• Read your invocation—preferably out loud to yourself—taking the time to understand each word.

• Breathe slowly as you let yourself project into it, and feel the power of the archetype that you are invoking.

• Feel the bliss of being mentally magnetic through the clarity of your intention and emotionally magnetic through the infectious power of your desire. Sit quietly in the emotionally magnetic state for as long as you can.

• Make a resolution to notice this attraction consciousness sticking with you throughout your day.

Here are a few suggestions for how invocative prayers might be phrased (feel free to borrow from these examples and customize your own as well):

Sample Morning Invocations

May I notice all the magical moments today, as life unfolds synchronistically and perfectly, according to Destiny's plan.
As I face an important decision, I invoke the power of Courage, so that my choices will not be distracted by fear.
May Wisdom guide my decisions today; may the wisest choices become clear to me.

I am creating the mental and emotional space to tune in my intuitive sensitivity in order to make the best choices today. I am guided to the best paths of action.

Sample Evening Invocations

May the Dreamer bestow upon me symbolic dreams that I will remember and record, which will shed light upon my life and true Self.

Let my dreams flow tonight, and may their symbolic meaning bring me a greater awareness of who I am, my best direction going forward, and the most enlightened choices I can make.

Channeling the Archetype of Creative Power— Creative Manifestation Treatment

The Creative Manifestation Treatment draws on the Creative Power archetype to help you stay focused on fulfilling your highest priorities, empowered by an optimistic and creative attitude. This guided meditation is based on the work of Ernest Holmes, who founded the Church of Religious Science in 1927. I revised Holmes's original treatment, adding two powerful steps to support decision-making and action taking. Anyone of any religion can use the Creative Manifestation Treatment to attract and attain whatever their heart desires. I encourage you to edit and customize the one-page treatment, to make the language and substance work best for you. (You can easily download a text version for this purpose via Divination.com.)

How to Use the Creative Manifestation Treatment

Find a seated position where you are comfortable but alert, as you might for a meditation session. Take a few deep breaths, releasing with an "ah" or "om" sound on each exhale. When you are relaxed but alert and ready, slowly read your treatment to yourself, preferably aloud, or listen to a recording of it that you have made. When you are finished, stay in place and breathe. Feel the bliss of being spiritually magnetic through the clarity and power of expressed intention, and emotionally magnetic through the infectious power of the feeling. Finish with a resolution to take your attracting attitude with you throughout your day.

The following template is drawn from other variations I have used in the past. Edit it to suit your own needs:

Step 1: Recognition

I acknowledge Creative Power, the universal magnetic energy that unites and makes things whole. Divine power expresses itself as love, wisdom, and courage. It is reflected in the vastness of space, the sun around which Earth revolves, the beauty of nature, the joy of love and miracles. This unlimited resource operates according to the law of cause and effect that begins with attraction: first the image, then the declaration, and then manifestation. I know there is no limit to Creative Power.

Step 2: Identification

I am one with Creative Power, which surrounds me and flows through me. My breathing reminds me of my interconnectedness with all of nature, and I can feel the connection any time I close my eyes. Divine love and wisdom surround me and go before me, making my way easy and successful. I am capable of facilitating any results I visualize or feel. I don't need to know their exact form, but solutions appear quickly and easily. I deserve what is good for me.

Step 3: Declaration

I declare that I am now enjoying the realization of [my desire]. This feels [liberating, joyous and pleasurable, etc.].

Step 4: Thanksgiving

I give thanks for the fulfillment of [my desire], the joyful anticipation of which I am feeling already. I feel strong on my path. I am confident and full of faith, and my heart is filled with gratitude.

Step 5: Release

I let go of tendencies to control things, to worry, or to interfere by trying to shape results in a particular way. I accept that the law of cause and effect is operating on this treatment right now, even if my senses have no proof yet. I am attracting [my desire], and [my desire] is attracting me. The manifestation of this, or something better, is in process. Creative Power is synchronistically producing the perfect results for me with perfect timing. I am letting go of trying to control things and surrendering to the good that is my destiny. My "faith" is my intuitive sense of the manifesting process that is happening behind the scenes right now.

Step 6: Feeling It—Emotional Magnetization

I am letting myself feel the presence of what I have declared, which is in the process of manifesting. As I let this feeling radiate throughout my entire being, I become emotionally magnetic.

Step 7: Decision-Making and Timing—Action Steps

I make the right moves at just the right time, starting with better decision-making that taps my intuition, intellect, and receptivity to good advice. I make and follow up on commitments to myself. In the dance of life, I am taking good steps in a timely manner. As long as I am in connection with Creative Power, I know I can't go wrong!

After you're finished reading the Creative Manifestation Treatment, stay in place and continue to breathe. Feel the bliss of being spiritually magnetic through the clarity and power of your expressed intention, and emotionally magnetic through the infectious power of the feeling you get when you project your imagination onto a clear vision. Resolve to take this sense of your spiritual attractiveness with you throughout your day.

Archetypes provide a powerful source of inspiration, guidance, and power for the visionary decision-maker and make room for personal evolution and transformation when we begin to understand them. Interpreting their appearance in dreams and learning to deliberately invoke archetypes adds power and momentum to your Hero's Journey.

8

The *Book of Changes* Divination System

There is no *yang* without *yin*, no *yin* without *yang*, and one is constantly in the process of becoming the other.

—**Monk Yun Rou**

Perceiving the meaning in coincidences and other anomalous signs is a function of intuitive sensitivity. When we maintain an awareness of what's most important to us, synchronistic events just seem to occur more frequently. But, still, we can't just order up signs and omens at the precise time we may need their guidance most. Fortunately, special tools can generate meaningful coincidences for you and help your conscious mind decipher the meaning. These tools are called divination systems.

In this chapter, we explore the *I Ching*, or *Book of Changes*, one of the Taoist classics, as well as the world's oldest and most revered divination system. This Taoist construction is based on the dualism of yin and yang, which is used to codify and explain how things change and evolve—physically and socially. Every phenomenon or situation has both yin and yang aspects, which constantly interact with each other.

Yin can be described as the feminine principle—pointing to various phenomena and energies as the moon, water, earth, subsistence, and receptivity. In the I Ching system, a yin aspect is symbolized as a broken line. Yang is the masculine principle, including aspects such as the sun, fire, heat, heaven, creation, and penetrating assertiveness. In the I Ching system, a yang aspect is symbolized as an unbroken line.

We have all seen the circular yin-yang symbol, with inverted paisley shapes that illustrate the way yin and yang are fused and interconnected, mutually supportive, and flipping or flowing into each other. Historically, it was posited that if yin arrived at an extreme it would then flip into the yang state, and if yang reached an extreme it was converted into yin. This event is symbolized in the I Ching system as a "changing line," ready to flip into the opposite state. Changing lines are the exception and, using the coin toss method, are represented by three of a kind—three heads or three tails. The duality of yin and yang and how they can morph into each other helps us to get a feeling for the primal forces of change that shape our lives, the overall significance of I Ching hexagrams, and the advisory meaning of changing lines when they happen in a reading.

ANATOMY OF A HEXAGRAM

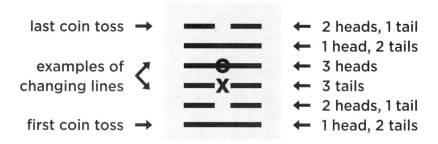

last coin toss →		← 2 heads, 1 tail
		← 1 head, 2 tails
examples of		← 3 heads
changing lines		← 3 tails
		← 2 heads, 1 tail
first coin toss →		← 1 head, 2 tails

The I Ching supports intuitive decision-making by operating on its set of sixty-four archetypes with the help of a synchronistic pattern that is created by the tossing of coins at the same time as we are thinking about something of importance. (If you desire more detailed information on how the I Ching reflects and maps out life changes, see my *Visionary I Ching* ebook, which provides detailed instruction to help with understanding and using this marvelous tool.)

Divination systems are not dark arts or fortune-telling gimmicks, as skeptics may assume. Divination has gotten a bad rap because of the erroneous assumption that its purpose is to predict the future, which has led to its appropriation by—and association with—hucksters, gypsies, and fortune-tellers. As a result, Western religions eventually got around to condemning divination—despite several biblical verses where Yahweh favors divination and even mandates its use.

Historically, the Israelites of the Bible, as well as their Christian and Muslim offshoots, viewed God as the agent of destiny, and used divination techniques to stay in tune with divine will. In addition to sacrifices and other rituals, the Bible mentions at least two divinatory practices in positive terms. The primary one appears in a number of Old Testament stories where Yahweh tells the Israelites to perform a decision-making ritual using the sacred runes of the High Priest, called the "Urim and Thummim."

The exact composition of the Urim and Thummim is not known, but scholars believe they were sacred dice, perhaps made of precious gems. They were stored in a pouch behind the high priest's "breastplate of judgment," which he wore when seeking divine guidance for legal judgments and strategic decisions of state. There is no way to confirm the exact details of how the Urim and Thummim were cast or read. However it worked, the Bible makes it clear that divination was sacred and that God was behind the answers it produced.

My earlier book, *Divination: Sacred Tools for Reading the Mind of God*, lists all the biblical verses regarding divination, positive and negative. In my research, I discovered there are more passages that look favorably upon divination than those that condemn diviners and astrologers. Since there are occasions where Yahweh actually chooses to provide answers or direction via the Urim and Thummim, it is interesting how the fundamentalist dogma keepers of the church have condemned divination so vehemently.

In the first century, as he was defining what became Christian dogma, when Bible and church were set up in the fourth century, Paul described an ability to decipher God's plan as the "gift of prophecy"—a form of channeling available only to faithful believers. Nowadays, thanks to universal access to the classical systems of divination, anyone who approaches the effort with sincerity can connect directly with Infinite Intelligence.

Since I had been a software executive, after the idea of I Ching software came to me, colleagues would ask, "Do you really believe in this stuff?" I knew where they were coming from—a culturally biased viewpoint engendered by religious interpretations of sin, fear of the Devil archetype, skepticism, and so on. I would carefully explain that no beliefs are required—because the real purpose of divination is to activate and support the intuitive sense. You just try it and see if it works for you. It is not a crystal ball that you have to believe in.

Stimulating the intuition around problems that logic can't handle is a superb reason to use the I Ching or any other authentic divination system. Anyone with a sincere interest and an open mind can use a divination system that offers a balanced set of archetypes (like the I Ching or tarot) to support creativity and decision-making—without having to believe in anything. All it takes is an open mind that is free from fear and a willingness to experiment. Either it works for you and stimulates your intuition or it doesn't . . . simple as that!

Because tarot readings—another archetype-based system—offer so many more permutations, interpreting the intersecting archetypes requires a bit of academic training. The even greater complexity of astrology means that being able to deliver an astrological reading requires even more instruction. Unlike tarot or astrology, the I Ching is simple enough that, with the help of a good interpretive text, anyone can easily learn to consult it themselves.

The *Visionary I Ching* app is a good place to start if you're looking for a compact and easy-to-use version of the I Ching. Available in the iTunes and Android App stores.

Through his friendship with Richard Wilhelm (the most famous translator of the I Ching from the Chinese), Carl Jung became intimately familiar with this Taoist divination system. He used and studied the I Ching for decades. In his foreword to Richard Wilhelm's famous translation published in 1951, Jung explained that the I Ching works on a synchronicity principle that operates on the set of sixty-four archetypes. He saw the I Ching as a way for individuals to leverage the archetypal dynamics of humanity's collective unconscious.

How the I Ching Works

According to legend, King Wen of Zhou formulated the I Ching as we know it some three thousand years ago. Nowadays, most people consult the I Ching by tossing three coins six times (sorting yarrow stalks was the older method) and recording the way they land in a six-line pattern called a "hexagram." Based on the pattern that the user casts, the I Ching points to one of the sixty-four archetypes, each of which has multiple possible permutations, or "changing lines." Jung wrote that the I Ching interprets an "inner unconscious knowledge that corresponds to the state of consciousness at the moment."[1]

Jung saw the I Ching as a reliable way to gain psychological and spiritual insights into changing conditions—not by taking a problem apart and analyzing its components, but by viewing a situation in the context of a seamless whole. "There is no need," Jung wrote, "of any question which imposes conditions and restricts the wholeness of the natural process. . . . In the I Ching the coins fall just as happens to suit them."[2]

When you write down your situation, problem, or dilemma and then focus your mind on it, you enter a state of receptivity to whatever pattern the casting of the coins reveals. As Jungian psychotherapist David Richo writes, "Oracular, ego-transcending wisdom of the archetypal Self emerges from deep in the psyche. The Delphic priestess has always been sitting here inside us, but we may never have traveled far enough within ourselves to consult her."[3]

By tossing the coins for a pattern that the conscious mind can't control, you inject a seemingly random element. But since you are the one who is tossing the coins—presumably in a focused, expectant state—the ritual takes on a personal aspect. The way the coins land is coincident with whatever you concentrate on. By casting the coins, you are creating a coincidence that can be interpreted and plumbed for meaning. Since all the archetypes reside within the unconscious, the casting of the coins calls out one aspect of your shared humanity for particular attention.

Given the intuitive stimulation that comes of this synchronistic experience, a new idea, thought, or solution to your issue or dilemma is better able to pop into your conscious mind. As the synchronicity principle explains, events suffused with connective portent may have no apparent causal relationship, but they are not just random. An intersection of events that triggers a sense of inner knowing is meaningful, and the two entities coming together stimulate yet a new reality (a new idea or sense of direction) within the conscious mind. Think of how two people who come together intimately form a third entity of the relationship. By the ritualistic casting of coins around a focus, you deliberately produce a meaningful coincidence, using the I Ching as a method of "applied synchronicity" to stimulate your intuition around a dilemma or matter of concern.

Activating the intuition is the true purpose of divination, which can provide wonderful support for creative thinking and timing. Beyond such practical use, the I Ching is a philosophically elegant representation of a sophisticated, holistic point of view that credits a cosmic order that is beyond human understanding.

The Creative and the Receptive

Taoist sages compiled the I Ching to gain better access to the Infinite Intelligence they called the "Tao" through a system and ritual that produces a meaningful coincidence. They perceived that the divine resource generously supported human creativity, nurturance, and balance between yin and yang energies. The first hexagram of the I Ching—entitled "Heaven" or "Creative Power"—is the hexagram in which all six lines are yang, with no yin lines at all. Yang is that outgoing "make-it-happen" energy quality. If you receive the first hexagram in a reading, the message is pointing toward outwardly expressing your creativity.

The second hexagram, which my *Visionary I Ching* refers to as "Receptive Power," is the one that consists of all yin lines. The Receptive was considered equally as important as the "take initiative" energy of Creative Power. In its balanced structure, the I Ching system reveals how the Taoist originators of yin and yang equally valued the feminine, "attract and let it happen" side of manifestation. The Receptive represents the power of coming into form and relationship, the power of containing or holding energy and of supportive nourishment.

Note how each of the dual aspects—the dark yin and the light yang—has a dot of the other within itself. This symbolizes the fact that nothing is ever completely yin or completely yang. Letting the yin and the yang complement and flow into each other—as artfully symbolized throughout the ages by the yin-yang symbol—constitutes what is known as the Tao, or the Way. So too, the I Ching embodies balance, with a structural elegance that is based on an equal mix of yin and yang lines.

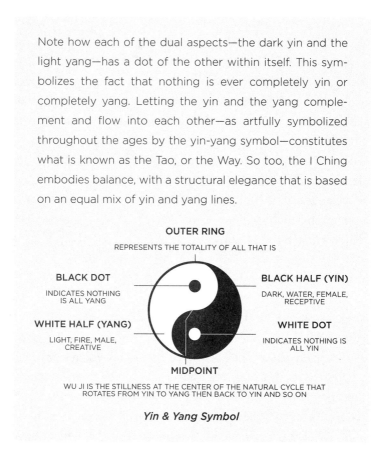

OUTER RING
REPRESENTS THE TOTALITY OF ALL THAT IS

BLACK DOT
INDICATES NOTHING
IS ALL YANG

BLACK HALF (YIN)
DARK, WATER, FEMALE,
RECEPTIVE

WHITE HALF (YANG)
LIGHT, FIRE, MALE,
CREATIVE

WHITE DOT
INDICATES NOTHING IS
ALL YIN

MIDPOINT
WU JI IS THE STILLNESS AT THE CENTER OF THE NATURAL CYCLE THAT
ROTATES FROM YIN TO YANG THEN BACK TO YIN AND SO ON

Yin & Yang Symbol

In the Taoist view of the universe, humanity is a bridge between Heaven and Earth—between inspiration and insemination on the one side and reception or fertility on the other. This dance between the yang and the yin—the outgoing, creative yang force and the receptive, supportive yin—is central to the VDM approach. Like an artist or a juggler, the human being mediates between heaven and earth. The executive skill of creative decision-making is a powerful example of this balancing act, and this exercise of leadership and power largely determines whether greater harmony or greater chaos collectively prevails in human affairs.

In many ways, the Visionary Decision Making process involves the interaction of the creative and the receptive. Receptivity to dreams and synchronicities for inspiration and guidance stimulates creative thinking and movement. If our intuitive sense is unblocked and sensitively tuned to receive signals of meaning, it is acting as the mature feminine principle, which is not only receptive but also discriminating.

Our hyper-yang patriarchal culture—so biased in favor of action over contemplation—honors Creative Power but gives short shrift to Receptivity, which is equally important. Taoist philosophy, as expressed in the Tao Te Ching and the I Ching, is more balanced because it predates the egocentric attitude and cultural biases of patriarchy. It is philosophically sophisticated—especially as it aligns with Nature.

How to Approach the I Ching

Your frame of mind when approaching the I Ching is a crucial factor in its effectiveness. Sometimes people turn to the I Ching when they feel anxiety, doubt, or frustration. If you are feeling emotionally upset by life changes outside of your control (which is most of them), it's easy to be blinded by fear. Unfortunately, fear easily dominates consciousness and blocks intuitive intelligence when you need it most. When your hands are involved in the act of casting the coins, make sure your mind and heart are focused on your issue of highest concern and your desire to know the truth, no matter what it may be.

To set the tone for a fruitful experience, prior to any I Ching consultation, begin your ritual by centering yourself. Enter a meditative mindset (as discussed in chapter 7) that supports your sincere desire for truth and wisdom. Perform whatever centering technique or ritual works best for you. Do your best to enter a state of focused relaxation.

Be clear about what you hope to learn or achieve. Possible goals could be making an important decision or reducing stress around confusing or challenging changes in your life. These are not the goals of the ego, which always wants to make things happen. A centering practice is an intentional process that helps move your ego out of the way so your mind can receive deep guidance. This is valuable in itself.

For some people, taking a soothing bath with candles is a good way to calm down and prepare for an I Ching session. After you relax, consciously let go of any attachment to receiving a specific answer or outcome. Commit yourself to caring only about truth. By giving the ego a "vacation" from its usual preoccupations, you increase receptivity to archetypes that can inform your conscious mind and support your decisions and actions.

Some people prefer a relatively elaborate ritual at a certain time of day, special garments, an amulet, or even some form of chanting. You don't need to go that far, but it can be a good idea to set aside a special space. This doesn't need to be an indoor fountain with palm ferns and Buddha statues, but if that feels right and you have the resources, inspiring art can be supportive. An inspirational photo—perhaps of an ancient temple, a natural landscape, or a divine image—is a portable device that you can take with you to support serenity. Simply lighting a candle, burning incense, or taking a few deep breaths with your eyes closed can facilitate focused relaxation. Choose what feels the most comfortable for you. The information you receive from a reading comes from within you, not from the external environment.

Before you cast a reading, take a few moments to affirm your allegiance to what is real and true. This is the most important intention affirmation: "I am letting go of my desire for any particular answer. I am open and committed to better understanding whatever is true." Confidently adopt the attitude that everything will work out the way it is supposed to. This will be the case whether or not you understand the reason now.

Once you've entered the proper frame of mind, you can begin consulting the I Ching. Only consult the I Ching when you feel balanced, open, and clear enough to receive the wisdom it provides.

Formulating Your Query

Approach an I Ching reading with the kind of question or issue you might present to a wise counselor or mentor. No matter how good the advice, you are the author of your own decisions. You always have agency and the way things turn out is up to you. In my story, the advice I received from an I Ching reading inspired me to create a multimedia version of the I Ching itself. The I Ching acted as my muse, but I was responsible for the decision, and it was a scary one on many levels. Even though I had never considered the idea of designing software—or starting my own business, for that matter—inspiration coupled with intuitive vision led me to venture forth and invent something that seemed worthy of my time and energy, even if that meant taking what felt like enormous risks. I consulted the I Ching regarding my life's mission at a time when I needed outside-the-box clarity and extra motivation to make a bold leap of faith.

It's important to ask the kinds of questions that get you the responses you need and can trust. You wouldn't ask an electrician how to change the transmission fluid in your car, nor would you ask a mechanic for stock tips. Likewise, divination systems like the I Ching are designed for certain kinds of questions. The process works best if you are looking for insight, wise advice, or a sense of which way the wind is blowing with regard to changes in your life. The I Ching is not designed to deliver data, yes/no answers, or predictions (although a reading will often point to trends or probabilities).

The wording of your query is important because it influences your mental state as you perform the casting ritual. Ask for guidance in the form of, "What is the best approach to take in relation to this situation?" It is not necessary to formulate your issue of concern in the form of a question—in fact, that can be problematic because it is so easy to ask the wrong kind of question. Just hold a specific subject in mind at the beginning of the process, or write down one or more keywords to represent the situation, person, or decision that is on your mind. The tangibility of writing down the subject of focus will help produce a clearer reading.

After you have had a chance to glean the primary gems of insight from a reading, receiving thoughts that stimulate new ideas and a broader perspective, you will be able to make a better decision. You have now taken a humble step toward a future aligned with who you are meant to be—that is, your destiny.

There are two classes of divination queries: the big picture and the snapshot. Big-picture questions work well when you are not in crisis but are interested in personality traits or trends in your life. My vocation-oriented query mentioned above is an example; another might center on compatibility with a person with whom you are having strong feelings. Beware of overly broad questions such as, "What is the meaning of life?" Although it is philosophical and can be used to inspire meditations, the I Ching was not designed to explain too much.

A snapshot type of query works best when you need to make a decision for a specific dilemma, a new approach, or just a bit of good advice in the moment. When dealing with an immediate problem, it is skillful to ask the I Ching about the attitude, method, or approach to take, rather than for details about what is going to happen. Avoid asking for data like, "Where will I get a job?" or "Who is the partner of my dreams?" Notice the difference when these issues are rephrased: "What is the best course of action for finding a satisfying job?" and "What should I look for in a suitable partner?" If you present the appropriate kinds of queries, you are likely to have a beneficial and satisfying reading.

As mentioned, while humans fantasize about being able to foretell the future, divination systems don't really work for queries looking for predictions. However, they can provide insights that give you a better sense of direction, along with pointed advice based on archetypal patterns and timeless wisdom.

The I Ching is most helpful when life presents important problems beyond the ability of logic to resolve. Questions about relationships, timing, and dynamic negotiations fall into this category. Career and work-related questions are also popular topics for I Ching consultations. For instance, people who are wondering what is next after transitioning from a job might be looking for ways to improve their career or may be seeking wisdom about their true calling. Such questions focus on the individual's connection to the outside world, passion, purpose, or vocation.

Self-improvement or introspection are also good reasons to cast a reading. Such readings can reflect on an individual's connection with themselves, their goals, their dreams, or their destiny. Many people cast the I Ching as part of their daily meditation. Because I Ching readings have always provided such good reflections for them, author and entre-preneur Charles Jennings and his artist wife Christine have made it their habit to cast the I Ching every New Year's Day for the past forty-five years, just before their annual good luck dinner of black-eyed peas. According to Charles, these readings provided "an insightful mirror for reflection on our lives, seen from a year-to-year perspective." Occasionally, Charles would consult the I Ching when facing a crucial business decision. In those readings, he said, "the oracle was not telling me what to do, or pre-dicting the future in any specific way. But it was always helpful in getting me to look at my situation in new ways."

That someone like Charles Jennings, running modern high-tech and cybersecurity companies, could find intuitive value in a book thousands of years old is a testament to the timeless wisdom of the I Ching—and the importance that proactive business leaders attach to any tool that might support their intuitive intelligence.

Sometimes people naively ask an oracle about how other people feel or will act. This is a common example of an inappropriate query. Even when you would like to inquire for or about someone else, the oracle can only respond to your energy and your issues—such as fear of confronta-tion, insecurity, or lack of trust—and will not be able to reflect anything about another person. Remember, you are the one tossing the coins and generating the hexagram that synchronistically turns up!

Perhaps you wish to inquire about another's intentions because you're feeling jealous, afraid, hopeful, or shy? Or maybe you just want to help them. In any case, the I Ching will only reflect what is going on for or inside of *you*. You can find meaning in a reading by examining your own feelings. If a friend or loved one is asking you to do a reading *for* them, direct them to *The Visionary I Ching* ebook, point them to instructions that may still be up on Divination.com, or help them find some other resource that shows how to easily consult the I Ching.

Remember that the goal of a reading is not to predict the future. Your destiny is yours to create through decisions and actions. The primary purpose of an I Ching reading is to help you understand situations better in order to make more skillful decisions with better timing. Even if all you get is one creative new thought, the I Ching has done its job!

The Real Meaning Lies between the Lines

The I Ching text was not designed to give a literal answer to any question. No matter which version you use, the benefits depend upon intuitively reading between the lines (with your query in mind). Rather than being a limitation of the I Ching, this is its real purpose. This is how it activates the intuition using archetypes that represent powers within you. The I Ching stimulates and empowers creative decision-making from the inside out.

Although the I Ching sometimes does provide specific advice, a reading more often points to a new direction or expanded perspective for you to consider and contemplate. Sometimes, all a first reading does is stimulate a new idea that helps you to better sharpen your query, which can then lead to a more refined experience in a subsequent reading. The idea is not to control anything but to gently nudge your intuitive intelligence to "think outside the box," giving rise to new ideas and inspiration.

Often, what first pops into your head captures the core message or central truth. However, if the meaning of a reading isn't immediately clear, take a break and come back to it. Read between the lines, again without attachment to receiving a certain answer or jumping to conclusions. Keep in mind, an oracle's response could possibly be about another issue on your mind that's more pressing than the question you posed.

One I Ching user I know described the perplexing results of a reading he received when he asked about his failing marriage. When the meaning of the hexagrams escaped him, he sought deeper meaning. Every succeeding layer only seemed more confusing. Later, looking back on the results, he found that the titles of the hexagrams he had gotten had provided an answer to his question—one he had refused to hear because of his attachment to receiving a certain answer in a certain way. Only with time and reflection was he able to digest the true meaning of the hexagrams he'd received.

It is helpful to take notes when consulting the I Ching, so have a pen and paper or your electronic device of choice at hand. (The *Visionary I Ching* app conveniently allows you to cast a hexagram using a smartphone or tablet, read about your hexagram, and save it for later review.) Saving your readings in a journal of some kind lets you evaluate and compare them in the future. Take note of your full experience—including the details of your ritual and approach, your interpretation (a sentence or two that summarizes what the reading reflected), and the result (the aftereffect of the decision you made following your reading). Over time, an I Ching journal will give you a broader perspective on the patterns in your life. The overview will help you to get clear about situations that routinely bring up certain hexagrams, reflect on how your readings have impacted your decision-making, and improve your ability to use the I Ching.

As you become more experienced, you'll find the future hexagram feature to be useful. The future hexagram is derived when the "changing lines" you may have cast (in the coins method, this is when you get three of a kind) are flipped from yang to yin, or vice versa, to produce a new hexagram. More detailed information about changing lines and the simple procedure of deriving the future hexagram is presented in *The Visionary I Ching* ebook and on Divination.com (currently). While the I Ching provides insight and advice based on timeless wisdom, the future hexagram offers a glimpse of how the present situation will evolve if you follow the counsel of your reading. In this way, the I Ching also supports predictive intelligence. Some readings do not include any changing lines at all, which indicates that the situation you inquired about is relatively stable for the time being.

It is not always easy to discern the quiet voice of intuition—or give it credit—but we need intuitive intelligence in order to make the best decisions. Sometimes we need to go back to the well more than once to get the clarity we need. But getting in touch with intuition to achieve clarity of purpose is central to the achievement of success and happiness. The skillful use of an authentic divination system like the I Ching can help you avoid major missteps. I encourage everyone who is willing to give it a try to approach divination sincerely with an open mind, heart, and soul.

The I Ching Encouraged Me to Become an Entrepreneur

When I was VP of marketing for that high-tech software company, I worked long hours, but I had a high-paying career that supported a lively social life and a nice home for myself and my son. All in all, it was a good place to be, and as far as jobs went, I was fortunate. The thing that was missing was *meaning*—a sense of personal mission or compelling sense of purpose. I had a good career, but according to Dan Millman, author of *The Way of the Peaceful Warrior*, I was not yet aware of my *calling*—an avocation that I would be inspired to do whether it paid handsomely or not.

Approaching the age of forty, I was at a crossroads with no clear sense of direction. I could see that many of my peers were also zooming through busy lives on autopilot, making a good income, but without the passion, excitement, and drive that comes from an inspired vision and an aroused heart. I didn't want it to be that way for me. I didn't want to feel empty.

Despite notable success marketing its first product, our research and development department's subsequent products were doomed from the start. As the one in charge of marketing and sales, which had become lackluster as we worked to sell products the market didn't want, I became the corporate scapegoat for the flagging sales revenues. I found myself suffering "slings and arrows" of office politics, largely instigated by the CEO, who was the chief engineer as well as founder of the company and who would never admit to poor design decisions. I was at a loss as to how to respond to the backbiting and passive-aggressive hostility coming at me from all sides. I was losing respect for the CEO and felt pessimistic about the company's culture—or product line—ever improving.

Because of all the stress, I actually started lugging my heavy I Ching book into the office for emergency use, just to keep my head about me—a support I had never resorted to at work in the twenty previous years of using the I Ching. Although it was a hassle, it did provide some moral support and guidance I badly needed to stay balanced in the turbulent and confusing situation at the office. I had a lot of fear. Accordingly, I would make sure to meditate for a few minutes to let go of attachment to any particular outcome before I turned to the I Ching for some supportive or wise counsel.

From multiple I Ching readings around this time I received the same message: make a break and move on. At that time, Portland, Oregon, had few executive software marketing positions, and I had no opportunities lined up. I didn't want to relocate, so leaving my job to find another that would be just as good in Portland would require an enormous leap of faith. I was "stuck," the I Ching told me, and I needed a "breakthrough." So, one fine day, when a senior director of the company, whose place it was to advise the CEO, came to town for a company meeting, I moved through my fears, made my decision, and executed it by turning in a letter of resignation.

Destiny can work in strange ways, and what happened next took me by surprise. The director, an older, mature, and accomplished high-tech guy whom I respected, called me in and asked what it would take to keep me from leaving the company. I was surprised by the question. By then, I was so stressed out that, despite all uncertainties, I had almost dismissed any possibility of things working out. I asked him if I could sleep on it, and when I got home that night, I turned to the I Ching again. This time I got hexagram 60, "Limits and Connections." This recommended biding my time while reasoning through issues and making plans. Not a signal for immediate bold action.

At work the next day, I submitted my conditions for my continued employment—which included more than I thought I could get—expecting that they would reject my stipulations and I would then have to move on. But the director agreed to everything and even offered me a 10 percent higher raise than I had requested! When I asked him why, he said they wanted me to stay and be happy. Impressed by this vote of confidence, I accepted the offer with a smile, saying, "I can't be bought, but I can be rented." We all laughed, and the tension was broken (for a while).

I thought that this was the "breakthrough" referred to by the I Ching. I felt that I was resolving the issues and moving forward productively, instead of just bolting when the going got rough. Ironically, however, the most significant aspect of me having used the I Ching at work was a seed that the experience had planted in my mind, which would soon stimulate a real, life-changing breakthrough.

Lugging the large book to work and finding a private space to toss three coins had been cumbersome. As a result, it occurred to me that it might be possible to create an interactive I Ching experience via multimedia running on the Macintosh—the first graphical computer to go mainstream. Pursuing this line of active imagining, I began to visualize how a Mac might be programmed so that a mouse could perform the work of casting a hexagram in an "energetically authentic" way compared to a person tossing three coins six times. I also could see how the computer would take care of the busy work of recording the results, looking up and displaying the text of a specific reading, and so forth. Building on this new product vision, I also imagined producing a new version of an I Ching experience with new text that would be more relevant to modern life.

The more I visualized the possibilities, the more I liked the idea of using a multimedia-capable computer with a mouse (like Macintosh) to deliver easier access to the intuitive stimulation of the I Ching in an engaging way. After all, I mused, casting an I Ching reading has a lot in common with a computer game. Certainly, both are interactive. I searched for existing I Ching software, but I could not find it anywhere. Rudimentary versions had been programmed onto huge computers at MIT and other places, but there was still no such software available for personal computers, or anything like it. The thought occurred to me that perhaps there wasn't a market yet. On the other hand, I knew that there was at least an enthusiastic market of one—myself. Developing anything that would work might require the investment of my savings, but I thought there must be others like me who would appreciate a modern I Ching program. The creativity of it was so compelling, I felt strongly moved to take the risk.

It was obvious that a computer could easily handle the mathematics of casting the six-line I Ching hexagram. The bigger challenge would be how to use a mouse to replicate the tossing of three coins six times in a way that allowed the user's energy to determine the outcome. A random number generator routine that spit out an entire hexagram would be simple and fast to program, but it would not be, to my way of thinking, *energetically authentic*. (Note: Almost all the other I Ching software or web developers who copied our work took the easier programming route, in which the computer did the casting.) I felt strongly that, in order for the software to be "energetically authentic," the user must be the agent doing the casting, not the computer. I was also intrigued by the possibility of combining a user's query with beautiful graphics and peaceful sounds. I thought a bit of soothing multimedia would help the user stay focused and set the mood of a calm, meditative state of mind while they cast their reading.

As an overall vision of using a computer to provide "ritual space" for consulting the I Ching began to gel in my mind, I had a "Eureka!" moment, excited by the vision that was taking shape. My natural curiosity was getting revved up and so were my creative juices. In that moment, I wasn't thinking in grand terms of destiny, or even thinking about a business plan with an exit strategy. Hell, I was overlooking considerations of my material well-being! I was going to spend my life savings on what most people would have considered a hare-brained scheme, but . . . I was mightily inspired. After all, the project was an intersection of two major fascinations of mine—the I Ching and multimedia.

Even at the time, the urge to invest all my resources on such a far-flung idea seemed illogical and foolhardy. And yet, I was too excited not to think about trying and finding out. It would be a creative adventure at the very least, and there was certainly no way to do market research. Even then, I instinctively knew what Steve Jobs later explained—when it comes to new kinds of products, people don't know what they want until they see it. So, it came down to how willing I was to take the biggest financial and career risk of my life just because I was fascinated with an idea for an esoteric invention. I was excited—and scared to death.

I took some time to meditate on this big question. I mentally prepared myself to consult the I Ching about whether to risk time and money and career to try to produce an I Ching program that I couldn't even be sure would work. Closing my eyes and invoking both love and nonattachment, I tossed the coins for a reading. The hexagram I got back was "Enthusiasm," with changing lines that flipped into a future hexagram entitled "Abundance." I felt clear that the I Ching was encouraging me to create a software version of *itself!*

Having used and studied the I Ching for more than forty years now—including authoring a new modern version—I have experienced time and again the power of an I Ching reading. Readings help me rise above the black-and-white, all-or-nothing thinking that the ego so easily gets caught up in. If nothing else, learning to use the I Ching has helped me understand the importance of open-mindedness, intention, and attitude. Authentic divination reflects and clarifies one's intention as much as it dishes out advice or wisdom. Although I do not depend on the I Ching for every decision I make, I still can consult it if I need to expand my perspective beyond the capacity of human logic. It's like traveling to a foreign land, feeling an empathic resonance with people of a different culture, and coming back with what my favorite travel guide, Rick Steves, says is "the best souvenir . . . a broader perspective."[4]

This profound Taoist divination system has helped me learn to more skillfully navigate time through the changing conditions of mind and body with timely decision-making. Emperors and sages used the I Ching for thousands of years in essentially the same way that I do—as a strategic decision-making tool to help them see the bigger picture, make better choices, and execute strategic plans with better timing. It is not necessary to use the I Ching to implement or benefit from Visionary Decision Making, but if you are open to the possibility, it will give you one reliable way to tap Infinite Intelligence.

9

Execution and Timing:
Answering the "When" Question

A vision without the ability to execute it is probably a hallucination.

—**Stephen Case**

The ordinary man is involved in action, the hero acts. An immense difference.

—**Henry Miller**

As Czech statesman Václar Havel so cleverly put it, "Vision isn't enough unless combined with venture. It's not enough to stare up the steps unless we also step up the stairs."[1] We have to take action, to do something. This is where conscious and deliberate decision-making comes in.

Earlier in this book we explored how to answer the "What" question, as in "What is my best next move?" with regard to any situation, dilemma, or important decision. But getting an answer to the "what" question is only half of the strategic decision-making process. You still need to plan and commit to a course of action (or nonaction, in some cases), time your actions right, and execute your plan. Execution is the setting of things in motion when the time is right. Without well-timed execution, the potential of even the most excellent decision may go unrealized.

Here are the four steps to implementing a visionary decision:

1. Determining *what* is the best next action you can take
2. Committing to that action
3. Deciding *when* to make your move
4. Executing your decision by moving forward confidently, without looking back or second-guessing yourself

Take Your Time Getting to the "What"

So many of us greatly suffer from the "hurry sickness" feeling that we have too much to do in too little time. But when it comes to making the decisions that will affect the long-term future, it's important to take as much time as is needed. Remember, intuition cannot be rushed. And be careful not to confuse strong impulsive urges with genuinely intuitive hunches. In addition to checking for synchronicities and messages in dreams that may come your way, use logical techniques like the ones in chapter 5 to winnow your best options down to two or three. Remember my counselor's admonition that there are always more than two solutions to any problem. Reality is never just black and white, so stay open to a small range of inspiring but plausible possibilities.

Even when you think you know the best solution, sleep on it before you finally decide your next move. Let the fruits of your brainstorming steep in a subconscious dialogue with Infinite Intelligence while you sleep. If the decision is important but not urgent, give it as much time as you can. In the meantime, record any dreams that you can and list all the synchronicities that you notice.

Never let anyone (especially someone trying to sell you something) hustle you into making a decision prematurely, especially when it is not really urgent for you. You may think of yourself as a resolute individual and uninfluenced by the dominant, authoritative forces at large, but no one is immune to social pressure. Ironically—if only because it gives you more time for intuitive processing—all big decisions of a personal nature are arguably made just before the window of opportunity closes. Always consider *when* a decision has to be made to give yourself maximum pondering time. This will usually lead to a more creative (and practical) solution. Whether your decision is of a personal nature or on behalf of a group, it is often best to wait a bit and decide not to decide . . . just yet.

Learn to invoke the power of impulse control and delayed gratification, even when it comes to decision-making. Get comfortable with saying, "Not right now" or "Probably not, but I'll think about it" or "Let me sleep on it." You can also try telling the other party that you need to confer with a supposedly higher authority—your spouse, an advisor (even if the advisor is an inner archetype, like the Sovereign), or some vague "board" of advisors. When important values are at stake, take as much time as you need to make the best decision in a way that feels right to you. When it comes to decisions that affect you more than anyone, other people's priorities take second place, even if they are "experts" . . . or your investment bankers. Sometimes it is necessary to assert yourself and defend your boundaries to secure the time you need, but you have a right to it. You are the CEO of your life, and you owe it to yourself to never be rushed into an important decision.

If you feel that you are inside a cauldron of change wherein a breakthrough decision absolutely needs to be made, create as much mental and emotional space as possible to support your intuitive receptivity. As noted earlier, avoid letting yourself succumb to the temptation of making important choices while under the influence of strong emotional reactions to fears or desires. And try to adopt an optimistic point of view. Studies have proven that a positive mood is associated with effective decision-making. If you are feeling rushed or overwhelmed, find a relaxing way to turn your attention to something else. Give your intuition a better chance to kick in around an important decision by taking a nap, meditating, watching a movie, going out for a walk, or distracting yourself by running an errand.

The VDM Meeting Technique

Sometimes the ramifications of a pending decision are complex and overwhelming, or there is the extra pressure of a hard and fast deadline. Making an important or strategic decision requires concentration. Fear of making a big mistake can keep you up at night, making it difficult to concentrate during the daytime. If you feel stuck or virtually paralyzed, schedule a VDM Meeting with yourself every morning for as many days in a row as necessary. Consider your options around the important matter every single day—until you are ready to make a decision and commit to a course of action.

It's best to schedule VDM Meetings as early as possible in the day. Try to make them your *first* item of business in the morning until you have had enough of them to reach clarity. This aligns with recent research, which suggests that morning is the best time to make decisions for most people due to human biorhythms.[2] You don't need a set length of time for your VDM Meeting, but forty-five minutes to an hour gives you enough time to review and reconsider your options using techniques like these:

- Review your viable options, as singled out by the weighted-pros logic technique.

- Read a guided meditation script aloud to yourself to put you into a positive and receptive state of mind. If you are not able to do this because of interruptions or emotional interference, stop the process and reschedule a VDM Meeting with yourself early the next day.

- Invoke the Sovereign archetype to support yourself as the chief executive decision-maker of your life.

- Invoke the archetype of the Sage and summon a letting-go state of egoless mind. You may feel empty and vast as you open yourself up to creative potential, like the fertile Void of Creation that existed before the Big Bang, when all things were possible.

- Do a short I Ching reading for one last reflection, asking for perspective on your decision. Use three coins and the hexagram lookup feature in *The Visionary I Ching* ebook or the *Visionary I Ching* app on a smartphone or tablet.

- Optional: Meet with one or two of your most trusted and objective advisors and share your latest strategic ideas with them. Keep the focus on decision-making.

- Be your own CEO and make a final decision on your best next move. Move forward, or step back, or do nothing and be patient as matters undergo changes on their own. It is quite possible that, unless you're procrastinating, doing nothing for now might actually be the best move!

As you become more experienced with the process, you will rarely need more than one or two VDM Meetings to make a decision, except when there are too many complex factors for one person to sort out by themselves.

The Power of a Signed Agreement with Yourself

If you have paid close attention to synchronistic signs and omens, consulted your dreams, met with advisor(s), or consulted the I Ching, your best option has probably become clear by now. (If not, keep repeating these steps until the option that best balances inspiration and plausibility blossoms within you.) You will have answered the "what" question and made up your mind about the best next move to make. Now that you have made that decision, you need to *commit* to a course of action. A tremendously supportive ritual for doing this is to write an agreement with yourself . . . and sign it.

Since this agreement is entirely between you and yourself, your statement of resolution can be short and to the point. No need for fine print. In addition, announce your decision to any key advisors to further solidify your commitment. At this point, set fears and considerations aside, and boldly take a stand. You have deliberated long enough, analyzed the options, and created enough peace and quiet for your intuitive antenna to be operative. Now is the time to summon forth your inner chief executive and declare your decision.

Even with all this preparation, making meaningful commitments when the time comes is not easy. In the case of strategic or lifestyle-changing decisions, there can be substantial risks. For example, major investment decisions are often based on recommendations from financial professionals. However, studies show that few financial advisors beat the market average after taking fees. So, these decisions informed by an "expert" still feel anxiety-inducing to the loss-averse emotional brain of the average investor. You don't want your excitement to turn into buyer's remorse. Nevertheless, to seize an opportunity, you have to commit yourself and make a move, in spite of trepidation and the temptation to obsess on all the things that could go wrong. (It's a safe bet that Mr. Murphy of Murphy's Law was not a great investor!)

A common misunderstanding about commitment is that it should precede and motivate one's efforts. But this is backward. A commitment is the outcome or byproduct of inspiration or passion, not its goal. A desire to conform to some ideal of commitment for its own sake should never drive a decision. When we are drawn upward by a higher affection, we are inclined to make whatever level of commitment is necessary to realize the goal. A solid stance—based on understanding your situation and accepting yourself unconditionally—is always the best position from which to make the right move at the right time.

Never force a commitment. If a commitment feels too difficult for you right now, either the time is not right or you are not ready. Avoid making a commitment because you think you *should* or trying to force a vision to manifest because you believe it is "the right thing to do." Your current self may not be the idealized self your ego wants to claim, but it is your real self right now. Sheer desire plus willpower is not going to improve circumstances if you are not totally honest and real with yourself.

Make a commitment to action when you feel motivated by an authentic and passionate desire. This will not just be an impulse, but a drive that gains strength inside you. It will not be the result of pressure from an outside influence or an internal "should" driven by your inner Critic or Perfectionist subpersonalities. It is crucial to know the difference between what the highest parts of *you* truly want and what someone else wants, even if that person is close to you. This is especially true if that "someone else" happens to be the internal (or external) voice of parental figures.

Focus on What You Want, Not on What You Don't Want

Commitment expresses itself through declaration and following through with focused attention. What we pay attention to in life is a choice and a crucial aspect of the decision-making process. The game of golf nicely illustrates the power of what we turn our attention toward. According to the best instructors, the process of hitting good golf shots requires making a commitment to the result you are aiming for, rather than focusing on any of the things that could go wrong. For instance, if you are focused on avoiding hazards like a pond or sand trap, your shot will invariably seek one out because, even though you didn't want it, your swing follows your focus. As this clearly demonstrates, whatever we focus on is what we subconsciously expect . . . and what we expect is what we will get. The best way, therefore, to avoid hazards is to single-mindedly focus on the target, commit to the shot you have in mind, and then trust your swing (your decision-making). In golf as well as life, a steady target-oriented approach produces confidence and efficacy.

The power of commitment grows with a focus on your target. Your vision is energized by your passion (in golf, to complete our example, this could be a strong desire to play better or score well). Make the commitment and become the change you want. Hold on to your vision. Hold on to yourself. Derive strength of purpose by channeling archetypal Sovereign energy as the CEO, King, or Queen of your own life.

For any major decision, the very last stage is making a firm commitment to accept the consequences of your decision whatever they may be. Formalizing the commitment in the form of a written agreement can be a powerful and positive way to do this. To help, I recommend writing an agreement with your Self (the Self archetype) that goes something like this:

Dear Self,
I hereby make the following commitment to you:
[write a short description of your decision]
I am letting go of fear and doubt, and I resolve to do my best to
    implement my decision with power and grace.
Signed: _____   *Date:* _____

Once you have signed an agreement with Self, don't second-guess it. You've taken your best shot at formulating the best decision; that part of the work is done. Don't keep replaying options in your mind. Visionaries are those who have developed enough confidence to start making their own strategic decisions without doubting themselves. The primary cause of the worst financial decisions I made in my life was a lack of confidence in myself, and deferring to the judgment of others with more academic credentials.

With the energy you've invested in the VDM process, you have done as well as you could under the circumstances. Second-guessing or climbing a wall of worry will only unbalance you and possibly cause you to sabotage a brave decision by making a more fearful one. The past is one of the things in life that we can never change. The strategic route is to focus on creating the future, mustering our confidence, and being receptive to support wherever it is available to us.

Answering the "When" Question— The Timing Part of the Decision Equation

Once you have decided on and have committed to *what* your next move should be, you still need to answer one last, important question: "*When* should I make my move?" Making your best next move at the right time is the secret of becoming great at games like chess and Go—as well as strategic decision-making over a lifetime. An excellent sense of timing will naturally arise from the steady practice of more conscious decision-making that thinks ahead.

As said before, when it comes to the most important decisions, it's never advisable to rush. On the other hand, if you don't implement a strategic decision in a timely manner, the window of opportunity will pass. So, *how* can you know when the time is right to execute a decision and start taking action?

There is no purely logical way to answer the timing question. Logic can help address the question of when to make your move, perhaps through a review of the past to discern trend lines that might repeat in the future. But such a projection is not enough to negotiate big shifts or life-changing decisions that represent creative departures from the patterns of your past. There is no pat formula for perfect timing.

Deciding when to make the next move is almost entirely intuitive. When it's time to effect dynamic action, a feeling in your gut (or however intuitive signaling works for you) can provide the signal you need. Rather than impulsively plunging toward the instant gratification of an appetite or desire, we need to invite intuition into the process and give it the space it needs. If your mind is quiet enough to perceive it, an intuitive signal will arise.

When you follow your intuitive instinct, you get a visceral sense of being in the flow, in sync with life. This is similar to the blissful feeling of being in *the zone* during athletics or dancing, negotiating a win-win deal, or cocreating a relationship. Of course, because intuitive signals can be subtle, making a move may still feel risky to the ego. And, sure, you will make some errors—especially when you mistake an emotional reaction for an intuitive feeling.

Learning to activate intuition is a trial-by-error process. Progress may be three steps forward then one step back for a while, but as you make fewer emotional decisions and more conscious ones, you will create a life of greater abundance and joy. Because timing is an intuitive decision, it will improve the more you tune your conscious mind in to intuitive sensitivity.

That's right—become more intuitive regarding the "what" questions, and you will automatically develop better timing around the *when*.

Using the I Ching to Improve Timing

As we saw in chapter 8, the I Ching was designed to help us see how things go together in time in order to synchronize decisions and actions accordingly. For the ancient Chinese, using the I Ching was a sacred practice, much like when the Greeks visited the oracle at Delphi. The I Ching, when consulted with sincerity and openness, generates synchronicities that are relevant to the seeker's state of mind at the time. Sometimes its reflections are crystal clear; sometimes it speaks in riddles like at Delphi. Using the I Ching can help us transcend our linear conception of time and invoke a sense of enchantment. It can shed light on new possibilities to give us a broader point of view, expanding our insights beyond the current focus of our conscious minds to reveal important patterns that our egos hadn't considered.

In the case of a timing question, it works best to frame your I Ching query in the present tense. Try asking something like, "What is the best approach to take to [the situation or relationship] now?" Then look at the response you receive to see which one of three directions that it might be pointing to. Just like it is taught in the martial arts—the philosophy of which is based on Taoist classics like the I Ching—there are three options: When it's skillful to assert oneself, when it is advisable to do nothing, and when it is best to retreat (or run like hell).

Bide Your Time

Good timing doesn't mean that something must happen immediately. Sometimes just waiting for the right moment and doing nothing is good timing in action. This point is beautifully illustrated in the Hermann Hesse classic *Siddhartha*, where the main character becomes enlightened and finds inner peace by mastering three skills: meditation, fasting, and *waiting*.[3] For decision-makers, waiting is an important ability. We always have the option to take our time when implementing an important decision.

Experienced intuition produces well-timed decisions—knowing when to say yes, when to say no, when to sleep on it, when to go for it, and when to delay gratification and wait it out. Daniel Goleman's groundbreaking research on "emotional intelligence" sheds light on how we can balance the right and left sides of the brain. Emotional intelligence shows up when we are receptive to good advice from trusted sources, and it provides a rationale for delaying gratification as a marker of personal maturity and good timing. The antithesis of emotional intelligence is compulsive or addictive behavior. You can be sure that when addictive impulses kick in, good timing becomes virtually impossible.

Perfect timing is the ideal, but who is to determine perfection? Philosophically, we realize that synchronicity is taking place all the time, even if we don't perceive it yet. From a cosmic point of view, things unfold perfectly according to some grand pattern that we cannot fully understand. Sometimes this includes the moves we make and when to make them. Even if we make an imperfect decision—some kind of relative "mistake" that produces an educational lesson—that might be exactly what we need right now. When it comes right down to it, the only way to perceive perfect timing is by *feeling* it. The modern expression "I'm not feeling it" captures the essence of perceiving good or not-so-good timing. Unless you are feeling your intuitive sense, you should avoid executing major decisions.

Pull the Trigger, Then Let Go

When you realize that you are clear and feeling it, it is time to execute. Call forth the inner Hero's fierce resolve, which the process of making big decisions naturally builds up to. Call the shot and give yourself (and any delegates you may have) the command to make it happen. At this point, you have set things up so that you can put one foot in front of the other, take one step at a time, and let the Universe (or your staff) take care of the details. The situation will change before your eyes, whether you try to control the way it takes shape or not. Let go of managing details and let the chips land where they may. Breathe a sigh of relief that you have risen to the occasion, and don't look back.

Making significant decisions causes extra stress to the extent that we put pressure on ourselves by becoming attached to results, including the way that we think results should occur. After making and executing a decision, it is time to let go and relax, knowing you have done the best you can. Letting go of worry or of "sweating the small stuff" allows you to feel an ecstatic sense of freedom. You accept that you made the best decision under the circumstances.

Now you are in position to make more, smaller moves—intelligent tactical moves that support your strategic decision. These don't require an abundance of intuition to figure out. You can usually take one logical step at a time. Things will change in front of your eyes, whether you try to control every little thing or not. So, don't try too damn hard! Do your tasks, delegate to others if you can, and let go of attachment to an exact form as change occurs. Exercise unconditional acceptance and go bravely with the synchronistic flow.

10

Perseverance and Mastery

Success is sweet, but it usually has the scent of sweat about it.

—**Anonymous**

Perseverance furthers.

—*Book of Changes*

Executing a bold strategic decision is not a one-time action or a single move in a new direction. The execution of long-term decisions must be renewed day after day to give the strategy a chance to thrive. That is why perseverance is a character trait that I emphasize when speaking to students and entrepreneurs.

"Perseverance furthers" is the most common sentence in the I Ching, serving as a necessary reminder that reaching a destination can sometimes require us to maintain a gritty determination. Even then, in spite of our best efforts to be creative and quick, destiny always plays out in its own good time. The timing of providence is usually not fast enough to suit the eager imagination or the anxious ego, which is why it is important that we make it a point to renew our daily commitment to heartfelt strategies.

When people commit to a plan of action on the basis of inspiration or love, a fierce determination can arise inside of them, despite all the risks and challenges. After I launched my first enterprise, I remember gritting my teeth and bravely repeating to myself, "I will never give up!"—especially when the going got tough. When faced with daunting circumstances or the threat of bankruptcy, I would repeat my determination mantra, put my head down, and focus on taking care of business. Fortunately, I had learned and developed valuable business skills I could keep busy with and put to good use.

In his bestselling book *Outliers*, Malcolm Gladwell shows how the life stories of innovators like Steve Jobs and Bill Gates demonstrate that mastery of skills is a key indicator of success. True mastery, argues Gladwell, takes ten thousand hours of practice.[1] During the first fifteen years of my own software career, when I worked for others, I put in over ten thousand hours at direct marketing. This gave me a core competency that was invaluable for my startup. Mastery is a combination of this kind of preparation plus a gritty perseverance. As Abraham Lincoln famously said, "I will prepare and someday my chance will come."

Nevertheless, even with strong competencies, a healthy intuition, and a passion for your calling, business survival for a bootstrap enterprise is bound to be a struggle. It's extraordinarily difficult for a startup to survive even a few years, especially if it lacks financial backers. As my story attests, I know from personal experience that the challenge of keeping things afloat can test every ounce of one's resourcefulness, determination, and perseverance—not to mention the ability to sleep at night.

In spite of the hardships, there is nothing more rewarding than following your muse and doing something meaningful to you, something that engages your heart. The power of an inspired calling—coupled with intuitive decision-making and good timing—is the true source of "good luck." People who have mastered a skill and developed a knack for good timing may seem to be merely lucky to a casual observer, but if you scratch the surface, you will find that their success probably has much more to do with the mastery of skills and great decisions. Our culture and our brains are continually affirming inherited raw talent and the good luck of successful people while downplaying their hard work, good decision-making, and the road blocks they have overcome.

In addition to a positive and expectant attitude, these factors take years to develop, but at least their development is subject to your will and under your control. Part of our learning is to understand the synchronistic aspect of timing. When you master how to recognize and use synchronicity to improve your own timing, you will be that much further ahead in the game.

Defying good business logic and the advice of my peers, I clung to my belief that the world could come to appreciate computer-assisted divination systems. In the beginning the only thing I knew for sure was that at least one reasonably sane person wanted it—myself! The *Visionary I Ching* app is fairly popular these days, but in 1989 I was one person on a short list who appreciated the idea of I Ching software, the likes of which had never existed. I supported my resolve with an invocation like this: "Oh, Spirit of Divine Providence, if I am the only one who likes what I am creating, and if I am the only one who benefits from using it, let that be enough for me." This was my prayer—my perseverance prayer.

As daunting as the expensive and exhausting project of developing a new kind of software was, the very idea of bringing the I Ching to life in a modern way energized my passion. I accepted the challenge. It also occurred to me that if a computer could be used to cast an authentic I Ching reading, there would be other elegant applications to be discovered. My sense of risk was offset by the realization that, at the very least, this was an exciting adventure that would grow me—like an initiation into a mystery school. I was inspired by the challenge of using modern technology to make psychologically sophisticated ancient spiritual technologies more easily accessible in an engaging way.

Armed with encouragement from the I Ching itself, I created my own luck by taking the risk of allowing Infinite Intelligence to work through me in support of an offbeat inspiration. Sometimes, a period of great difficulty or dissatisfaction holds a hidden blessing, and that had been my situation. My job, as prestigious and well-paid as it was, had become a source of great unhappiness. I wanted creative freedom.

My difficulties at work forced me to turn inward at a time when I was ready in terms of skills—but also psychologically and emotionally—to discover my calling and build something new. I perceived that there would be a synchronous elegance for me in producing an accessible, interactive I Ching experience that had been prompted by the feeling of gratitude I personally had for the I Ching, which I had been using for twenty years.

Because it was inspired by a desire to invent products and services that supported my broader vision, I called the company Visionary Software and gave myself the title Chief Visionary. Our original company slogan was "Creative Freedom through Vision and Humor," which was printed on the first Synchronicity packages that appeared on the shelves of software stores back then. When I sold the second version of the business after eighteen years of ups and downs, my original vision had evolved to produce much greater levels of creative freedom than I ever had imagined. In the process, I learned that being inspired by a vision and maintaining a sense of humor are two elements of successful risk-taking that keep you from going crazy. If you are willing to be open and pay attention to what's going on inside and around you, you never know what the future has in store. Listen to yourself and put your energy into the things you want to do rather than just what's popular or profitable in the short term. The universe will speak if you commit to listening.

For me—perhaps more than most—becoming an entrepreneur was all about trusting my intuition, because there was no way to rationalize a decision to develop I Ching software in 1989. In truth, my peers were dumfounded that I left an executive position in a growing industry to take on such a wild and chancy project. They didn't understand my passion for the I Ching or my visions of multimedia, and could not relate to my determination to invest everything I had to create and market such a program. But I was determined to give it a try. In the process, I would learn that, even when supported by enthusiasm as fervent as mine, the day-to-day work of manifestation requires exceptional levels of determination and perseverance. Grit is at least as crucial for successful outcomes as inspiration and talent.

A Tale of Grit

Even before the Synchronicity program was finished, getting my unique software product onto store shelves was a critical goal. In 1989, there actually was such a thing as software stores, and Egghead Software was the largest chain in the world with over two hundred stores. It was one of the only retail outlets that carried programs for the Macintosh computer, which had about a 5 percent share of the personal computer market at the time. Survival as a software developer of a consumer product for the Mac depended tremendously upon getting onto Egghead's shelves for the holiday buying season. Egghead's deadline for placing a large purchase order was the end of September.

In March of 1989, as we were nearing the completion of the Synchronicity program and product, I was trying to make contact with a fellow named DJ, who was the merchandising manager of Egghead's Macintosh division and its only buyer. As with any bootstrap entrepreneur, it is critical to get profitable sooner rather than later, and convincing DJ to place an order had become absolutely critical to the survival of our fledgling enterprise. Having spent all my savings and just keeping it all together on my consulting income, I knew I didn't have the resources to stick it out another year unless we ramped up sales.

It was not easy getting on the phone with DJ. In fact, it was virtually impossible. His schedule was incredibly hectic, because his unit had to spend $60 million per year in marketing funds from Microsoft, which controlled 80 percent of the software business at that time (including Mac office software). This made him a busy man in a high-pressure situation—and I could feel it—but empathy for DJ was not going to save my company. Only a large purchase order for my strange little product could do that!

DJ was young, arrogant, and extremely overloaded. But I persisted. Since he literally never called me back, I began ringing his extension throughout the day, every day, only leaving a message once a week or so. (There was no caller ID in those days, so he didn't know that I was pursuing him.) My hope was that one of these times he would pick up the phone. One evening in May around 6 PM—after the end of normal office hours—I had the impulse to try his extension one last time that day. Lo and behold, he answered the phone, probably thinking it was his current wife. From that point on, I called him every couple of days at 6 PM, hoping he would pick up. In this way, I succeeded in getting a conversation with DJ about once every two or three weeks for the next several months.

Ultimately, he found our unique new product interesting. Like most Mac aficionados at the time, he thought of himself as a pioneer and he wanted to stay abreast of the latest software technologies. He liked the idea of putting his stamp on something. He agreed to let me send him a beta review copy of the Synchronicity program. Thus began a long, laborious, and sometimes tortuous back-and-forth. When I was fortunate enough to get him on the phone, he would invariably create new hoops for us to jump through.

Some of his demands were outrageous. For instance, he insisted that we include a little rubber frog in every box, as a nod to our multimedia effect of randomly croaking frogs in a Japanese garden. (Just for fun, I trademarked Random Frogs, so that we were the only software that could ever offer this special feature.) Increasingly desperate to win his approval on that large initial order, I was in no position to argue. I did everything he asked (including procuring a couple of thousand expensive little rubber frogs) without audible grumbling. The seasonal ordering deadline was drawing near and I was running out of money. It was a stressful period of uncertainty, made all the worse by DJ's attitude of casual arbitrariness. As the deadline got closer, I was having nightmares of going bankrupt and losing everything.

One day when I got a hold of him, DJ sardonically asked, "How is it that I seem to talk to you more often than I talk to Microsoft?" With a wry smile on the other end of the line, I replied, "I don't know . . . must be the luck of the Irish!" The good news was that he kept talking to me. He was beginning to soften. But the clock was ticking and time was running out for our little company. I knew that if I could not get DJ to place an order soon, Visionary Software would go bankrupt. Our survival depended on one person—the fickle Mr. DJ.

September arrived, but still no order, not even an indication from DJ that he was leaning in that direction. And it was on my mother's birthday, September 17, that I received dreadful news when I called for DJ. "He is no longer with the company," I was simply told. I was devastated. It was a dark night. Perseverance furthers, eh?

One week later in the mail, I received a purchase order for a thousand units of the Synchronicity program for placement in all two hundred Egghead stores. Placing that order had been DJ's last official act. Perseverance *had* furthered! This order from Egghead was the only thing that kept us from going bankrupt that first year. (Interestingly, DJ came to work for me a couple of years later as a consultant, and we became friends. I officiated at his wedding—and I'm pleased to report that he is still very happily married. Let's hear it for synchronicity!)

Thanks to a gritty determination, I had not given up, and the business had survived a major hurdle. After investing so much blood, sweat, tears, and fears, if my little business venture had not survived that first year, I may have never pursued a big creative dream ever again. Certainly, my life would have been hugely different—and probably much more limited—as a result. Was this a "miracle"? Depending upon your definition, I suppose so, but I also know perseverance played a huge part. The vision to see for yourself what others don't, an inspired sense of dedication, and the intuitive intelligence to make wise decisions, are all parts of the matrix of success. But a determined persistence is the glue that binds and holds the manifestation process together. As they say in twelve-step programs, "it works if you work it." And, as Einstein supposedly put it, "It's not that I'm so smart, it's just that I stay with problems longer."

The Role of Sacrifice

The concept of personal sacrifice is not popular, because it raises the fear that we might lose something we already have. Nevertheless, sometimes we face choices that are mutually exclusive. One of the costs of manifesting what you want is that you may have to make some room for it by letting go of something else. Sometimes you have to be willing to sacrifice your pride, comforts, and security to achieve a higher level of success, as my story demonstrates.

The kind of persistence it takes to launch a new enterprise from scratch involves a tremendous amount of sacrifice—much larger than most people are willing to make. I know that I paid a high price—and not only in terms of long hours, frustration, and recurring fears of catastrophe. I also had to swallow my pride when dealing with the ridicule of people who thought I was crazy. And, as noted, I dealt with the whims of at least one person who had the power to waste a tremendous amount of my time and energy and to possibly devastate my hopes and dreams.

No matter what you want to manifest, life will offer many distractions. It is often essential to give up some comfort or pleasure to focus on an important decision or task. This sacrifice is made easier when your heart is involved, as you are attending to a higher affection. Inflamed by a passion for my creative vision, I was motivated to sacrifice time, energy, a social life, and practically my firstborn son for the cause. I was so in love with my venture that I committed myself to it and took it all the way. In the process, I effectively sacrificed being available for a serious relationship commitment, which was also something that I wanted. But I was effectively already "married"—to my dream.

Energetically, I was not available for a deeply intimate relationship. It would have been helpful to have an understanding life partner, but like an artist obsessed, my heart was absorbed with my creative passion. It may be possible, but I think it must be quite difficult to develop and maintain an intimate partnership and family while also devoting oneself to bootstrap entrepreneurship. Unless relationship partners share the same vision and have complementary skills, it would require a mate willing to sacrifice a substantial portion of her or his own needs in support of the person who feels compelled to risk everything to get a startup off the ground. That would be noble, but it is a lot to ask of anybody!

This brings up the question of sacrifices that are made by people who make it their mission to support or take care of others. They might give themselves for love—or lots of other possible reasons. If they are driven more by their loving nature than by a fearful sense of duty, their efforts will create great happiness for themselves as well as those they can help. To voluntarily choose to serve or support others is a noble vocation in itself. In the yogic tradition, one of the four original yogas is called "karma yoga," the chosen path of selfless service. Someone following this path lives in harmony with his or her purpose, or dharma. This yoga is for those who find joy in being of service, perhaps while living an ordinary life working and raising a family. Mother Teresa is the extreme poster child for karma yoga in our times, devoting her life to serving the poorest of the poor and dedicating herself to alleviating the sufferings of others.

As long as it is freely chosen, a path of selfless service is also entrepreneurial in spirit. In the self-absorbed world we live in, it's quite an independent choice. If providing services or resources for others is one's aptitude and true destiny, it is a high calling that deserves recognition, reward, and power, because it is so vital to the success of any relationship or partnership, enterprise, and society as a whole. At the very least, being of service is a vocation that cultivates acceptance, humility, and unconditional love—qualities that support a deeper sense of meaning and fulfillment. Selfless service embodies an interpersonal or social definition of success. Anything that expands and deepens your heart is *a risk that grows you* and ultimately a movement toward happiness.

We always make our choices in life according to our strongest values at the time. We may need to let go of something that we like or enjoy very much, but which has become a lesser desire. To devote ourselves to a lofty purpose or goal and summon the required determination and perseverance, our mission must be our primary focus. Staying aware that you may need to make tradeoffs, involving pruning some of your desires, will help you make more conscious decisions and feel less conflicted when you do. Letting go of a desire or attachment for the sake of a stronger goal or greater good is a sacrifice that enhances self-esteem and is an important aspect of the Hero's Journey. A wise counselor once referred to this letting go as the "expulsive power of a higher affection."

Patience and Delayed Gratification

> Do you have the patience to wait
> till your mud settles and the water is clear?
> Can you remain unmoving
> till the right action arises by itself?
>
> —Lao Tzu

The practice of patience is a form of sacrifice—the letting go of an immediate desire in favor of a higher-order desire that may take time and effort to develop. The art of patience is helped by accepting that there are things we can control and things we can't, and allowing questions to pose themselves without judging or fixating on control. Patience is a major challenge in our hectic world, plagued as we are by hurry sickness. In order to escape the pressure of making important decisions, our fragmented attention is easily diverted to omnipresent novelties like entertainment or gossip.

In today's world, people crave instant attention, affection, recognition, and self-assurance. For some reason, we tend to confuse quantity of attention with quality—even though the differences are easy to recognize. One of the causes for such confusion is that social media holds high importance these days and perpetuates impatience around hard work or self-improvement. The unfortunate result of scattering our attention is an inability to wait much for anything without experiencing anxiety. Furthermore, our ability to fully enjoy an activity may be compromised by the hurrying habit of thinking about what's coming next and getting ahead of ourselves rather than living in the moment. We find it impossible to fully enjoy the present when we are preoccupied with multitasking or anticipating what's next.

Those who have patience will enjoy greater opportunities of understanding and will increase their ability to create possibilities for something better to happen. Patience transforms obstacles—even a rejection or failure—into possibilities. People who embrace a patient attitude are better able to accept situations, let go of expectations, and move forward taking one conscientious step at a time.

Delaying gratification is a deliberate practice of patience, letting go of the ego's desire for immediate gratification. The ability to control one's impulses is a foundational trait of strong character, emotional intelligence, and wise decision-making. Otherwise, this world of constant distraction will toss you about and have its way with you. Delayed gratification is a sacrifice worth making if you believe that your eventual fulfillment will not only happen, but will happen in a more satisfying way because of your investment in letting it happen according to its own good timing.

Grandma's Law

As a single parent, I tried to pass the lesson of delayed gratification on to my son. I called it "Grandma's Law" and it went like this: "Sure, you can have some ice cream . . . but only after you finish your green beans." It was a lesson that was imposed by my mother at a young age: do your assigned tasks first, before going out to play. Specifically, I invoked Grandma's Law with my son to persuade him to make a habit of doing chores and homework on Saturday, reserving Sunday as his full day set aside for play, rather than the other way around.

Learning Grandma's Law early in my own life helped me experience the efficacy of delaying gratification. By getting the work out of the way, by preempting deadlines, I was less stressed, I felt good about staying ahead of the game, and ultimately I thrived in school and as an entrepreneur. A nice bonus of putting work before play is that when the time for leisure comes, you enjoy it more with less anxiety because you are ahead of the game, without tasks hanging over your head until the last stressful minute.

Be Receptive to Good Advice

Everyone has opinions, and people enjoy giving advice to friends and colleagues. Unfortunately, as much as we may resonate with friends emotionally, they rarely make objective advisors. This is especially true when it comes to strategic decisions that involve big changes or staying on track through the ups and downs of a calling that they don't understand, can't relate to. After all, your friends like you the way you are—that's why they are your friends! They are naturally resistant to seeing you change because it threatens the relationship as they know it. Look to friends for moral and emotional support, but seek elsewhere for objective feedback and strategic advice when it comes to manifesting a bold new vision.

A primary function of a board of directors is to advise the CEO or executive director. Directors of large companies are paid handsomely to attend meetings and perform advisory roles. In a startup company, however, there is usually a small, unpaid group of otherwise busy people on the board. I had learned from my previous ventures that it is difficult to get high-quality, experienced advisors to sit on the board of a startup company lest legal liabilities arise, especially when there is no compensation or insurance involved.

When I started Visionary Networks, my second venture, I decided to take full legal responsibility myself and do without a board of directors. In Oregon, one person is legally able to fill both of the only required seats, president and secretary. Instead of trying to assemble a real board of experienced directors who were willing to take on some legal and fiscal responsibility, I chose to assemble an advisory board of two. I asked two successful entrepreneur friends—both of whom had already succeeded at software development and publishing—if they would help me in a "low-risk" advisory arrangement. It would involve neither legal liability nor a lot of time. I offered to give each of them 1 percent of the company's stock, to be issued immediately, and all they had to agree to was to meet with me once a week to go through my decision-making agenda with me. On top of that, Visionary Networks would buy us all lunch! These two guys, already successful software entrepreneurs, had served on my first board of directors. They were both inclined to help and agreed to my unusual proposition. Thereafter, the company would treat me and one of them to a lunch meeting to discuss strategic decisions, which we did mostly separately every week until we sold the company eight years later.

The agenda of both weekly meetings was always the same: to go over the most important decisions that I was facing as CEO. On occasion, I would show an advisor a list of the reasons or benefits I had formulated for each of the options that I saw before me, so that we could discuss and weigh them together. Both of these fellows were analytical types whose perspectives complemented and balanced my inspiration-driven approach to corporate strategy. I called them "No Men," because they were the furthest thing from the proverbial "Yes Men." They almost enjoyed shooting down my too-many creative ideas. I like variety and want to do everything! "That doesn't move the meter, dammit—focus!" they would each remind me.

Under an agreement I had made with myself, I had decided that I would not make any strategic decisions unless I got at least one of my No Men to agree it was worth a test. I was not legally obligated to abide by their advice, but this was a discipline I imposed on myself to govern my rambunctiously creative right brain.

During that eight-year period, I actually only made one major decision that both of them advised against. That financially risky decision was to acquire the domain name Tarot.com. Ironically, buying that five-letter domain turned out to be one of my better business decisions, becoming worth a fortune over time—which shows how the exception does indeed sometimes prove the rule.

Over the years, my advisors were generous and patient—two qualities that eventually paid off handsomely when I sold the company and wrote them each a check for $200,000. And that was in addition to eight years of free weekly lunches!

You can recruit your own advisory board without giving stock away, although options linked to successful results could make sense if your venture is a corporation with stock. Or if you use your advisors judiciously, you could pay them for meetings (plus lunch) or find another way to reward them beyond the satisfaction they might derive from mentoring you (which is enough in some cases, depending upon their motivation and needs). In any case, make sure you select people who are willing to tell you what you need to hear, not what you want to hear. Being confronted rarely feels comfortable, but what you are looking for is sound advice, not fuzzy feelings. That can come later—in fact, over the years both of my advisors became close friends.

When looking for advisors, consider who will balance your personality and skills. And it's especially good if they have a record of success in a comparable field. Former executives are often interested in mentoring. Another option is to retain an executive coach, especially if you can find one with experience related to your field. A coach will help make sure that you are making conscious decisions and following through on the commitments you've made. However you set it up, it's good to have advisors who can focus on helping you make strategic and tactical decisions, as well as providing moral support to help you persevere through the challenges that will arise.

Although I was originally hired at a computer center to work as a low-paid secretary, my career was jumpstarted by the fact that Dan, my boss, was a graciously willing mentor for me. He saw my potential and was impressed by my enthusiasm in the way I picked up the ball and did what I could to learn everything that could be helpful to him. He permitted me to go beyond the job description to do more for him, even taking me to trade shows as part of my education in software marketing and sales. Even though I made mistakes, he empowered me to take on any responsibilities I felt ready for. This was an invaluable gift for which I am ever grateful. Even though I was never promoted to a higher position in the two years I worked there, I developed skills and catapulted myself into a career as a "software marketing specialist." And my next job paid twice as much.

Perseverance is made so much easier when you have an active and available support system. Some people prefer to go it alone and try to do without help as much as possible—perhaps to prove something—but they are only making life more difficult than it has to be. Perhaps they think they shouldn't need anyone's help, that they should be able to do it all on their own. Or maybe they don't feel they deserve the time and careful attention of others.

A refusal to seek and receive guidance from advisors and mentors usually stems from an ego-based need to prove oneself, which, I theorize, could be the outgrowth of a history of sibling rivalry or insecure parenting. Sometimes people fear that they won't get enough credit for results if their decisions and actions are informed or improved on by the input of others. This all-or-nothing thinking can come from stubborn rebelliousness, an inaccurate self-assessment, or a prideful need to prove one's specialness. Either way, it's the immature ego trying to prove itself as not needing any help or wanting to be thought worthy of special esteem.

Independence becomes self-defeating when it gets to the point where your need to assert your autonomy is so great that you are not receptive to help from willing and qualified sources. Failing to accept support due to insecurity only leads to worse decision-making, which leads to more insecurity and so on—a perverse downward spiral. Persevering is never easy, but being receptive to the advice of mentors and wise elders can help tremendously. We all need support.

Personal Support Groups

While I was pursuing the aloof and elusive Mr. DJ at Egghead, it was a day-to-day challenge to sustain my faith in my vision. I needed moral support and operational advice, but I didn't exactly know where to turn. Operating from a vision that was ahead of its time, I couldn't expect the average person to understand multimedia software, the I Ching, or how I envisioned one enhancing the other. Nevertheless, feeling the need for support, I joined a Mastermind group at a church where I volunteered as meditation minister.

Mastermind groups are over a hundred years old and experienced something of a resurgence in New Thought circles during the 1980s. The purpose of such groups was to help their members clarify their visions and support each other. Of course, part of this was helping to dissolve doubts people hold about what they deserve and whether they are up to the challenge of achieving their goals.

The five other people in my Mastermind group were the only people at that time who were aware of my efforts to get a purchase order from DJ and how important it was to my company's survival. This weekly meeting was my only source of support or encouragement. Even though the other group members didn't really understand what I was trying to do, they helped me keep faith in myself . . . and my right to have a vision of my own. These supporters could not provide practical business advice for a startup software company, but I benefitted greatly from their moral and emotional support. The ability to receive support—whether intellectually or emotionally or financially—is a central requirement of ongoing VDM. Find a place where ideas can be exchanged and tested, mentors found, and support networks formed. Backing yourself up with a support group is a great way to accomplish your goals and will help you persevere.

Whoops . . . Knowing When to Pull the Plug

Perseverance involves adapting to conditions that are beyond our control, but even this has its limits. Your vision may be off in terms of scope or timing. No matter how strong your determination, an idea that is too big or too far ahead of its time is not going to take off anytime soon. Examples of this abound. Take the world of alternative energy. Nobody disputes the fact that cold fusion is a wondrous concept. Unfortunately, we are nowhere near being able to produce it. And, even if one had the scientific aptitude and skills to make it work, the scope of the project would require hundreds of millions of dollars, which is far beyond what a lone scientist or creative genius could raise. Learning to accept and being able to manage a high probability of failure—psychologically as well as financially—is an important part of the entrepreneurial mindset. In a sense, knowing when to pull the plug is confronting failure head-on, which is only possible if we stay humble. Don't keep a bad idea on life support because it is too painful to admit that your timing was off or you did things in the wrong order. Live and learn!

When I developed the first divination software, it was at least ten years ahead of the marketplace and, after a few years, my first startup went bankrupt. Fortunately, I was in a position to develop the same idea ten years later when the world wide web was taking off as a platform for marketing and e-commerce. After I sold the company in 2007, people would remark how perfect my timing was! That was true with regard to the sale of the company, but the timing didn't feel great during the fifteen prior years, when I was struggling to hold things together. The new management team of three MBAs, who bought the company in service of their superior business vision, drove it into the ground and I walked away with nothing but a hard lesson. But there is no doubt how far off my timing about divination software had been. There is a time to call it quits, or at least take a long break. As the lyrics of the song "The Gambler" put it, "You've got to know when to hold 'em, know when to fold 'em." Sometimes in failure, the most important thing you gain are the lessons you learned, and if that's all you get, that's okay. Lessons that are truly learned are a huge advantage going forward.

Regrets Be Damned

Perseverance is a forward-looking quality grounded in faith for your vision. When you are too focused on the past, perseverance will suffer.

This can take the form of holding on to feelings of regret, perhaps over unfortunate decisions you have made. Regret can be thought of as holding on to negative judgments of the past. But this is totally nonproductive. A feeling of regret is only a useful signal that there is some mistake for which you need to forgive yourself. It is a residual emotion that inhibits personal growth. Properly grieve what is irrevocably lost, try and take a lesson from it if you can, and then let it go so you can focus on new possibilities.

We all need to let go of regret, perhaps by taking refuge in the belief that everything happens for a reason. Who are we to say that our mistaken timing or some unforeseen obstacle was not necessary to lead us toward a critical piece of learning or a new opportunity, a stepping stone helping us on our path forward? What if you missed a train but met your lifetime partner on the platform? Would you classify that as a regrettable mistake? Or was that destiny working itself in inscrutable ways? We need to maintain respect for life's mysterious ways.

It's impossible to notice new opportunities or make great decisions when we indulge in regret or self-recrimination or harbor doubts about our worthiness. Holding on to feelings of embarrassment or shame ultimately disempowers us and makes us feel more desperate. Despair leads to more self-defeating decisions, and so on, in a downward spiral. Let's improve our ability to forgive ourselves for the educational mistakes of the past—starting now. Embrace your vulnerability and know that you can rectify past regrets and turn mistakes into educational blessings. It becomes easier to stop judging yourself when you remember the wonderfully mysterious way that the universe tends to bring everything back into balance again and again.

To the surprise of some people I know, I say that I have no regrets. Of course, I have made plenty of mistakes. But when a feeling of regret begins to arise, I take it as a signal that I need to learn something, forgive myself, let go, and move forward with as much faith in myself as possible. This habit of self-forgiveness opens the mind and is a prerequisite to fully learning from whatever comes next. Once you have forgiven yourself—

and have made amends to others, if necessary—there is no reason to hold on to negative memories of past mistakes. Just forgive yourself and move on, knowing that even though you may have made mistakes, you did the best you could have done under the circumstances. Accept yourself completely with all your imperfections. Focus on feeling grateful for the lesson and resolve to make better decisions going forward. Letting go is a freeing process, liberating your soul's creative imagination to soar again. Look forward!

So, don't fret too much when you make mistakes. They are going to happen. If a decision does not play out the way you intended, restart your brainstorming and decision-making processes, beginning with a fresh review of options you have now. Things change, sometimes rapidly. Give thought and energy to the practice of conscious decision-making, like an Olympic athlete steadily perfecting her or his form. Perseverance and resilience play huge roles in the manifestation process.

The Challenge of Unconditional Acceptance

A prerequisite for perseverance is unconditional acceptance—of ourselves, others, and whatever is happening—whether we totally understand what is happening or not. We never do. Our peace of mind can be disrupted by a pressing desire to know *why* something has taken place, especially if it is something that we didn't want or expect. Caught up in resistance to the way a situation has turned out, we demand an explanation. Unfortunately, questions like "Why did this happen to me?" are a waste of time and our attention. Sometimes we just need to accept the fact that the way things are working out may not be comprehensible for the time being. Coming to a full understanding of why something happened cannot be forced, no matter how urgently you might want to know.

If we get stuck on the "why me" question, we are keeping ourselves off balance. We need to develop unconditional acceptance—of ourselves and the way things are. The higher challenge is not to figure everything out, but to accept life and our role in it unconditionally whether our limited brains can now make sense of it or not. This is humility—to roll with the punches, get back in rhythm, and regain our balance by accepting everything, including the limitations of our own capacity to know all the answers.

Paradoxically, acceptance is the most powerful catalyst for change. Now, this is not the same as resignation. When we accept people and situations just the way they are, we allow them the space to evolve according to their own temperament or nature. Joyful acceptance is a simple and beautiful aspect of love. Resistance or lack of acceptance, on the other hand, stimulates conflict and polarization and adds suffering to pain by building up the emotional charge. (Just ask the parent of a teenager!) Remember, reality is your friend. Avoiding it is a powerful defense mechanism in which a situation becomes too much to handle and you simply refuse to experience it. Keep in mind, denial is normal and we all engage in it at times. If we keep finding ourselves in the same negative situation and clueless as to why, then we are undoubtedly in denial about something. Look for the red flags and question your assumptions and you'll be on your way to breaking a negative cycle. As Lao Tzu, most famous of Taoist sages and author of the Tao Te Ching, is said to have observed, "Life is a series of natural and spontaneous changes. Don't resist them; that only creates sorrow. Let reality be reality. Let things flow naturally forward in whatever way they like."[2] Trying to get the universe to give you answers on demand is like going out in the backyard and pulling on a bush to make it grow faster. The effort to force things only harms the plant. Instead of always trying to force changes to happen the way your ego thinks they should, try thinking of yourself as a fledgling Warrior of acceptance and let it develop however it will.

Calling up the Warrior archetype in this situation helps me connect with the strength needed to accept the things I don't understand or don't like, because unconditional acceptance is not easy. I include "fledgling" to remind myself that I'm always a relative beginner at this—I am not great at it and may never be. Although we love to know, demanding answers is not only unrealistic, it is arrogant. As we develop in wisdom, the adage "The more you know, the more you know you don't know" becomes more true to us and supports our capacity for unconditional acceptance.

We would all like to change things, including other people—if only to help them adapt to and share our favored ways of seeing and doing, our schedules, our lifestyles. And sometimes we are anxious to change things fast. But perseverance is about learning to flow in time—bobbing up and down like a surfer waiting for the right wave at the right time. To persevere with alertness intact, we need to be comfortable with some degree of ambiguity. Mastery at life requires that we be nimble and improve our ability to change speed or direction, which helps us respond intelligently to the waves of change as they rise and fall, rather than losing ourselves in the undertow.

From Perseverance Arises Resilience

Although I eventually achieved business success, I experienced financial failure twice—once as a foolhardy young investor and again in my first foray as an entrepreneur. Both times I lost my entire net worth and slid into debt with nothing to show for it other than hard lessons learned. As a fledgling and undercapitalized entrepreneur, I suffered many awful dark nights of the soul—sleepless nights filled with self-doubt and dread. With hindsight it was clear that I made the same fundamental mistake both times. You guessed it—poor decision-making! Due to my lack of self-confidence, I delegated the authority for my most important financial decisions to others whose hierarchy of values was different from mine. Starting over from these devastating financial mistakes was extremely painful. I felt guilty and ashamed. I suffered deeply. It took me a long time to recover and come to acceptance each time, but I had to do it twice before I sufficiently learned the lesson about the importance of trusting myself and my intuition, and being true to my own values.

Both times that I failed financially, I had taken a huge risk with the objective of monetary return. Taking risks is important. It is something our inner Hero is wired for. But it was only after I pursued a vision that was more about meaning than money that I came out ahead, including financially. Unfortunately, it's not easy to take one's focus off money when debt collectors are circling. Perseverance in extreme circumstances requires heroic acceptance and strong resilience.

When you accept that everything, including mistakes and failures, happens for a reason, it becomes easier to delay gratification, make sacrifices, and rebound from missteps. Developing resilience is like a muscle memory of the mind—remembering that you can handle setbacks and bounce back. Resilience comes from a sense of growing mastery coupled with perseverance.

Summary of VDM Process

In Part II we have focused on developing Visionary Decision Making skills. Don't feel you need to adopt every technique or practice I have presented. Just as carpenters and mechanics develop a liking for certain tools, I encourage you to try them all to discover which ones work best for you. Before we move on to philosophical perspectives in Part III, let us just pause a moment to summarize the process of making a visionary decision.

1. Train yourself to be on the lookout and notice synchronicities, dream symbols, hunches, and random ideas that pop out of the collective unconscious. Some of these may seem miraculous. That's fine. Carefully take note of them as they come within the range of your hunter's perch and record them for reflection and analysis as needed.

2. Call upon your intuitive intelligence to decode the *meaning* that synchronicities, hunches, and archetypal dream symbols may hold for you. Meditation and mindfulness practices are excellent ways to filter the mental and emotional static that can block intuitive receptivity. Once your mind has settled down, you can also generate and interpret meaningful synchronicities using the I Ching.

3. Consider ideas and hunches picked up by your intuition relative to your hierarchy of values and your personal priorities. Evaluate your best choices right now from a short list of feasible options that become apparent. Ask yourself, "What is the best next move for me to take in this situation when the timing is right?" Make as many VDM meetings as you need to contemplate this until you receive a clear answer. Persevere in this process by applying both logic and intuitive gut feelings about your values. Sort (and re-sort) your options until you are clear about the best next move for you to make. Commit by signing a written agreement with yourself.

4. Focus on receiving a clear answer to the "when" question, the timing part of executing your decision. Fiercely act on your best next move as soon as your intuitive mind feels the timing is right. Feel it with excitement and pull the trigger. Send out necessary communications. Delegate what you can. Set the wheels in motion. Let the inner CEO execute!

5. Be prepared to accept the outcome of your decision without regrets or second-guessing yourself. Once you have executed the decision, don't look back. Do not invite comparisons or indulge in buyer's remorse. You did the best you could to make the most skillful decision possible. Then you bravely executed your decision by moving forward in the face of uncertainty. By making a bold move in an intuitively informed way, you have done as well as anyone could have done in your position.

6. Persevere. Maintain awareness of your highest priorities and execute the visionary decision and renew your commitment to it over and over again, day by day. Be patient. You can't make a plant grow faster by tugging on it. Let the sapling of your vision grow with confidence, knowing that if you don't let yourself get too distracted, your daily nurturance will ensure that it flowers and bears good fruit.

Part III

Philosophy and Lifestyle

11

Belief Engineering

There is nothing either good or bad, but thinking makes it so.

—**William Shakespeare**

The power of thoughts has been widely researched. In fact, major schools of psychology posit that thought precedes both feelings and actions, even if only by a split second—during which an enlightened insight could spontaneously activate or paranoid thoughts compulsively take over. Fortunately, most adults have learned to control their worst impulses, which is a way of defining adulthood.

Cognitive behavioral therapy (CBT) is one of the most popular—and effective—therapeutic interventions for depression and anxiety. The first principle of cognitive therapy is that your feelings, emotions, and moods are created by your cognitions, or thoughts. Cognition refers to the way you look at things—your perceptions, mental attitudes, and beliefs.

CBT teaches that we generally feel the way we do right now because of thoughts we are thinking. When we are feeling depressed, for instance, our thoughts are dominated by a pervasive negativity. In this case, we perceive not only ourselves but the entire world in dark, gloomy terms. What is even worse, the feeling of depression gives rise to more dark thoughts. It doesn't take long before we come to firmly believe things are every bit as bad as we imagine them to be.

A bleak vision sustained over time will create a lingering sense of hopelessness. This feeling may be the result of illogical thinking, but it feels so real that we can convince ourselves the distress will go on forever. CBT helps us see that the negative thoughts which cause emotional turmoil nearly always contain gross distortions. Although these thoughts appear valid, we can learn that they are irrational or just plain wrong, and that the twisted thinking is a major cause of our suffering. It goes to show us how powerful our thoughts can be!

Feelings derive from thoughts and then fuel each other in a spiral, upward or downward, depending upon the quality of our creative thinking, positive or negative. Depression is the downward spiral that CBT was invented to cure, but the principles apply in either direction. New thoughts are powerful to begin with because they give rise to feelings and emotions, but thoughts become most powerful—in a negative way—if they spin and coalesce into stubbornly held opinions and beliefs.

Humanity seems to suffer from a stubborn learning disorder which is a combination of close-mindedness and self-righteousness. The addiction to being "right" about one's opinions or beliefs can fuel ideological fervor that threatens peaceful coexistence among humans as well as between humans and nature. Lest our individual and collective egos continue to run amok, we must learn that we can be too sure of ourselves and our current ideas. We need to be free to learn and grow—to get more creative and to come up with better solutions to our biggest problems as a species living on a fragile planet.

Mentally, we are wired into a world of vast media networks (including propaganda channels that call themselves "news," pretend to be objective, and malign other media as "fake") that traffic in strong opinions and conspiracy theories. It seems that just about everyone has got a strong opinion these days, and the internet gives anyone who wants it a megaphone to argue with—anonymously and often abusively. How is it that people consider their current opinions so worth fighting for? So much more important than empathy or conflict resolution? Why have human beings slaughtered millions of people and fought so many wars over matters of custom or belief? Something crazy is going on when we identify with beliefs to such an extent, taking them and ourselves so seriously.

Just because we want something to be true, just because we want to believe something, is not justification for so adamantly adopting a belief. We must always ask ourselves: Why might our ego want us to believe it? Does it simply make us feel better? Does it make us feel righteous or superior? Does it feed some view of ourselves as victims, entitled to recompense? Does it support our fears, including a fear of being taken advantage of? Or does it reflect reality in a way that is helpful to our consideration of possible responses and courses of action? We must always question our motivations before we adopt and argue too strongly for any position.

An ancient Zen proverb admonishes, "Cease to cherish opinions." From the Zen point of view, *all* our beliefs are opinions. Beliefs are not sacred. They are not worth fighting over or dying for. They are not a ticket to some heavenly realm. Nor do they entitle us to indulge ourselves in prejudicial rage and take it out on others. From a spiritual point of view, what you think and what you believe are not nearly as important as how you behave and how you treat yourself and others. Your beliefs are simply your current operating assumptions, based on the best perceptions you can make right now given your intelligence, learning, upbringing, conditioning, and experience. Who do we think we are to argue so virulently? Putting too much weight on personal opinions is just a way of puffing up the ego. Understanding this embarrassing fact helps us be more humble, as well as open and flexible. When we don't take ourselves too seriously, we can take a moment to remember how much we don't know. This humility makes it easier to allow our beliefs to evolve based on new learning, to operate on the basis of better, more useful assumptions, and to preserve the neuroplasticity of the human brain into old age.

Self-help author Catherine Pulsifer declared, "What we believe becomes who we are."[1] And who we are changes as we grow. Since beliefs have a major impact on everything we say and feel and do—including every decision we make—it is important to become highly conscious of what our beliefs really are. Considering that so much of our worldview can take shape before we have a capacity for critical thinking, knowing what you believe may not be as easy as you think, but it's vital to be aware of the beliefs that you identify with and rely on to make decisions. Every belief is a choice—one that we are making now for the first time or just a repetition of one we made long ago. Remember that ultimately reality is our friend—not just an external factor that we should try to mold around egocentric fantasies. Reality is life itself, which is not dependent on our stories, ideas, or opinions. When we resist reality, we suffer. When we are in alignment with truth and good timing, reality becomes our best ally.

Many of our beliefs are such deeply ingrained assumptions that we take them for reality and are hardly aware of them. Ironically, their very invisibility has the effect of making these kinds of beliefs even more influential on a subconscious level. We seldom take time to reconsider some of our most basic assumptions about who we think we are, how to get our needs met, and how best to cope with not getting them met. Nevertheless, for the sake of making better decisions going forward, we need to take conscious ownership of whatever we believe, because our assumptions will determine the kinds of choices we will make. In this sense, beliefs are useful and important.

Carol Dweck, a psychologist researching workplace dynamics at Stanford University, writes: "We usually assume that skills, motivation, and drive are the most important determinants of success. Now we know that belief and mindset are often at the heart of that drive."[2] We leverage our beliefs—especially self-confidence, which is a faith in our own capabilities and resourcefulness—whenever we make a momentous, visionary decision. Such personal empowerment, however, runs counter to our general cultural conditioning, including the indoctrination by dogmatic religions that have imposed forms of magical thinking and fearful biases onto human consciousness for the last two thousand years. Even if you are not religiously trained, ideologies have had a tremendous influence on you, on all the cultures of the world, affecting the governance—and self-governance—of every man, woman, and child.

In the normal course of events, we operate on assumptions that make sense and work for us. To use a simple example, if I don't believe I can walk up to the speaker's podium, my body will act out the mind's belief: it will stiffen, I will not be able to move my legs freely, and I may stutter when I start speaking. If I unknowingly take a placebo believing that it is going to make me feel better, that is likely to work just because of my belief. Not just our bodies and brains, but also our character is affected by what we believe about who we are and what we are supposed to be doing. As Dr. Dweck put it, "Beliefs matter, beliefs can be changed, and when they are, so too is personality."[3] And beyond the personal level, human beliefs have a profound impact on our species and planet.

Believing in Yourself and in Your Own Intuitive Sense of Things

Nobody has explained the conflict between blind acceptance of beliefs and trusting one's intuition better than the Buddha, as I learned during one of my first meditation retreats in Sri Lanka in 1982. Our meditation teacher, Ayya Khema, told the group a story that served as a conversion experience for me. It is recorded that during the latter period of his life, when he was a wandering teacher, the Buddha arrived at the village of the Kalama tribe to give a talk to the villagers. Early on, an elder politely asked, "Excuse me, sir, but we are confused. Every few weeks, another teacher passes through our village. And all too often he tells us something that contradicts what a previous teacher said. At that point, we hardly know what to believe. Do you have any advice for us about how to resolve this?"

The Buddha replied, "Your confusion is understandable and my advice is simply this: Don't put your faith in teachers. Don't put your faith in scriptures or tradition. Don't put your faith in authorities. Don't even believe what I'm telling you right now—unless it rings true for you . . . in your heart."

There are many brilliant Buddha stories, just as there are marvelous stories about Jesus, Lao Tzu, Mohammed, and other enlightened teachers. (The Buddha's teaching period lasted thirty-five years, and he was teaching in a highly literate society, so even though he lived about six hundred years earlier than Jesus, many more stories survived.) This one struck me like a ton of bricks. At age thirty, this was the first time I had ever been taught that my spiritual good had to do with trusting my own judgment rather than strict obedience to dogma, the adoption of orthodox creeds, and a self-denying form of humility.

In my strict Catholic upbringing and thirteen years of parochial school, I had always been told what to think and believe, as well as how to behave and what *not* to do. We operated under an impression of God as an omniscient ruler and judge who was recording every move we made, and even counted a lot of normal *feelings* as being sinful (like anger toward one's parents, for instance). To top it off, we were taught—as children of all fundamentalist religions are—that to doubt the teachings given by our church or temple is to be tempted by the devil, and all such traitorous thoughts needed to be summarily dismissed and suppressed, lest we lose our soul.

The discourse to the Kalamas contradicted everything I had ever been taught on this front. The Buddha's injunction to trust one's intuition was not only unique in my experience, but it had that powerful ring of truth that he referred to. It was a startling new teaching for me, but it felt like wise advice compared to blindly holding on to what I had been taught as a child. This lesson inspired me to learn as much as I could about intuition and how to better cultivate and trust my own intuitive sense. It also led to a lifetime practice of examining and reevaluating old beliefs that influence my ability to clearly perceive reality and make the best decisions for myself and those in my care.

Trusting subjective judgment brings up the general question of truth and whether it is ever possible to be absolutely objective. Physicist Werner Heisenberg's uncertainty principle, a groundbreaking discovery in the realm of quantum physics, provides profound insight, as it proved that the subatomic activity of particles and waves is altered by the act of observing them. Because of this so-called observer effect, nothing can be perceived or accurately measured in a fixed or absolute way because the act of measuring changes things. Nothing our senses can perceive is permanent or ever the same.

Extrapolating from Heisenberg's scientific proof of a lack of fixedness in the world, we can conclude that nothing (including whatever we believe strongly) can ever be proven. This radical idea may seem absurd or even frightening at first (even though he could not refute it, Einstein himself had trouble accepting it), but it can also be liberating, as it supports greater cultivation of intuitive intelligence and creative freedom. As the cautionary scientific aphorism goes, "absence of evidence is not evidence of absence." Some rationalists claim to require evidence to believe anything, because they don't trust feelings, including intuitive feelings. It seems that those who cannot feel must measure. And, for them, what cannot be measured is unimportant, does not exist.

Now, let's not misunderstand—beliefs are important. Even if they exist within the context of our limited capacity for knowing, useful operating assumptions are necessary to get anything done. Rather than clinging to unchanging articles of faith, however, we do better to learn how to activate our intuitive intelligence and choose what we believe according to what truly makes sense to us. In the context of Visionary Decision Making, this is a synergy between what passes the test of logic—as being plausible—and what just feels right in our gut. When it comes to the creative process, intuition is more powerful than conviction, which is quite the opposite of what we are taught as children by moralistic authorities. In this respect, the VDM paradigm can be seen as an exciting call for personal freedom. As biologist Bruce Lipton put it, "I was exhilarated by the new realization that I could change the character of my life by changing my *beliefs*. I was instantly energized because I realized that there was a science-based path that would take me from my job as a perennial 'victim' to my new position as 'cocreator' of my destiny."[4]

How We Adopt Our Beliefs

Making observations and forming beliefs is a human's adaptive response to living in a complex and socially interactive world. A child's mind is wired from birth by its give and take with caretakers (especially mother) and starts forming conclusions almost from birth. We make conclusions because life would be too overwhelming if beliefs were not formed to help us make sense of what to expect, how to feel safe, etc. When we are totally dependent, we instinctively trust that our parents know everything and will take care of us. In the process of this coadaptation, the child automatically adopts the beliefs and traits of its caregivers.

This is the social price of belonging to a family or tribe. As we grow up, it's virtually effortless to hold on to the beliefs that we were taught when we were too young to know any better. There was hardly anything conscious about the way we picked up our core beliefs. We contracted our beliefs like we might contract an illness. After they were passed on to us, we came to identify with them and they became part of us. Then we grew up to defend our adopted beliefs tenaciously, with fervor.

Beliefs are important, as we shall explore below. It is a primordial human need to make sense of things, and our beliefs will stick even after they've stopped serving us well. In fact, once you are used to believing something, you'll filter out any evidence that pops up to the contrary (this is known as "confirmation bias"). Look back on your own life and notice some of the ways you have gone through life creating experiences that match your beliefs. Self-limiting decisions have influenced practically everything you've done. If you want to start making the best strategic decisions going forward, you need to be willing to reconsider what you currently think is true, so you can grow beyond the limitations imposed on you by beliefs that you adopted when you were a toddler.

The legal system stipulates that ignorance of the law is no excuse. In a parallel way, ignorance of your beliefs and how they control you is no excuse for the way your life turns out. It is incumbent upon mature, self-determining adults to become conscious of and reevaluate beliefs that were formed in childhood. Of course, it is your right to retain beliefs adopted at any age, especially if you consciously make the choice to do so. But adults cannot get away with conveniently blaming bad decisions on what they were told by parents, teachers, ministers, or bosses. That runs contrary to the definition of "adult."

Get to know yourself and take full ownership of what you believe as soon as possible. Your success and happiness, the meaning of your life, depend on it. Later in this chapter, I will show you how to upgrade your beliefs, how to develop new "visionary beliefs," and how to replace old-to-the-core beliefs with the ones that are more up to date and will work better for you going forward.

The Value of Beliefs

Beliefs, or operating assumptions, are important from a practical point of view, even if they are not sacred or the key to salvation like the dogma-centric religions declared them to be long ago. A debate has raged since the first century, when Paul of Tarsus, in the early days of the movement that would eventually become known as Christianity, extolled "faith" as the key to salvation rather than "good works." Paul was referring to "faith" in the belief that Jesus rose from the dead and that he would redeem you if you pledged allegiance and atoned for your sinfulness. What he originally meant by "works" was the strict observance of Jewish law and the traditional rituals. In fact, St. Paul advocated letting go of the requirement for several Jewish rites (like circumcision) to facilitate his zealous efforts to convert Gentiles.

After the formation of Christianity at the Council of Nicaea (325 CE), "faith" came specifically to mean believing in and adhering to the newly assembled Bible and the Nicene Creed—a codification of beliefs that formed the dogmatic basis of the organized church. The process of choosing which books to include in that Bible and the Nicene Creed—the first required "credo" for "believers"—was organized and sponsored by Constantine, the pagan Roman emperor who called the council and ratified a faith-based Christianity as a state-approved religion. "Works" eventually came to mean charity and helping others, but in terms of winning the heavenly reward, faith has continued to reign supreme according to church teachings.

The idea that we are saved on the basis of what we believe and profess to believe—rather than on how we behave or whether we do good things for other people (which even pagans do)—was central to Christianity when it was formed 1,700 years ago, and this position has maintained currency in the most powerful religions on earth ever since. According to this point of view, to be "saved" from eternal damnation and torture, one needs to pledge allegiance to stone-age scriptures and the orthodox beliefs derived from them. Trusting oneself is considered the sin of pride and must not be allowed lest it lead to "heresy" and damnation. Free-thinking has been vigorously suppressed throughout the ages—under the penalty of ostracism or excommunication, and even torture and gruesome execution. This case for the supremacy of a set of beliefs is an idea that has fueled totalitarian empires, countless wars, and millions of executions. Isn't it time we fully exercised the hard-won freedom to question, test, and upgrade our beliefs?

It Doesn't Matter How Strong Your Faith Is

Believing something with all your might—and even converting others to accept your articles of faith—does not make what you are believing any truer. Taking refuge in orthodox beliefs might make one feel better or more secure, but these kinds of convictions will not proactively contribute to personal fulfillment. Faith is not the magical shortcut to salvation that ideological religions would have you believe.

We are not "saved" by believing one thing or another. In terms of fulfilling your destiny—your purpose in living—useful beliefs are important in order to make the right moves at the right time, but supportive beliefs—no matter how strongly felt—cannot do the trick by themselves. Despite promises of eternal life, rigid convictions that aren't allowed to be doubted—along with a meek acceptance of the suffering they may produce—are not pathways to worthwhile freedom. Ultimately, there is no freedom from responsibility.

The most empowering form of faith, the one that helps most, is the one that helps you save yourself, known as *self-confidence*. The word "confidence" in Latin means "having faith in yourself." Of course, your Self is connected to all that is, including Infinite Intelligence. In that sense, to believe in yourself is to accept that Divine Intelligence flows through you and empowers you. In this sense, believing in yourself is one faith that will help you to evolve and glean wisdom from your experience. Confidence encourages you to experiment and *take the risks that will grow you.*

A disciple once asked the Buddha how he would know the Truth if he found it. "You know the Truth, because the Truth works," the Buddha answered. A belief worth maintaining is one that makes sense to you and also actually *works* to help you get what want according to your chosen value system. Believing in yourself works. Have confidence and faith in your intuitive intelligence and your resourcefulness—your direct access to the vast resource of Infinite Intelligence that is always there for you.

You will become a superb decision-maker if you make it a point to review and upgrade all your beliefs throughout your lifetime. Your confidence will increase as you let change happen and change with it. Committing yourself to learning what beliefs are most effective for you, voluntarily putting your faith in them until proven otherwise, and owning your avowed beliefs are self-empowering acts of personal responsibility. This is the purpose of belief engineering . . . and it works!

A Special Category: Core Beliefs

You may think that you are aware of what you believe, but that is often not the case. As pointed out above, some of our perspectives have very deep roots, deeper than our memory. From the day we are born, we do our best to make sense of the world by interpreting things and forming conclusions (in other words, beliefs) that support our needs for safety and nourishment. Because you formed these deep impressions at a preconscious age, a category of beliefs below your awareness resists becoming conscious and therefore can hold sway over you for a lifetime. These are referred to in personal development circles as "core beliefs."

The tendency to automatically identify with deeply held beliefs is insurmountable as long as they remain unconscious. They feel like they are part of you, rather than just one way to look at the world. And core beliefs are reconfirmed throughout our lives by selective evidence, as we focus on the events and feedback that seem to support them and ignore evidence that contradicts what we already feel to be true. This is the well-known phenomenon of "confirmation bias," which explains the incredible conditioning power of beliefs. Without serious introspection, core beliefs make us automatically interpret events in ways we accept without question. As they reside in the personal unconscious, they play a huge role in limiting our possibilities, our ability to be fully present in reality, and opportunities for us to evolve. Because they are invisible to the conscious mind, and surreptitiously influence our behavior, core beliefs exert a constricting effect on intuitive receptivity and decision-making, without us ever knowing it.

Let me offer an example of a core belief that long affected my own life. Probably around the age of three I formed a conclusion that I needed to be perfect in order to get love. This was based on my experience of being objectified by, and having an insecure attachment to, a wounded mother—which led me to the conclusion that love is something that must be earned. This dynamic led to decades of pressure and anxiety, and made me look for opportunities to work really hard to win a few crumbs of intimacy. Until, at age twenty-nine, I became aware of the pattern and how it was holding me back, I carried this self-limiting assumption and expectation into all my relationships—always trying to be as "perfect" as I could be in hopes of winning a few scraps of love. In relationships, I sometimes struggle with this old wiring even to this day. I have spent a lot of energy rewiring this core belief in this lifetime.

Not all core beliefs are negative or limiting. Those who were brought up with good enough parenting have a secure attachment style and may have a core belief that they can depend on unconditional love no matter what. If so, this is a good thing and good to know and celebrate, because it is self-supporting and a platform for personal growth. It is even more powerful if you are conscious of the belief.

Whatever the case may be, make the effort to become conscious of your core beliefs as soon as you can. It doesn't matter what experience or conditioning gave rise to them. Some are hard to accept, but you don't need to know why it happened that way. Though piecing together an understanding of what happened to us before we developed a capacity for memory may help at times, it's not necessary to totally understand the why of it, just the what. (Poor parenting is almost always covered up and denied by the parents. This is part of the reason that people develop a functional blindness to their own defects and may not be consciously suffering, except that they are stuck. Suppressing shame, they cannot resolve their problems because they cannot see their problems.) However these insidious beliefs came to be, you were an innocent child and it's not your fault that you adopted beliefs that work against you and don't serve others. As young children, we believe almost everything we are taught, but everything we learn isn't true.

Becoming aware of unconsciously held core beliefs will liberate you from getting stuck or finding yourself at the mercy of blind spots. Fortunately, whatever your old beliefs may be, once aware of them you can upgrade them to help, not hinder, you on your path. When we develop a greater self-awareness, we become more aligned with our highest aspirations, which inspires greater self-mastery and confidence. We derive hope and encouragement from recent discoveries in neuroscience, which prove that even emotional patterns wired in helpless desperation as children can be rewired in adulthood. It's not easy. It can be the work of a lifetime, but it's worth the effort and it's never too late.

Upgrading Your Beliefs

It behooves us to make it a habit to question and test *everything* we believe and ascertain whether our current beliefs are helping or hindering. Doubt is not an evil tool of Satan, except from a black-and-white, self-righteously fundamentalist point of view. Doubt has a positive discernment role to play and is an important tool in recovering your true self by breaking the spell of every false message you ever took in. We need to delete or upgrade beliefs (like apps on a smartphone) that are no longer up to date, realistic, true, or helpful. Belief engineering means trying out new beliefs. It's perfectly OK. Consciously testing new operating assumptions, like a new set of clothes, is a strength of character.

One of the considerations of belief engineering is practical: How well will a particular belief support a proactive mindset and contribute to better decision-making? How well will it work? Will a certain belief empower or disempower us? Use a combination of intuition and logic to figure this out with doubt as an instrumental tool of logic in this process. Doubt enables us to consider other options and perspectives and helps us strive for clarity about what can be achieved and what cannot. Galileo called self-doubt "the father of all invention." Let doubt inspire you with its inherent ability to spark creativity and energy. Even though it involves some personal work, consciously reevaluating what makes sense to you and what needs more study is a philosophical requirement for self-actualization, maturity, and wisdom.

Your beliefs spawn your feelings and choices, which means you need to choose your beliefs if you want to successfully direct your own life. No matter what anyone else says—including powerful religious or political establishments that scare people into conforming to orthodoxy (I call this indoctrination "totalitarian mind control")—you can invoke the Warrior archetype to defend your boundaries by helping you let go of beliefs that hinder your success and happiness, no matter what anyone else might think. This especially includes the belief that we will be damned if we question or dare to doubt our indoctrination. You may be judged or condemned in certain quarters (good riddance), but in support of breaking free, I am reminded of a saying common to twelve-step support groups: "What you think of me is none of my business."

Let's take one example of an entrenched belief: "I never follow through on anything, and I am unable to finish what I start." Carrying this belief will almost guarantee that you will never complete anything in a timely manner. *Remember: The subconscious mind is always trying to prove itself right, no matter what beliefs it consciously or unconsciously holds.* Thankfully, there is a simple technique for "flipping" a self-defeating belief. First, restate it and convert it to something like this: "I am a capable person, and if I keep working at this step-by-step, I *will* finish this project." This is a realistic idea that your brain can accept. If you repeat this revised assumption to yourself several times when the self-defeating belief kicks in, you will begin to approach tasks and projects with more confidence and less stress.

People who hold the notion that they are incapable of finishing things were not born with this belief. At some point, without realizing it, they formed an explanation—perhaps according to critical remarks one of their parents made—and accepted that it must be true. Then, of course, their powerful subconscious is wired to make them live up to it! It's not our fault as young children, but when we put our faith in lies, we give them power, and soon those lies are ruling our lives.

Fortunately, new brain science has disproved the notion that "you can't teach an old dog new tricks." Early neuroscientists believed that the brain was not capable of regenerating itself. It was thought that after a certain age brain cells could only die off or be destroyed. Now, with the help of new brain-scanning technologies, scientists have established that the human brain has amazing "plasticity" and remains adaptable for our entire lives. On a physical level, strongly engrained beliefs are strong memories that have developed into a set of neural networks in the brain. The concept of neuroplasticity is an important and hopeful development because it demonstrates the possibility of transforming troublesome neural networks, to be able to revise automatic thought processes, behavioral patterns, and second nature–like feelings. No matter how old you are, you can grow new neurons and train your brain. Discovery and learning need never end. You are not stuck with your current programming, that which you think you know right now.

Belief engineering starts by becoming more consciously aware of what you tell yourself, and then changing that internal dialogue for the sake of better decisions and better results. When you mindfully maneuver your attention from being the old (automatic) self to becoming a conscious observer of old patterns, you recondition yourself to be able to make better choices, demonstrate different behaviors, and experience different feelings. Once you realize and fully accept that your beliefs and actions are your responsibility, you know that it is okay to change them. You are an adult, so take responsibility now. After all, either way—actively or passively—you are choosing and responsible for your own beliefs.

Exercise: List Your Core Beliefs

Take a moment and write down one or more beliefs you ascribe to—including one that you think you might hold subconsciously—that could benefit from reframing. Across from each one, write out what a revised, more productive or supportive assumption might be.

Keep a small copy of your list on your fridge, in your wallet, or on your computer desktop. Let it grow. Upgrading old beliefs is like training a puppy to go outside: consistent reminders on a regular basis.

Having a hard time coming up with ideas? The following lists areas of life where people often have a self-limiting core belief:

- **Your talents and capabilities:** "I'm no good at that stuff anyway, so why would anyone hire me?" Antidote: "I am capable of mastering anything I am interested in learning."

- **Your worthiness to be loved:** "I'm only lovable if I am perfect/make lots of money/look beautiful," etc. Antidote: "I accept myself unconditionally. I am my own best friend and will never abandon myself. I appreciate my own kindness and resilience."

- **Your luck:** "Nothing turns out right. Everything bad always happens to me, so I shouldn't even try." Antidote: "I am far luckier than I know. I can improve my luck starting now."

- **Your world:** "People always take advantage. It's foolish to trust anyone I don't know very well." Antidote: "By allowing myself to give others a chance to be good with me, I expand my circle of friends and supporters."

The Pitfalls of Magical Thinking—Too Good to Be True

The fact that we ultimately are responsible for our beliefs does not mean that we should make them up, believe whatever is most convenient, or adopt whatever makes us feel good—even though people do these things all the time. Strategic decision-making is not powered by starry-eyed and impractical magical thinking. The ego thrives on assumptions that support the narcissistic fantasy that the world should provide you with what you want because you want it so badly. Fantasy can inform vision, but beyond that it is never a basis for strategic decision-making, because it undermines clear thinking and good judgment.

Magical thinking can take different forms: believing what you want to believe, imagining that you can get something for nothing, or expecting to get lucky because you think you are so special that you deserve it. Some magical thinkers believe that all you have to do is visualize an object of desire and hold it in your mind's eye to attract it, and somehow it will pop into your life. The famous law of attraction teaches that you pave the way for getting what you want by believing that it is possible and becoming energetically receptive to its manifestation. In effect, you will attract what you desire to come to you.

There is certainly truth in the power of attraction. For one thing, we are always more likely to notice things that support us getting what we desire. And there is a subtle magnetizing effect exerted through held thoughts and feelings. But as true as the law of attraction is, attraction alone is not enough. One needs to be wary of magical thinking, how the craving ego will create arguments and find "evidence" to support the effortless fulfillment of desires. It's highly unlikely that things are going to unfold according to any plan or schedule of ours. We may get what we want, but its form might well be different than what we imagined. Unfortunately, for those who demand an easy, perfect solution, the process of manifesting what we want requires discipline and almost always some sacrifice or measure of delayed gratification. Your satisfaction and personal growth will benefit from an ability to appreciate the fact that what you want may turn out to look different than what you'd imagined.

The pitfall of succumbing to magical thinking is not just the domain of a hip counterculture. It permeates decision-making at all levels. Consider the words of Eileen Shapiro, the author of *Make Your Own Luck*:

Magical thinking in business (and life) decisions may reduce anxiety—and maybe that's why it appears in so many business plans—but it's a poor way to bet. If the odds are slim that your current set of bets will get you where you want to go unless a major miracle intervenes, you might want to reconsider whether more bets in the same vein are just bringing totally atrocious odds down to new odds that are merely horrendous. Magic thinking is widespread in all kinds of bets—corporate bets, career bets, and life bets. Once you spot it in your bets, you have the power to change your destiny by either changing your bets to ones with better odds of achieving your goals—or changing your goals to fit your actual bets.[5]

Magical thinking is a form of all-or-nothing thinking that leaves out consideration of the unpredictable nature of change, which makes it costly. On more than one occasion, I personally learned this lesson the hard way. As mentioned in chapter 6, I took a sabbatical to visit spiritual centers around the world when I was twenty-nine. To free up my assets for the trip, I sold my house, my two cars, a rental fourplex, and most of my other property. An investor friend convinced me that I should let him convert everything I had into gold and silver commodities trading (his specialty), which was at sky-high valuations at that time. Due to what was later termed "irrational exuberance"—a sure symptom of magical thinking—it looked like the upward trend in precious metals was never going to end (arguably because of inflation fears, and so forth). This was a smart investment, a "sure thing," my new financial advisor assured me. In my naiveté, I put my faith in him. Easy money.

With no experience as an investor and not feeling qualified to trust my own judgment in that arena, I delegated a vitally important decision to someone else. Another losing factor was that I felt no personal connection to what we were investing in—it was entirely based on my desire to make money while I took off on a sabbatical of self-discovery. Unfortunately, as it turned out, the precious metals market had reached its apex with nowhere to go but down (way down). The market value of gold and silver was almost totally wiped out, including my investment. While I was on my long pilgrimage, unbeknownst to me I lost my entire financial net worth, and ultimately gained an expensive lesson on the negative potentials of magical thinking.

Betting and losing all my money revealed how wishful thinking can be motivated by the desire for a quick fix, a shortcut. I learned how trying to get something for nothing has a security-oriented, fear-based motivation lurking in the shadows, a sort of "Please rescue me" fantasy. Truly creative risks may have a dreamlike quality too, but they are driven by heartfelt passion, rather than a desire to score a magical win or escape an uncomfortable situation. I have learned to apply critical thinking and healthy skepticism to any prospect that seems too good to be true.

There is a huge difference between impulsive decisions that depend upon miraculous solutions and bold decisions derived from a visionary approach that is rooted in who you are. To feel heartfelt passion, it is necessary to trust life and trust yourself. Trust is always a risk that requires some courage, which itself requires adopting an optimistic point of view. (Pessimists don't take risks, if they can avoid them.) Optimism depends on beliefs that make sense to you and support the creative possibility that you are betting on. The Visionary Decision Making process reinforces useful and effective operating assumptions that favor the kinds of risks that will grow you.

Visionary Beliefs

As discussed, the beliefs we hold are strategically important, even if we can't exactly prove them. They fuel our capacity for everything we do, physically and mentally. "Visionary beliefs" is the term I coined for *provisional* beliefs that a person can try on for size to see how effective they might be, and adopt them as operating assumptions to see how well they work. According to my definition, visionary beliefs must be intuitively reasonable—in other words, they must make sense to you—but you don't need to subscribe to them, or claim that you believe them, while you are trying them out. Just give them a chance.

The following are visionary beliefs I have experimented with, which I found to be effective and accurate for me. You might consider trying them, or some version of them, to manifest better results for yourself going forward.

Visionary Belief: Change Is a Friendly Force

We are living in a period of accelerating change that can easily feel chaotic. It is the instinctive tendency of all animals, including humans, to react to sudden changes as if they are threats. Indeed, throughout most of human existence, there *were* life-threatening dangers. Our nervous system is programmed to fight, flee, or freeze at a moment's notice. A hair-trigger reactivity kept us safe in a world that included saber-toothed tigers, for instance. Unfortunately, we are still wired this way, since we have not changed much biologically in the last hundred thousand years. Even today, when we are triggered by fear, we can barely think, only react. But once we develop the discipline, we can intervene with the beam of conscious awareness known as *mindfulness* coupled with a sophisticated intuition that is more realistically tuned to the challenges of modern times. When you are in tune with yourself and reality, you just know what to do.

Fortunately, the risks we take today rarely, if ever, involve life-or-death, split-second decisions. In the absence of constant danger from predators, we are free to become more creative and develop potentials that go beyond merely ensuring survival. Rather than feeling threatened by it, the most creative individuals opportunistically regard change as a friendly force, and these people end up serving as evolutionary change agents. They create enough space to be alert for synchronistic signals and new opportunities, so they can make visionary decisions and take the risks that will grow them and help them support themselves and their people no matter what. Learning how to navigate and manage change—

the overall goal of the VDM approach—empowers them to blossom as creative risk-takers and develop a better sense of timing in the process.

In this time of rapidly accelerating change, change management skills have become crucial. In the process of learning to more skillfully navigate change—and sometimes to facilitate it—we come into alignment with the rhythms of life. When things click, we can feel the universe as a supportive realm that wants to help us—at least to the extent that we are willing to cooperate and synchronize with natural cycles. With a deep sigh of relief, we hold on to the belief that everything we need will be provided or made available. We just have to tap into Infinite Intelligence with its treasure trove of resources that are always there waiting for our download—in the form of creative ideas, signals to guide our way, archetypes of wisdom and power, and much more.

People who see change as friendly rather than threatening are more optimistic and more likely to enjoy the ups and downs of life. To better embrace change, most of us could develop a more fluid relationship to time. People who fear change essentially want time to stand still. Their constantly frustrated wish is for the security of a fixed and stable universe that they can control.

The mechanical division of time into hours, minutes, and seconds—brought about by the recent invention of clocks—clogs up the spontaneous flow of life energy. To fully relax into the now, visionaries find ways to free their minds from the domination of linear, measured time. They understand the high value of "time-outs" to intentionally loosen the domination of modern society's overcontrolling mechanical approach. This is good, but in fact there is nothing to escape, because if we take our eyes off the clock, our experience of time has a natural plasticity. When we enjoy life, time seems to go by quickly. When we resist, it seems to crawl.

As many great teachers have shown, the secret of joyful living is to become more aware of what is happening in the one time that is real—the present moment—and not dwell on the future or the past. To improve strategic thinking and decision-making, we need to let go of trying to control things long enough to give our intuition a chance to activate and be receptive. Our capacity for joy will also expand when we live in the present moment.

Visionary decision-makers do their best to stay aware of how life is in flux. The ultimate time-management solution is to develop a lifestyle where we can transcend the measuring and parceling of time and relax into our intuitive sense of timing. Easy does it. (Don't worry; this becomes much easier in Stage Three.) Good timing, a fundamental component of every major decision, is the secret of surfing the never-ending, unpredictable waves of change. Nothing ever stays the same and nothing lasts forever. These are immutable laws that nobody can dispute. Why pretend it can ever be otherwise? When we come to regard change as a friendly force, the success brought about by our improving sense of timing will provide encouragement to cultivate more intuitive intelligence and wisdom.

Visionary Belief: Infinite Intelligence Is a Resource That's Always Available

When, as a bootstrap entrepreneur, I was asked if my company had any investors, I might have smiled and replied, "Oh yes . . . my backer has infinite resources." And then I might have explained that I was referring to Divine Providence, or what I refer to in this book as Infinite Intelligence. In chapter 4, we saw how the divine realm of powers and heroic archetypes, which Jung called the "collective unconscious," can be approached as a resource rather than as a mighty God-King who judges our behavior and controls our fate, whom we might entreat for favors.

Psychologically or spiritually, Jung's concept of a larger mind with unlimited creative and supportive resources that is always available when we choose to tune in is a reassuring belief. As many addicts come to understand, we need the help of a higher power to achieve the level of freedom we strive for. Individual willpower, no matter how strong, is never enough all by itself. To evolve and prosper, we humbly accept that we need the help of Infinite Intelligence, which contains the supreme archetype of Creative Power. We are grateful that this help is always available to us if we just pay attention to it and tap into it. Bottom line here: once you learn how to tune in via your intuitive sense, Infinite Intelligence can provide everything you need to be creative, productive, successful, emotionally agile, and even happy.

Visionary Belief: I Deserve to Have What I Want (and What I Want Is Good for Me)

Achieving success and meaning in life requires believing in yourself, that what you want is possible, and that you deserve it. Some of us—especially children from large families or those who had wounded parents—came to believe at an early age that our wants and needs were a burden and that it was selfish to even express them. (As one of seven, this was my experience, and even more so for my parents when they were children, who came from families of thirteen and fourteen children, respectively.) The visionary belief that you deserve to have what you want helps you be more open and forthright and actually ask for it. If you believe you *don't* deserve to live out a positive destiny, your subconscious mind will never allow you to manifest it. Your inhibition could be in response to negative beliefs based on unconscious guilt and shame, cultivated by child-rearing in some religious cultures. You will need to upgrade such core beliefs to become able to receive love and cultivate the greatest good.

Taking charge of your beliefs requires self-confidence, which produces positive changes in attitude. Learning to trust yourself, your intuition, and your interpretation of what things mean builds your self-confidence. As your decision-making gets better, you will enjoy better results by making the right moves at the right time, which will in turn increase your efficacy and further your confidence.

Self-confidence arises from discovering your natural talents and then practicing them until you achieve a level of mastery. As we saw in chapter 2, skills that grow from your personal fascinations are the ones that you will be most inspired to develop. During Stage One of life, when self-discovery is top priority, we follow and learn everything we can about whatever fascinates us the most. In the process, we develop skills and, eventually, if we persevere and put in our ten thousand hours during Stage Two, we achieve a level of mastery. Then we are truly in position to create our own luck! As Louis Pasteur so aptly put it, "Chance only favors the prepared mind."

When it comes to the power of attraction, nothing is more attractive than self-confidence, because powerful and positive energy is magnetic. When I invoke the Sovereign archetype—the authoritative aspect of noble character who likes to "take care of his or her people"—it seems that I become more attractive. Why? Well, for one thing, everyone likes to be taken care of! A paradoxical result of generosity is that when people realize they are being cared for and looked after, they are happy to oblige a patron or sponsor. They appreciate him or her and want to reciprocate. Essentially, proactive generosity makes relationships hum. The most effective way to get what you want is to use your intuition to understand what others want and then give it to them or help them get it.

Generosity in business is good policy. We usually think of generosity as a personal trait, but considerate and empathic customer service increases goodwill and sales by building better relationships. Embedded policies of generosity can take many forms. The way my fledgling business used our minted micropayments currency to give a birthday gift to our users is a fine case in point. Another illustrative example was how I instructed our bookkeeper to pay every invoice the same day we received it from a vendor, using the online Billpay feature of our accounting software. I told him that, even though business schools teach students to take full advantage of Net 30 or Net 60 terms on receivables, and that this was going to cost our cash flow a little bit, it would be worth it by providing an extra bit of relationship insurance. I felt this was a small price to pay for goodwill earned with vendors that might pay off during times of tight cash flow.

The Synchronicity Belief: There Are No Accidents

One can hardly state this visionary belief better than Jungian author Robert H. Hopcke in his book *There Are No Accidents*:

If we bring a symbolic attitude to our lives, searching out the meaning of what happens to us and thereby allowing our own capacity to make wholeness out of the random and disparate events of our lives, then . . . no matter what happens in the plot, wherever the setting, whoever the characters, major or minor, we will see that indeed, there are no accidents in the stories of our lives.[6]

The intuitive notion at the heart of VDM is perceiving the Universe's perfect timing—even if our half-asleep minds cannot perceive its perfection or, conversely, just take what happens for granted. For the sake of better decision-making, we experiment with the belief that there are no accidents . . . and start paying more attention. We choose to believe that there is a reason for what happens, *even if we don't know the reason yet*. We choose to believe that the universe is imbued with an intelligent way of doing things that is just beyond our current ability to comprehend. We choose to trust in Infinite Intelligence.

Our decisions will no longer depend on—or wait for—finally figuring out the reasons why something happened. Perhaps we will look back at some future date and understand, but it is not our job—or within our ability—to know everything on demand. That's too much for human consciousness to expect. We just need to make enough sense out of things to make a slightly better decision as to our *best next step*. That's it . . . that's the best we can do! Making better decisions step-by-step in the absence of perfect knowledge—with the help of some courage and an activated intuition—is the sauce of personal development and the achievement of success as you define it.

Living a synchronistic life involves cultivating acceptance and wonder while letting go of judgment and resistance to the way things appear. This includes accepting your karma (substitute your concept of cosmic justice here) by taking some refuge in the belief "what goes around comes around." We have to pay our dues sooner or later. Even then, sometimes the worst nightmare can turn out to be the greatest blessing. You never know. For instance, when I was twenty-two years old I was arrested for possession of LSD at a house party that got raided by police, and I was hauled off to jail tripping on acid. I thought I was dreaming, having a nightmare.

Unbeknownst to me, getting in serious legal trouble (for the crime of "illegally stimulating the central nervous system against the peace and dignity of the State of Oregon," as the affidavit read) facilitated my destiny. My friend Jack, the minicomputer programmer and my *Spacewar!*-playing partner, interceded with Dan, the director of the computer center, to hire me to type documentation for their software products and to go to court for me as my new employer, both of which Dan did, largely out of compassion for my plight. Being hired as a secretary of a computer center directly led to my software career. It made the difference between me being sent to prison and getting off with probation. The point is that my worst nightmare turned into a career I was destined for!

You never know, so why not accept that, as long as you keep faith in yourself, everything will work out one way or another? The synchronistic point of view renders difficulties—even desperate straits like going to jail on acid—easier to accept and surmount. It does away with the unnecessary kind of suffering that results from resisting the way things happen. When this visionary belief is working for you, you will feel grateful for the little miracles taking place. You will also benefit from remembering that there are no accidents—only occasional failures to discern the larger unfolding pattern.

As my story attests, a belief in meaningful coincidences is useful for expanding your vision and can help your timing. Noting and appreciating synchronicities highlights the expansive scope of what is possible, as well as the grandeur of Infinite Intelligence. Respect for synchronicity serves as a bedrock for more creative thinking and superior decision-making. If we pay attention and look for it like a hunter, synchronicity will prove itself. The more we become aware of it, the more we can count on it. We unblock our intuitive antennas and open our eyes to what's happening on a level that is beyond the ego's control.

Synchronicities can mystically guide us to the people and situations we need so that we can wake up to new opportunities and better choices. My friend, author David Richo, touches on how synchronicity is perfect timing when he writes, "Everything that happens to us is synchronicity because everything fits perfectly into our step-by-step advance toward a fulfillment of our potential."[7]

As we take advantage of the insights we derive from synchronicities that we notice, we will realize with joy how perfectly everything is unfolding in our lives according to a higher logic. We still have to do the work—we have to make the decisions and execute them with timely action. But awareness of the magic of synchronicity makes the job easier and transforms our experience of life—with all its inevitable ups and downs—into a more rhythmic and meaningful journey.

Visionary Beliefs Create a Virtuous Cycle

Some of the visionary beliefs presented above may be new ideas. Try them on and discard them if they don't work for you. Even more ways of looking at things will occur as you apply conscious decision-making techniques. Once again, there are no prescriptions for what you should or should not believe. The only essential criterion is that your beliefs make intuitive sense to you and that they support better decisions and results. Accepting that humans are not equipped to understand everything, you adopt beliefs that make sense and reliably work for you after you try them out for a while and see what happens. On the basis of your own experience, jettison the operating assumptions that are not facilitating the results you want.

Upgrading your beliefs gives rise to a "virtuous cycle." Useful beliefs that make sense to you will support your ability to make better decisions and perfect your timing. When good things result, the upward spiral completes and reinforces the beliefs that have improved the more skillful way you are now approaching people and situations. Our beliefs not only impact our decisions but constitute a way of looking at things that conditions our attitude and (given healthy blood sugar levels) our moods. This, in turn, increases both the pleasure and effectiveness of all our thinking, feeling, and actions.

The overarching result of the synchronistic philosophy is a freer and more joyful life that attracts other people, as well as whatever you desire. This virtuous cycle culminates in a fresh philosophy, a better personality, and a more satisfying and creative lifestyle—with lots of benefits.

Serenity

Serenity is one of the most soothing benefits of beliefs that work. This is a state of relaxation born of equanimity—maintaining a balanced and even-keeled point of view—via acceptance rather than resignation. The famous Serenity Prayer sums up the essential strategy of visionary living: "May I change the things I can (by making and executing good decisions), accept the things that I cannot change, and develop the wisdom to know the difference."

Having arrived at a belief in synchronicity that is reinforced by your experience of better decisions, serenity will help you relax mentally and physically. Its psychologically soothing effect will feel like swaying in a hammock under the shade of two palm trees on a beautiful beach, or being a baby cradled by a loving mother. Devotional types might visualize Divine Mother sprinkling life with nurturing sparks of synchronicity during the day and full-color dreams during sleep. Things that happen become more interesting, as we open to the possible meanings contained in dark clouds and silver linings—and sometimes even in events that might have been dismissed as random. As serenity rules our minds, we stop sweating the small stuff, choosing to humbly accept the belief that there is a reason for everything. To the extent that we can leverage and take refuge in more evolved beliefs, everything will change for the better.

In summary, our beliefs are important because they are necessary and useful, not because they are right. We are called upon to be adults and to be conscious of, and responsible for, every operating assumption we claim and adopt.

12

The Synchronistic Lifestyle

The great and glorious masterpiece of humanity is to know how to live with a purpose.

—**Michel de Montaigne**

When we bring what is within us out into the world, miracles happen.

—**Anonymous**

Chaotic changes are in the air. Time seems to be going by faster and faster. In a world racked by environmental and social catastrophes—wildfires, flooding, hurricanes, and tornadoes—a sense of security feels hard to come by. Spoiler alert: there is no security. There never was. Nature's governing laws of impermanence and constant change have always seen to that.

The best way to predict your future is to create it . . . and the playing field is more internal than external. Nobody can do it for you. Forget about comparing yourself in any way. Don't be concerned with how popular you are, how much attention you can attract, or how many "Likes" you get. The inner game brings in the spiritual dimension. This is life's biggest game—and the one that takes the most guts. It's about channeling Creative Power and creating meaning for your life. It's about expressing your life-purpose in whatever joyfully satisfying way you can. These are things only you can define for yourself, an arena of decision-making where a hero's courage is often required. You are the hero on your particular hero's journey. There are dragons of fear to put to rest, there are mountains yet to climb. Considering that you have been reading this book, right now, your timing is good.

Synchronicity is the manifestation of perfect timing—the synchronization of everything that happens and all the changes in the universe. It is an elegant term for how everything is interconnected and how things come together in time. As we have noted, synchronicities are taking place all the time whether we notice them or not. There's value in becoming increasingly more aware of them, because they remind us of how interconnected everything is, as well as our place in an ever-changing world. There's even more value in learning how to leverage synchronicity in order to answer the call of Creative Power in our lives, which is what this book has been about.

Taking special note of synchronicity and serendipitous encounters has become integral to my perspective, providing me important feedback from the universe about thoughts, feelings, dreams, and goals. By allowing my intuitive sense to guide me more on where to go, what to do, and who to connect with, synchronicity has revealed clues and signs along the way . . . and I am not done yet. Greater awareness of synchronicity has helped me learn to trust myself and my intuitive intelligence.

While mystical awareness of synchronicity is a joyful experience in and of itself, this book is predicated on the radical notion that we can learn to use synchronicity to go beyond the occasional transcendent experience and consciously create a life that's optimal for us, a life that we want. Learning how to consciously leverage the synchronicity principle gives the visionary decision-maker a major advantage, while also developing a keener intuitive intelligence for increasingly better decision-making. It's a spiritual path, but it's a pragmatic one too.

Visionary beliefs supported by an empowered imagination aligned with your aptitudes, fascinations, and values provide a foundation for an expansive approach to problem solving and a playful approach to fulfilling your purpose. Given a solid foundation of self-knowledge, we can utilize awareness of synchronicity to pick up on signs that point us in the direction of the destiny we are cocreating—in coordination with Infinite Intelligence—and to make better and more timely decisions. As noted throughout this book, intuitive intelligence benefits enormously from paying attention to the little miracles that arise in the form of synchronicities, dream symbols, and hunches. Once we master the art of noticing them and deciphering their meaning, synchronicities can become a decision-making lever that reinforces a sense of being connected and in the flow. They become apparent more often, which feels as if you are attracting miracles to yourself. In addition, by using authentic divination tools like the I Ching, you can create synchronicities in the form of readings that stimulate your intuitive intelligence. The happy result of this approach to living is the evolution of what I call "the synchronistic lifestyle." Over time, as you learn to trust your intuition with healthy self-confidence, life becomes more miraculous.

Miracle-Mindedness

"There are two ways to live your life," an anonymous quote goes. "One is as though nothing is a miracle. The other is as though everything is a miracle." As you let yourself be supported by useful visionary beliefs, your mind will download creative power more easily, able to open up to and receive inspiration and guidance from Infinite Intelligence. This will be your experience of that new way of seeing the world this quote alludes to, which I call "miracle-mindedness." Few people have better exemplified a radically creative open-mindedness than Einstein, one of the greatest geniuses of the modern era. But even he didn't come by it easily.

A mechanistic worldview had ruled science and dominated thinking since Isaac Newton kicked off the scientific revolution with the laws of motion and gravity in the seventeenth century—that is, until Albert Einstein applied his intuitive intelligence and mathematical genius to venture into uncharted territories. Einstein had a mystical, playful way of perceiving how the world works. He was gifted at math, but his rare genius derived even more from his imagination and visualization skills. Even though he specialized in physics, his mind was capable of opening to the broadest planes of consciousness. He was a brave individual who adopted a fresh perspective free of the limitations of the imposing scientific paradigm he grew up with. His thought experiments tested novel viewpoints. He possessed the mental flexibility to entertain the possibility of revolutionary exceptions to the conventional ways of seeing, thinking, and believing.

Einstein's multidimensional imagination afforded him an extraordinary level of creative freedom. Very few can hope to match his level of genius, but anyone can achieve higher levels of inner freedom by adopting a miracle-minded approach. This attitude and perspective practically define the Visionary Decision Making paradigm and support the cultivation of the synchronistic lifestyle.

After sufficient practice, miracle-mindedness becomes the way one goes through life. An attitude of open-minded wonder begins to permeate perceptions and support background feelings of awe, humility, and contentment. You don't have to be perfect at this way of looking at things. It's not all-or-nothing. But to the extent that your conscious attention is allowed periods of such radical openness, amazing benefits and favorable outcomes will become more likely.

An ability to adroitly navigate life with the help of visionary beliefs brings with it an improved sense of timing. With a better sense of rhythm, you will be able to accept the mysterious aspect of life's unfolding patterns and ride the waves of change without as much inner resistance or fear. Such a courageous orientation—which you can consciously adopt if you are not held back by old, unconsciously held core beliefs—produces a feeling of excitement or adventure. This feeling state can trump the natural fear response to what's unfamiliar.

As you allow yourself to upgrade your beliefs, you will differentiate between working assumptions that serve your best prospects and unconsciously held beliefs that hold you back. Creativity-supporting visionary beliefs will give rise to a virtuous cycle featuring a broader awareness that evolves into a miracle-minded mindset and greater intuitive sensitivity.

Embracing synchronicity requires that you trust your intuitive intelligence and give it the freedom to probe synchronistic intersections and opportunities that arise holding creative potentials and new opportunities. There is something to learn from *everything* that happens—even happenings you didn't like or hadn't expected—not to mention seemingly miraculous events.

Make Life a Game You Win More Often

Sometimes we can be our own worst enemy. We get in our own way in an effort to avoid uncomfortable feelings. Pain is a normal part of life, but there is a difference between pain and suffering. The extent of our inner suffering is governed by attitude—and, more specifically, where we fall on the spectrum between acceptance and resistance. Resistance to realities is what causes mental and emotional suffering, not the pain itself (the way hypnosis relieves painful sensations proves this). We don't have to accept a position as helpless victims who are defending ourselves against possible dangers. We have the option to follow the example of the gods and turn life's challenges into playful sport—even if this sometimes means that five steps forward are followed by three steps back.

From the point of view of personal development and evolution, it helps to look at life as a game of strategy like chess or Go. Fortunately, your life is a game that you can't really lose—as long as you keep getting better at it. As with any game, winning depends on maintaining a positive attitude and exercising the skills you have developed. With your visionary beliefs supporting your active intuition, a virtuous cycle kicks in that reinforces a positive attitude. Maintaining a miracle-minded stance of positive expectancy will help you make more intuitive decisions. And, as in the workings of compound interest, even making slight improvements in your Visionary Decision Making skills will help you become exponentially more intuitive going forward.

When negative or catastrophic images tilt your mind toward the downward spiral of feeling depressed, the synchronistic point of view can act as a counterbalance. Try to remember that things are never as bad as they seem. The open-mindedness of an optimistic perspective allows images and magnetic feelings of healing, harmony, and happiness a much better chance to flow. As Charles Dickens wrote in the famous first line of *A Tale of Two Cities*: "It was the best of times, it was the worst of times." Like the glass half-full or half-empty, the one we choose depends on attitude.

Navigating life more intuitively makes everything more fun. You may even come to enjoy making big decisions (like a high-stakes gambler playing with marked cards). You will not only enjoy the superior results you get when you operate from beliefs that support what's meaningful for you, but you will enjoy the unfolding process itself. The high pleasure of participating in strategic decision-making and bold action reminds me of the Hindu concept of leela, a Sanskrit word that defines the playful way their deities operate in and on the world. Like Greek gods at sport, these archetypal examples of divine playfulness encourage us to maintain a childlike and good-humored attitude about life to the extent we can.

With a sense of rhythm like a graceful dancer or an athlete, you will feel increasingly more confident about the moves you make as you become more intuitively tuned in to the cosmic music. Being in the flow of good timing is exciting and fun—whether you are dancing, discovering new friends, or transacting business. Perfect timing is making the right moves at the right time. An ecstatic and energizing sense of rhythm develops the more you get in sync with the flow of change. Even a slightly improved sense of timing will greatly improve your odds of taking your best next moves with better timing than ever before. (This progressive evolution reminds me of *Groundhog Day*, that wonderful movie about life's learning processes.)

Benefits of Living Synchronistically

The benefits of the synchronistic lifestyle are multidimensional, inter-related, and huge, because they lead to greater joy and abundance in the most important areas of your life. The following are some of the major benefits of cultivating your intuitive intelligence and operating with a visionary level of awareness.

Creative Inspiration

Coming up with new ideas is always fun and exciting, but it requires that you unleash your imagination. This is too much to expect from yourself if you are too fearful, stressed, or preoccupied. To become more creative, we need to make a note whenever we have a hunch or notice a synchronicity, and then schedule ways to break out of our routines to create enough space to be able to contemplate the hunches and creative impulses that follow. Then we can cultivate fertile creative ground by tuning the intuitive antenna to the imaginative realm of Infinite Intelligence—perhaps with the help of mindfulness techniques like meditation or authentic divination.

As Marney Makridakis eloquently put it in her book *Creating Time*, "Creativity, meaning, and time dance together in an unavoidable, and rather effective, cycle: the more meaningful your projects are to you, the more likely you are to engage in them. Then, the more meaning you are experiencing, the more creative ideas you'll have for more mean-ingful projects. Meaning creates more meaning, and creativity begets creativity!"[1]

Give yourself a broader array of choices in any situation by ask-ing, "What if . . . ?" in order to bring up outside-the-box possibilities and to recognize alternative patterns. Once you get the hang of it, cul-tivating and maintaining a higher awareness of creative possibilities in your decision-making will increase your intuitive intelligence and add a highly pleasurable dimension to your life.

Confidence

Confidence is believing in yourself and your right to your particular Hero's Journey and unique contributions to the world, no matter how humble they might seem in comparison to others who are getting a lot of attention. In reality, it is unwise to ever compare yourself to anyone else. Confidence arises from believing that you have a destiny that inspires and empowers you to exercise your will in risk-taking ways. Once you discover what fascinates you and what you love, as well as what you are naturally good at, you will more frequently notice synchronicities and inspired hunches related to those things. Your viewpoint can evolve from fear and scarcity-consciousness (for example, the fear that there won't be enough) toward abundant opportunities to learn and thrive.

Whenever meaningful coincidences arise, let yourself enjoy a delightful "aha" moment as you feel a sense of fulfilled expectancy and the encouragement to believe in yourself and your destiny even more. Confidence grows with the experience of good fortune, which attracts more good luck. This is especially the case when we are operating from a heartfelt place. As we have seen in my case, even though nobody else believed in my vision of authentic divination software, my confidence was inspired by a passion for what I was drawn to create, which made it feel like the right thing to do, supporting the courage to go for it in spite of my fears.

Contentment

Contentment is a ripened state of happiness that comes with wisdom. It is a harmonious feeling state that is almost entirely neglected in modern society's frantic grasping for consumption and stimulation. The attainment of contentment requires wisdom derived from experience, which is helped enormously by paying attention to archetypal patterns, fascinations, synchronicities, and dreams. Contentment arises from a deep feeling of gratitude supported by a combination of unconditional acceptance and compassion for yourself and all beings. As a state of mind, contentment is the sweetest, highest pleasure of abundance.

Wisdom

As you develop intuitive intelligence by fine-tuning your intuitive antenna to pick up signals, insights, and inspirations, everything will take on a greater sense of meaning, which leads to the mature quality known as wisdom. Wisdom is the natural culmination of learning from experience. It takes time, but, once cultivated, it helps us to balance taking care of our individual selves with attending to the greater good of all. Things get out of balance when our point of view is too narrow or self-obsessed—a constriction of consciousness that can happen due to lack of self-esteem and/or an inflated sense of self-importance.

It is important to be able to call upon a strong ego that is ready to defend boundaries, but the ego should never be left in charge. The ego-self is most properly a "lieutenant" who needs to take direction from the higher level of consciousness, sometimes referred to as the spiritual Self. The ego does not make a good general. Forming an appropriate relationship between your ego and the rest of creation is the beautiful fruition of self-knowledge. An inscription on the ancient Oracle of Delphi once read, "know thyself." And as Lao Tzu put it long ago, "Knowing yourself is the beginning of all wisdom." Know your place in the world that is your home. Know that you are a valuable part of creation.

Grace

Grace is the happy coincidence of receiving what your heart desires, even before you think you deserve it. The gift of grace often comes in unexpected ways to a mind that is receptive. When grace is present, it inspires gratitude for Infinite Intelligence and creative power. When grace descends in the form of synchronicities, intuitive hunches, and good karma, the process of receiving it reminds you that the universe is a friendly place. The universe will provide everything you need as long as you cooperate by being true to your heart, paying attention, and remaining receptive.

The grace of synchronicity highlights the fact that your efforts alone are not enough to achieve your heart's desires. We are connected to all that is, totally interdependent with all of it. Intuitive intelligence helps us remember this. If we define heaven as a state of freedom and joy to be experienced during this lifetime, the blessing of grace is at its core. The grace of Spirit or Heaven is available to us to the extent we stay tuned. In a state of gratitude, we learn to trust the universe. Jungian therapist and teacher David Richo put it so well: "Grace is the higher power than ego at work in synchronicity. This power seems to have heart, that is, to want what is best for our growth."[2]

Grace is operating in your life when you are in sync with your destiny. Here is another personal story that provides a good example. In the earliest days of running our website offering I Ching and tarot readings, I got a call out of the blue from a man who said he owned the domain name Tarot.com, wondering if I would like to purchase it from him. When I asked how he found me, he said he had purchased a copy of the original Synchronicity I Ching software some ten years earlier and had been following my efforts ever since. He contacted me because he liked the authenticity I brought to my divination software and websites. He had a personal interest in divination, he said, but his Tarot.com and I-Ching.com websites were little more than a hobby. Despite other offers, he thought that I might be in a position to buy and put these domain names to the best use. He told me that he had a solid offer of $42,000 cash for Tarot.com, which made me gulp because, as valuable as such a name might someday prove to be, the figure seemed well beyond the reach of our little company. At the time we were barely keeping it together and didn't even have a line of credit with a bank.

Since he admired the way we produced our authentic interactive divination experiences, I asked if he would sell it to me for a lower price. Without hesitating, he replied, "I'd rather not." Not knowing how on earth I would get the money, I still didn't hesitate, "Okay, we definitely want it, but one last question—and please don't let my asking this be a deal-killer—would you be willing to let me pay it off in twelve monthly payments?" I took a deep breath and started thinking my letting-go mantra while silently waiting for his answer. It seemed like an eternity before he finally replied, "OK, I guess so." Believe me, this seemed like a miracle! (As it turned out, I paid him off within five months, and the Tarot.com domain name is now probably worth a million dollars.)

You attract grace when you are in alignment with what fascinates you or what you love, when you are in sync with your authentic self, and when you use your intuition to take risks in alignment with the flow of change. It is a wonderful feeling to realize that when you commit yourself to what you love, you are more likely to receive the support you need.

The Hero's Journey and Your Glorious Destiny

Destiny can be thought of as the intersection between passion and purpose. Ideally, your destiny is reflected in a vision and goals that outline your Hero's Journey—the life that you are meant to cocreate with the help of Infinite Intelligence. Your destiny is your highest potential as a human being, featuring your unique mix of aptitudes and talents, your personal expression of productivity and contribution.

Your destiny is yours alone. It is *your* evolutionary path that unfolds with a vital assist from your skillful decision-making and mastery of skills. William Jennings Bryan had it right when he said, "Destiny is not a matter of chance; it is a matter of choice. It is not a thing to be waited for; it is a thing to be achieved."

The word "fate" is often used interchangeably with "destiny," but a useful distinction needs to be made. Think of fate as something predetermined by the past, while destiny is future-oriented, creative, and full of potential. Unlike fate, destiny is not passive and you are not its victim. Basically, it is your choice whether to orient yourself toward creatively cooperating with your destiny or bemoaning and resisting fate.

This is one of the central guiding decisions we all make for ourselves, over and over again.

The Roman goddess of destiny was called "Fortuna." She is the archetype that helps seekers steer the ships of their lives toward greater good fortune. In ancient statues and paintings, she is depicted holding a nautical rudder (used for steering) and a cornucopia of abundance. With Fortuna as your partner, you envision your destiny as a creative adventure. Under her influence, you will be guided toward superior decisions and better timing.

In contrast to Fortuna, the Fates were deities who were responsible for all the troubles that befell human beings. This included whatever "karma" people might have coming as a result of some inherited character flaw or past transgression.

The Fates were depicted in Greek and Roman mythology as spinning, measuring, and cutting the thread of a mortal's life. In a fatalistic point of view, your future is predetermined, and you are more or less a helpless victim in the cosmic casino of random luck. Resisting your fate—acting as if you have no control or influence over your life—temporarily lowers your intuitive intelligence and is never a basis for skillful decision-making. Victim-consciousness provides people with excuses to avoid responsibility and risk-taking. Ironically, it is negligence to your own best interests that will actually turn you into a victim—you'll be the victim of a victim mentality and its resulting passivity!

Moving away from victim-consciousness toward becoming the cocreator of your destiny is something you grow into. Start, or restart, now. Develop intuitive intelligence and decision-making skills to get what you want in a timely manner with the least amount of suffering. Life will offer you myriad opportunities to realize the expression of your Hero's Journey. No matter how modest or grand your destiny in this lifetime may be, you are called to play the hand you were dealt and fulfill your potential, whatever it is. You can't control everything that happens, but you can significantly tilt the odds in your favor.

Your Dance Partner, the Goddess Destiny

Making the right moves at the right time is a valuable art for everyone, but staying in sync with the music defines the art of performers like musicians and dancers. The art of responding with balance and rhythm to the chances and opportunities that the Goddess of destiny offers you is like following a lead in partner dancing. If you can be humble and receptive, and your ego lets go of trying to take over and lead, you can learn to follow the subtle signals of a good dance partner—in this case the Universe itself. If you tune in via your intuitive sense, it will lead by providing you turn signals in the form of inspirations and other forms of inner guidance.

As you trust your instincts and maintain faith in the goodness of life, you will become nimbler in the exercise of intuitive intelligence through Visionary Decision Making. Here are some ways that using the synchronistic awareness of intuitive intelligence is similar to dancing:

- Tapping into your intuitive intelligence requires you to stay on your toes and be light on your feet.

- When dancing with Destiny, use your intuitive sensitivity to follow her lead instead of trying to call the shots and letting Ego take over. Picking up dance signals via intuition is more like responding to a soft touch on the shoulder than a contest of wills. In the synchronistic lifestyle, you trust your instincts and feel the rhythms of the cosmic music.

- Your timing steadily improves with practice.

- As you learn to trust intuitive insights and hunches, you become more balanced and prepared to move in a new direction when you are guided to do so. How does Destiny guide you? Via synchronicities, dreams, hunches, and creative inspiration!

- A graceful sense of rhythm develops when you navigate life with an imperfect but improving sense of balance.

- As you navigate changes in your career, family, and relationships, you are tuned to the flow of energy. When you stay conscious of and connected to your priorities, you are less likely to bounce around from one crisis to the next.

Dancing is a perfect example of good timing in action. All of us, clumsy or not, are dancers poised in a physical, mental, and emotional duet with our calling, or destiny. Even good dancers will miss a step now and then, but with practice their dancing achieves a balance between a vision of what they want to do and the improvisation of "feeling it." They're clear about their desires and intentions, and they are comfortable with their ability to respond with agility in a world where they know anything can happen. It's the perfect metaphor for cocreation.

Learning how to move gracefully through life is a spiritual accomplishment, a milestone on the path. When we are in "the zone," we become like the proverbial person of the Tao—bridging the gap between the heaven of Infinite Intelligence and the world, as shown in the Tao symbol showing the balance of yin and yang energies flowing into each other.

When you dance with Destiny, even more profound experiences of meaningful coincidence arise, leading to more seemingly miraculous results. This is what happens when profound desire and concerted action are in alignment with what Plato referred to as anima mundi, the soul of the world. When you know who you are, and you have discovered what you are meant to do based on your personal fascinations, you are in sync. It doesn't matter if the manifestation of your dreams is challenging. You are too delighted in receiving all the support that helps you turn challenges into opportunities to let difficulties that arise set you back very much.

Destiny in Action

For one last story, I offer a wonderful example of synchronicity support-ing my destiny, which occurred shortly after I published Synchronicity, the first I Ching software. My fifteen-year-old son and I needed to find a new home that would be large enough to house us and accommodate my new startup business with the first few employees. I had located a beautiful, large house that was ideally located in the neighborhood of my son's high school, but I was concerned that my application would be turned down. For one thing, leaving secure employment to become an entrepreneur had affected my credit rating, making it even more difficult to compete in Portland's tight housing market. Still, I was hopeful until I went over to the place to apply in person and learned that almost a hun-dred people had submitted applications before me.

Nevertheless, I was able to meet with the owner of the house, whereupon she asked what I did for work. I told her I had just started a little Macintosh software business. I didn't expect her to understand anything about software (it was 1990, after all), but as it turned out she had just gotten one of those early Macintosh computers shaped like an ice cube and she was curious about what I might have developed that could run on it. Tentatively, I explained that my software product was a bit quirky—an interactive version of the ancient Chinese I Ching called Synchronicity, I told her. The expression on her face when she heard this was priceless. It turned out that she was one of the few very early buyers of Synchronicity. In fact, she told me it was the only software she had ever purchased . . . and she loved it!

We both realized what a remarkable synchronicity this was. Happily for my son and me—and the business—she took it as a sign and leased the house to me on the spot. A year later, she sold me that house. Thirteen years after that, profits from the business (which by then had outgrown the house and moved out years earlier) paid off the mortgage. I raised my son, as well as started and restarted the business, in that house over the next nineteen years. Early on, I took out a second mortgage on the house to make payroll. Later, the house supported the company as collateral for a line of credit with the bank. In my mind, that house is the home that synchronicity built. It was destined to support my work and my calling—and ultimately was paid for by it. How ironic and perfect is that!

Synchronicities like this—and having the Tarot.com domain come to me—arise to support you when you are following your calling and dancing with destiny. You still have to make good decisions and execute them, but it is so much easier when the universe helps out. And it will! As David Richo puts it, "Synchronicity is one of [the] forces of grace. It is the spur of the moment in that it spurs us on and it happens just in time for us to learn or make a move or grow in some new way."[3]

Living from the Inside Out

The Visionary Decision Making approach was not invented overnight. It represents decades of study and thought experiments, trial and error, risk-taking in the real world, and learning from lots of mistakes. It is the fruit of the long practice of insight meditation and authentic divination systems to awaken, stimulate, and support my intuition. It is a proven way to navigate the journey of life by staying open to your sense of direction in changing tides. It is a way to let Creative Power flow through you and support passionate action.

Over time, the exercise of intuitive intelligence through the practice of VDM will change your perspective and support the confidence you need to fulfill your personal and vocational destiny. It starts on the inside with knowing yourself, accepting yourself unconditionally, and learning to trust your intuition. A bit of courage combined with good decision-making and learning experiences eventually leads to greater wisdom. The experience of successes—even small ones—will support the strongest faith that a person can develop: confidence in yourself. Starting now, consider it part of your unfolding destiny to make better decisions for yourself and your loved ones, to play a healing role in the world. As a result of your commitment, watch it work out that way right before your eyes!

It's normal to stumble as you learn to dance, but if you keep practicing, you will develop a better sense of rhythm as you go along. You will enjoy the dance of life more and more. Make it fun. Start by playing more of your hunches. Let yourself be willing to go through the fear of making some mistakes. Go ahead, it won't kill you! Risk a bit of embarrassment, if that's what needs to happen for you to let go of fears of judgment or disapproval. You will learn that a little embarrassment is not the end of the world and often well worth it in terms of adventure and educational value.

Feel the fear and go for it anyway, recalling that fear and excitement are two sides of the same coin. Remember that no matter what predicament you've ever found yourself in, you've handled it, right? Or you know what you would have done differently. Take comfort in remembering that your own resourcefulness is a safety net that nobody can take from you.

Begin with small risks. Get revved up to practice more frequent risk-taking in little ways, to make the art of intuitive decision-making into a manageable adventure of self-discovery, evolution, and progress. If you are someone who tends to be shy, you could start introducing yourself to strangers—perhaps by asking directions even if you don't need them. Or you might take a dance lesson or acting class where you are required to interact with others in a graceful way. If you are extroverted, you can risk some of your time and attention by the practice of focused listening, or by interviewing another person and not interrupting them before they complete their reply. In general, try testing your intuitive impressions. Allow yourself to be guided by them to get a deeper sense of people you encounter—even people you think you already know. Take the risk of openly checking with them to see how often your intuitive hunches about them turn out to be right.

Acts of generosity and loving kindness are always excellent ways to take small risks (and contribute to social harmony at the same time). Make it a habit to perform at least one unconditional act of generosity every day, expecting nothing in return—not acknowledgment, credit, or even gratitude. How is this a risk? Because giving can feel like depletion to our ego if we forget all the resources that are provided us and stay mired in poverty-consciousness or a pessimistic point of view. Also, to the extent that we are not accustomed to donating time, energy, or money, to freely give any of these can take us out of our comfort zones.

While the practice of generosity is admirable in every stage of life, it defines and expresses the calmness and grounded character of a wise Stage Three. Once I transitioned from Stage Two, the "builder" stage, by selling my business, I founded a nonprofit I called the Divination Foundation (also known as IntuitiveIntelligence.org) to express my creative freedom in the form of books, blogs, and radio interviews. I wanted to give back by helping people to make better decisions through my research, interviewing, writing, and publishing. In addition to my contribution of time and energy in the form of nonpaid work, I also donate to worthy causes via my "giving budget"—a concept that has been around for millennia. Ancient Jewish law, for instance, mandated the tithing of 10 percent of one's income to charity. But giving isn't just about money, nor is that necessarily the best way. If you cannot afford to give support in a financial way, don't let anyone tell you that you *should* donate 10 percent or 5 percent—or any percentage—of your income. There are so many ways to support the collective good with time and energy. All forms of generosity are good. Perhaps the truth is best expressed by this proverb: "If you have much, give of your wealth; if you have little, give of your heart."

Let's Dance!

The more you trust your intuition around taking risks that will grow you, treating life like a game or a dance, the better your intuitive sensitivity will become. Even when you stumble, your understanding of yourself and other people—and human nature in general—will dramatically improve. You will discover that the more you trust yourself, the more confident and happier you become. Change is inevitable, and changes that happen outside your control can be frightening. But as you cultivate your natural intuitive intelligence, you will discover that you have the agility to ride unpredictable waves of change like a balanced surfer. Going forward, you may even be able to influence the shape of waves to some extent. In short, your creative influence will grow.

Situations fluctuate, opportunities expire, and relationships change form without asking permission. But armed with VDM practices and more functional operating assumptions, you will have the creative power to influence the flow of change more than before. Even slight improvements in coordination and timing will compound to exponentially greater abundance and joy in your experience of life, facilitating both your individual and the collective healing. Here's to cocreating good fortune—not only for your own sake, but also for the good of humanity and the natural world upon which our survival itself depends.

Beyond getting survival needs met, another vital aspect of personal happiness is being securely connected—to a partner, family, and community; to all of humanity; to nature and spirit. A secure attachment with family or community supports greater confidence and creative explorations. Beyond the needs for security and belonging, however, we deserve a chance to be successful or happy in ways that are significantly meaningful to us. Many studies have found that seeking meaning rather than happiness produces greater satisfaction. As a species, we just thrive on meaning. In making an effort to live your life with a sense of purpose, your learning capacity will expand throughout your lifetime, no matter how old you are. Your beliefs will evolve and change as needed, based on what you learn.

Being true to who you are and what is most important to you—together with a cultivated intuitive intelligence—will give you the means to make great decisions and find your best timing in every stage of life. Through your willingness to take the risks involved in following your destiny, abundance and joy will not only be more possible, but much more likely.

These days we are dealing with more rapid change than ever before. Let's develop our internal sense of security by becoming more resourceful and creative as we learn how to better manage change and make the right moves at the right time. Visionary Decision Making is the central skill and challenge—the challenge of a lifetime, the challenge of creating meaningful success on your own terms. May you awaken, activate, and learn to trust your intuitive intelligence. May you enjoy the thrilling adventure of your own unique Hero's Journey!

Acknowledgments

The lessons in this book took more than forty years to learn and four years to write. Although I fully expect more learning (and writing) to come in this lifetime, a book that covers such a large part of my life and significant lessons learned is an important part of my Stage 3 legacy. Like a long letter that a person might leave behind for a beloved descendant, I wrote the book to pass on teaching stories that encourage others to discover and live their dreams.

This book would have never come to fruition without the tireless support, project management, and superb editing skills of my executive assistant and copyeditor, Nayana Jennings. Nayana has consistently tempered my flighty dalliances with the Muse to help me stay on track and complete the book.

There has been so much other help along the way. Gratitude goes out to managing editor Lindsay Brown of Beyond Words and for editorial assistance from Brittany White. And hats off to our web developer, Susan Langenes, who has been doing a wonderful job designing and developing our websites, IntuitiveIntelligence.org and Divination.com.

The wise counsel and friendly encouragement of fellow author Catherine Ingram helped tremendously, as well as the support of several other friends who took a peek at the work in various stages and nudged me toward the finish line. And, of course, I am most grateful for the generous contribution of a foreword by my brilliant friend, John Gray.

A couple of years ago, when I was feeling stuck and having trouble motivating myself to finish writing this book, executive coach Michael Beck reminded me that my ultimate goal was not sales or profits (in fact, all proceeds go to support our nonprofit work), but to help people make better decisions for their own sakes. The only goal for me has been sharing hard-won wisdom with as many readers as possible who find this book. So, no matter how you came across a copy, dear reader, I thank you for being a receptive audience and helping to make this massive effort worthwhile. It would be a great service to me and to potential readers of this book if you would leave a review on Amazon and/or Goodreads. And, if there is an easy way for you to pass the book on, I heartily invite you to do so!

Above all, I am grateful to be alive on this beautiful planet at this time and to every day feel more fully how the boundless compassion—of God, Infinite Intelligence, or whatever archetype you prefer to visualize in your life—is holding us and backing us up. The presence of the higher powers that inform and guide us has been confirmed by the greatest teachers for eons. I am grateful to all the teachers. Benefitting from their legacy and learning to call upon archetypal powers has been a sublime blessing in my particular hero's journey—this evolutionary learning adventure we call a human life.

Anyone who wishes to contact me or the Divination Foundation may currently do so via the contact links on IntuitiveIntelligence.org or Divination.com.

Appendix A:
The Creative Manifestation Treatment

The Creative Manifestation Treatment draws on the Creative Power archetype (or, God) to help you stay focused on fulfilling your highest priorities, empowered by an optimistic and creative attitude. This guided meditation is based on the work of Ernest Holmes, who founded the Church of Religious Science in 1927. I revised Holmes's original treatment, adding two powerful steps to support decision-making and action taking. Anyone of any religion can use the version below to attract and attain whatever their heart desires. I encourage you to edit and customize the one-page treatment below, to make the language and substance work best for you. (You can easily download a text version for this purpose via Divination.com.)

How to Use It

Find a seated position where you are comfortable but alert, as you might for a meditation session. Take a few deep breaths, releasing with an "ah" or "om" sound on each exhale. When you are feeling relaxed but alert and ready, slowly read your treatment to yourself, preferably aloud, or listen to a prerecorded reading that you have made. When you are finished, stay in place and breathe. Feel the bliss of being spiritually magnetic through the clarity and power of expressed intention, and emotionally magnetic through the infectious power of the feeling. Finish the treatment with a resolution to take your attracting attitude with you throughout your day.

The following template is drawn from other variations I have used in the past. Edit this one to suit your own needs:

Step 1: Recognition

I acknowledge Creative Power, the universal magnetic energy that unites and makes things whole. Divine power expresses itself as love, wisdom, and courage. It is reflected in the vastness of space, the sun around which Earth revolves, the beauty of nature, the joy of love and miracles. This unlimited resource operates according to the law of cause and effect that begins with attraction: first the image, then the declaration, and then manifestation. I know there is no limit to Creative Power.

Step 2: Identification

I am one with Creative Power, which surrounds me and flows through me. My breathing reminds me of my interconnectedness with all of nature, and I can feel the connection any time I close my eyes. Divine love and wisdom surround me and go before me, making my way easy and successful. I am capable of facilitating any results I visualize or feel. I don't need to know their exact form, but solutions appear quickly and easily. I deserve what is good for me.

Step 3: Declaration

I declare that I am now enjoying the realization of [my desire]. This feels [liberating, joyous and pleasurable, etc.].

Step 4: Thanksgiving

I give thanks for the fulfillment of [my desire], the joyful anticipation of which I am feeling already. I feel strong on my path. I am confident and full of faith, and my heart is filled with gratitude.

Step 5: Release

I let go of tendencies to control things, to worry, or to interfere by trying to shape results in a particular way. I accept that the law of cause and effect is operating on this treatment right now, even if my senses have no proof yet. I am attracting [my desire], and [my desire] is attracting me. The manifestation of this, or something better, is in process. Creative Power is synchronistically producing the perfect results for me with perfect timing. I am letting go of trying to control things and surrendering to the good that is my destiny. My "faith" is my intuitive sense of the manifesting process that is happening behind the scenes right now.

Step 6: Feeling It—Emotional Magnetization

I am letting myself feel the presence of what I have declared, which is in the process of manifesting. As I let this feeling radiate throughout my entire being, I become magnetic.

Step 7: Decision-Making and Timing—Action Steps

I make the right moves at just the right time, starting with better decision-making that taps my intuition, intellect, and receptivity to good advice. I make and follow up on commitments to myself. In the dance of life, I am taking good steps in a timely manner. As long as I am in connection with Creative Power, I know I can't go wrong!

When you have fully read or recited this treatment, sit with the feeling (step 6) as long as you like. Feeling it is the most powerful addition I made to Ernest Holmes's original five steps. It makes you magnetic!

Remember to edit this treatment to develop a personalized version for yourself. (You can download the full Creative Manifestation Treatment from Divination.com in the resources section for easy editing.) Once you have found wording that feels potent when you speak it aloud, print it out and read it every morning before you start your daily routines.

Appendix B:
Visionary Decision Making Practices

Determining Your Hierarchy of Values (Chapter 2)

Dr. John Demartini uses the word "values" in a specific, practical, and measurable way. In the approach that he calls "hierarchy of values," the word "values" does not refer to ideals, moral codes, or entrenched beliefs. In Demartini's teachings, you can identify real values by simply analyzing how much time, energy, money, and thought you actually invest in them. Make a list of your current four or five major activities or preoccupations. Keep it as a file on your computer or smartphone, or keep a small printed copy in your wallet or purse. The idea is to keep the list somewhere you can easily see it, to regularly remind yourself of your top current values. (Sometimes, just knowing it is there helps, even if you don't look at it.) Edit and refine the list as you become more and more clear about your own unique hierarchy of values.

Tracking Synchronicities in a Journal (Chapter 3)

Keeping a synchronicity journal helps you take full advantage of signs that the universe provides. Whether on paper or in a digital file, make a point of recording meaningful coincidences—as well as dreams, hunches, and good ideas—that occur to you every day. If you have a smartphone or regularly use a computer, I recommend setting up a file on your smartphone, computer, or tablet.

Just having such a journal will make you notice more synchronicities, and more quickly capture the moment when a profound coincidence happens. Your physical "gut feelings," or that "feeling in your bones," will become sharper and more refined. The synchronicities you record will change your perspective and lead to new insights, relationships, and opportunities. Make a habit of entering all your synchronicities whether or not you understand their meanings yet. The significance of the people you meet and new potentials will become clearer as you go back and look them over. Add reflections and insights once a week as you attain a deeper understanding over time.

The Weighted-Pros Logic Technique (Chapter 5)

The fear of losing contains greater power than the hope of winning. To balance the emotional impact of loss aversion, I created a variation on Ben Franklin's pros-and-cons decision-making technique, which I call "weighted pros"—a practical approach that will help with any decision. When faced with a choice, create a simple table with your three best options across the top. For example, if your decision has to do with finding the right place to live, you might boil it down to three options:

rent downtown condo
buy house in suburbs
house-sit for friends

Instead of listing pros and cons below each of the options, list only its advantages. There are two reasons for only listing positives and not tallying the negatives: First, a con is usually an inversion of a pro. On an emotional level, the pro of one choice can seem more compelling when viewed as a con of another. It just seems to be easier for the human mind to focus on what it doesn't want rather than what it does want. Make a concerted effort to counteract that tendency by taking the fear element out of the calculation. Give each of the positives a weighted value on a scale of 1 to 10 (10 being the highest positive score), and then add up the total values for each column. The option that offers the highest value is your best logical choice.

Mindfulness of the Body Technique (Chapter 6)

Just take a minute right now: Pay a few moments of close attention to the feelings in your body. The feeling of your weight against the chair (if you are sitting), the feeling of your skin against your clothing, the subtle sensation of your nose hairs as you inhale and exhale.

When practicing mindfulness throughout the day, note your physical responses to information, people, and events that come your way.

Progressive Relaxation Technique (Chapter 6)

The technique works best when you're seated or lying down, but it can even be done standing.

First, tighten the muscles in the calf of your right leg. Hold the tension for five to ten seconds, and then let the muscles relax. When you release the tension in a particular muscle group, the muscle relaxes beyond its pre-tensed state. Repeat the process, isolating the muscles in the lower part of your left leg, and then work your way up your body, moving through the other muscle groups. By tensing and relaxing all your major muscle groups, you'll feel a stabilizing, grounding sensation throughout your whole body and clarity in your mind.

Mindfulness of a Letting-Go Moment (Chapter 6)

Close your eyes for a few moments and let go of whatever thoughts arise—noticing them but just letting them float by like passing clouds. Do this for a minute or two and notice the changes in your mind. Thoughts will keep popping up whether you want them to or not. Sooner or later, if you sit still long enough, you may experience a quieter, more spacious aspect of the mind, like a clear sky. In the meantime, as thoughts come and go, seemingly on their own, what makes them any more yours than passing clouds? Practice letting go until you have learned to slip into the natural mindfulness of our ancestors, free of having to pay attention to obsessive thoughts and worries that do you no good.

A Beginner's Meditation (Chapter 6)

Here's an easy way to begin a meditation practice: Find a spot where you can be alone and undisturbed for fifteen or twenty minutes. Sit comfortably in a chair or on a cushion on the floor, close your eyes, and concentrate on your breath. Bring your attention to the sensation of inhaling and exhaling, not with any special kind of breathing—deep or otherwise. Quietly watch the rise and fall of the breath, noting the subtle physical sensation of air coming in and out of the nostrils. Or note the rise and fall of the abdomen with each breath.

Sit still long enough to allow the chattering of your mind to simmer down, which can take up to fifteen minutes. Use an object of concentration, like the breath or the hum of a fan, and continue until your mind finds stillness.

I compare this slow settling down of the mind to how boiling water eventually settles after you take the pan off the burner. The flames represent the desires and attachments that stir up the mind. Even when you turn off the flames of desire, the boiling water will continue to churn before it simmers down. It takes a little time at first. This process can be frustrating to a novice, who may wonder if the settling will ever happen. But after just a little bit of patient practice, you will find that you can slip into a meditative state more and more quickly.

When first starting a meditation session, I suggest using a timer and committing yourself to sitting still—and only that—for twenty minutes.

Forget about achieving results (though you will). Psychologically, letting go of attachment to outcomes reduces a tendency to put pressure on yourself to do it right or to wonder if you are being successful at meditating. If you commit to just sitting still and stick to taking a daily "time out," you will start meditating—if only because as long as you are just sitting, there is nothing better to do! With practice, it becomes second nature to meditate wherever you are.

Mindfulness of Breathing Technique (Chapter 6)

Your breath is an excellent object of concentration because it is always there—when you are standing in line, when you are riding an elevator, and during in-between times throughout the day. It's discreet in that it is not obvious that you are meditating.

While it is also useful to maintain a formal sitting practice, you benefit from every possible instance of mindfulness throughout the day. Ayya Khema used to say that even a single moment of mindfulness is mentally purifying. The technique is simple: let go of rapidly changing thoughts and feelings by concentrating on your breath (or other object), while being open to and mindful of whatever arises in your field of consciousness.

The Letting-Go Mantra (Chapter 6)

Close your eyes and take a full breath, thinking the word *Letting* as you inhale and the word *Go* as you exhale. Repeat. When you reflect on the meaning of the two words, this mantra is reminding you to do what meditation is all about—letting go of attachment to thoughts and feelings that arise. Use the letting-go mantra anywhere and at any time. It helps instill inner peace and serves as a conscious reminder that letting go is the key to having a clear and open mind. In addition, letting go of your busy mind creates an opening for intuitive insights to alight like butterflies settling onto a sunflower.

Harvesting Intuitive Insights during Meditation (Chapter 6)

Meditation aims to let go for the sake of cultivating a transcendent consciousness. But another major benefit is greater intuitive sensitivity.

Considering the value of insights that arise during meditation, it can be useful to interrupt your concentration long enough for the left brain to record them. Rather than placing all the emphasis on just letting go of thoughts that arise, especially if you are facing a big decision, make a point to note insights that may come up during your meditation session.

To do this, you will need a pen and paper or a recording device. Once you've recorded an insight, let go of thinking about it—or anything, for that matter. Go back to focusing on your breath, mantra, or other object of concentration.

Although this approach to meditation is somewhat unconventional, I have found creative value in using meditation this way. Practicing mindfulness helps you develop an ability to hear the voice of intuition, which can connect Infinite Intelligence to your best interests.

Tracking Your Dreams (Chapter 7)

There is more than one way to keep track of dreams. Jung kept a notebook at his bedside, as many people do. Immediately upon waking, he wrote down what he could remember of his dreams. If Jung could have recorded his dreams using a voice recorder—as I prefer to do—he probably would have embraced the technology.

Record them as quickly as you can, without dwelling on what you put down. First impressions are most useful! Once you've recorded your dreams, you can start to interpret what they mean. The key here is to avoid self-censoring or second-guessing yourself. Let your mind generate free associations based on images you recall from the dream and record whatever comes up.

Even if you're looking for help with an important decision, don't narrow your interpretation to that specific issue—at least not at first. Be open-minded and receptive. Answers and insights may emerge in a different order than you expected.

Invocations and the Synchronicity Prayer (Chapter 7)

When you are going through major transitions, it is helpful to practice a daily invocative prayer ritual—not so different from the habit of saying the morning and evening prayers that many of us were taught as children. Return to the ritual of morning and evening invocations to stay more connected to Infinite Intelligence during the day and in your dreams at night. After you wake up in the morning, welcome a greater awareness of synchronicities throughout the coming day. Depending on what you intend to create or build or preserve, you can summon and activate other powers as well. At night, your affirmative prayer calls forth the healing and awakening power of dreaming.

To be more receptive to insights throughout your day, use the Synchronicity Prayer: "May I notice and pay attention to synchronicities that arise during this day. If I don't understand their meaning, I trust that it will be revealed in due course. In the meantime, I am grateful to notice the signals."

Compose your prayers in your own words and keep them in a file that you can edit on a computer, tablet, or smartphone. No matter how you choose to word your prayers, it helps to create a routine like this:

- Sit and breathe with a fairly straight back . If you need to lean against a cushion, wall, or back of a chair, that is fine. The mind tends to be sharper when we sit or stand in a balanced position rather than slumping or reclining. Take three deep breaths to let go of tension in your body. If you are not going to disturb anybody by doing so, try making an audible "ah" or "om" sound with each exhale.

- Read your invocation—preferably out loud to yourself—taking the time to understand each word.

- Breathe slowly as you let yourself project into it, and feel the archetypal power that you are invoking.

- Feel the bliss of being mentally magnetic through the clarity of your intention and emotionally magnetic through the infectious power of your desire. Sit quietly in the emotionally magnetic state for as long as you can.

- Make a resolution to notice this attraction consciousness sticking with you throughout your day.

Here are a few suggestions for how invocative prayers might be phrased (feel free to borrow from these examples and customize your own as well):

Sample Morning Invocations

May I notice all the magical moments today, as life unfolds synchronistically and perfectly, according to Destiny's plan.

As I face an important decision, I invoke the power of Courage, so that my choices will not be distracted by fear.

May Wisdom guide my decisions today; may the wisest choices become clear to me.

I am creating the mental and emotional space to tune in my intuitive sensitivity in order to make the best choices today. I am guided to the best paths of action.

Sample Evening Invocations

May the Dreamer bestow upon me symbolic dreams that I will remember and record, which will shed light upon my life and true Self.

Let my dreams flow tonight, and may their symbolic meaning bring me a greater awareness of who I am, my best direction going forward, and the most enlightened choices I can make.

Preparing for an I Ching Reading (Chapter 8)

Center yourself for a fruitful I Ching experience. A centering practice is an intentional process that will help move your ego out of the way so your mind can be receptive to guidance. (This alone is valuable.) Enter a meditative frame of mind that supports a sincere desire for truth and wisdom. Perform whatever centering technique or ritual works best for you prior to any I Ching consultation. Do your best to enter a state of focused relaxation.

It's also vital to be clear about what you hope to learn or achieve. Possible goals could be making an important decision or reducing stress around changes in your life that are currently beyond your understanding. These are not the goals of the ego that always wants to make things happen.

After you relax, consciously let go of any attachment to receiving a specific answer or outcome. Commit yourself to caring only about truth. By giving the ego a "vacation" from its usual preoccupations, you increase receptivity to archetypes that can inform your conscious mind and support your decisions and actions.

The information you receive from a reading comes from within you, not from the external environment. Simply lighting a candle, burning incense, or taking a few deep breaths with your eyes closed can facilitate focused relaxation. Choose what feels the most comfortable for you.

Before you cast a reading, take a few moments to affirm your allegiance to what is real.

Once you've entered into the proper frame of mind, consult the I Ching. Confidently adopt the attitude that everything will work out the way it is supposed to—for one reason or another. This will be true whether or not you understand the reason now.

Only consult the I Ching when you feel balanced and clear enough to listen to the wisdom it provides and to tap into your intuition.

Formulating Your I Ching Query (Chapter 8)

It is not necessary to formulate your concern as a question. In fact, it is less confusing to just make a note of what is on your mind—what dilemma, situation, relationship or decision you are working with. You can hold a specific subject in mind at the beginning of the divination process or just write down the name of a situation or a person you are involved with.

The tangibility of writing down your subject enhances focus and produces clearer readings.

Documenting I Ching Readings (Chapter 8)

It is helpful to take notes when consulting the I Ching, so have a pen and paper at hand or be close to your electronic device of choice. (The *Visionary I Ching* app conveniently allows you to cast a hexagram using a smartphone or tablet, read about your hexagram, and save it for later review.)

Saving your readings in a journal lets you evaluate and compare them in the future. Make note of your comments on the experience (including the details of your divination ritual and approach), your interpretation (a sentence or two that summarizes what the I Ching is reflecting), and the result (the aftereffect of the decision you made following your reading).

The VDM Meeting (Chapter 9)

If you feel stuck or virtually paralyzed, schedule a VDM meeting with yourself every morning for as many days in a row as necessary. Consider your options around the important matter every single day—until you are ready to make a decision and commit to a course of action.

Always schedule VDM Meetings as early as possible in the day. Make them your first item of business in the morning until you have had enough of them to get to clarity. There's no set length of time, but forty-five minutes to an hour gives you enough time to review and reconsider your options using techniques like these:

- Review your viable options, as narrowed down by the weighted-pros logic technique.

- Read a guided meditation script aloud to yourself to put you into a positive and receptive state of mind. If you are not able to do this because of interruptions or emotional interference, stop the process and reschedule a VDM Meeting with yourself early the next day.

- Invoke the Sovereign archetype to support yourself as the chief executive decision-maker of your life.

- Invoke the archetype of the Sage and summon forth a letting-go state of egoless mind. You may feel empty and vast as you open yourself up to creative potential, like the fertile Void of Creation that existed before the Big Bang, when all things were possible.

- Do a short I Ching reading for one last reflection, asking for perspective on your decision. Use three coins and the hexagram lookup feature in *The Visionary I Ching* ebook or the *Visionary I Ching* app on a smartphone or tablet.

- Optional: Meet with one or two of your most trusted and objective advisors and share your latest strategic ideas with them. Keep the focus on decision-making.

- Be your own CEO and make a final decision on your best next move. Move forward, or step back, or do nothing and be patient as matters undergo changes on their own. It is quite possible that, unless you're procrastinating, doing nothing for now might actually be the best move!

Enter a Written Agreement with Yourself (Chapter 9)

Formalizing a choice into a commitment by written agreement is a powerful and positive technique. I would suggest starting out by writing an agreement with your Self (the Self archetype) that goes something like this:

Dear Self,
I hereby make the following commitment to you:
[write a short description of your decision]
I am letting go of fear and doubt, and I resolve to do my best to implement my decision with power and grace.
Signed: _____   Date: _____

How to Upgrade Beliefs (Chapter 11)

Write down one or more beliefs, especially those you take for granted and never think about, that could benefit from reevaluation. Across from each, write out a revised, more productive assumption.

Keep a small copy of your list on your fridge, in your wallet, or on your computer desktop. Let it grow. Upgrading old beliefs is like training a puppy to go outside: consistent reminders on a regular basis.

Having a hard time coming up with ideas? The following lists areas of life where people often have a self-limiting core belief:

- **Your talents and capabilities:** "I'm no good at that stuff anyway, so why would anyone hire me?" Antidote: "I am capable of mastering anything I am interested in learning."

- **Your worthiness to be loved:** "I'm only lovable if I am perfect/ make lots of money/look beautiful," etc. Antidote: "I accept myself unconditionally. I am my own best friend and will never abandon myself. I appreciate my own kindness and resilience."

- **Your luck:** "Nothing turns out right. Everything bad always happens to me, so I shouldn't even try." Antidote: "I am far luckier than I know. I can improve my luck starting now."

- **Your world:** "People always take advantage. It's foolish to trust anyone I don't know very well." Antidote: "By allowing myself to give others a chance to be good with me, I expand my circle of friends and supporters."

Appendix C:
Visionary Beliefs

"Visionary beliefs" is the term I coined for *provisional* beliefs that a person can try on for size to see how effective they might be. According to my definition, a visionary belief must be intuitively reasonable—in other words, it must make sense to you—but you don't need to subscribe to it, or claim that you believe it, even as you are trying it out.

Change Is Your Friend

Change is a constant; there is nothing we can do about that. The two basic orientations toward change are fear or excitement. People who see change as friendly are more optimistic and more likely to enjoy the up-and-down flux of life. People who fear change, on the other hand, would like time to stand still.

To embrace change, we need to develop a more fluid relationship to time. When we enjoy life, time seems to go fast; when we feel resistance to something, it seems to crawl. When we come to regard change as a friendly force, we can learn how to navigate and manage it, and the success brought by our improving sense of timing will encourage us to cultivate our intuitive intelligence.

The Vast Reservoir of Infinite Intelligence Is Always Available

Individual willpower, no matter how strong, is never enough by itself to effect constructive change. To evolve and grow, we need to seek and accept the help of a higher power. (VDM simply refers to that higher power as Infinite Intelligence or Creative Power.)

Once we learn how to tune in via our intuitive sense, Creative Power provides everything we need to be creative, productive, successful, and happier. When I was a bootstrap entrepreneur and people asked if I had investors, I would reply, "Yes . . . my backer has infinite resources." (Of course, I was referring to that higher power.)

I Deserve to Have What I Want (and What I Want Is Good for Me)

If you believe you *don't* deserve to live out a meaningful and fulfilling destiny, your subconscious mind will not allow it to manifest.

Learning to trust yourself, your intuition, and your own interpretation of meanings does wonders for self-confidence. Self-confidence arises from discovering your natural talents and then practicing them until you achieve a level of mastery. Then you are in a position to create your own luck. As Louis Pasteur put it, "Chance only favors the prepared mind."

The Synchronicity Belief: There Are No Accidents

Living a synchronistic life involves cultivating acceptance and wonder while letting go of judgment and resistance to the way things appear. Recall the old expression, "Things are never as bad—or as good—as they seem." It's essentially true.

Be a warrior of acceptance and accept your own karma (substitute your concept of cosmic justice here), taking refuge in the belief that "what goes around comes around." You understand that there are no accidents—only occasional failures to discern aspects of a larger unfolding pattern. A greater awareness of synchronicity will ease the bumps and transform your experience of life—with its inevitable ups and downs—into a more rhythmic and meaningful journey. Enjoy!

Notes

Chapter 1

1. Bessie Stanley, "Success," *Brown Book Magazine*, 1904.
2. Jeff Bezos, "We Are What We Choose," May 30, 2010 Baccalaureate Remarks, Princeton University, transcript, http://www.princeton.edu/main/news/archive/S27/52/51O99/index.xml.
3. Eileen C. Shapiro and Howard H. Stevenson, *Make Your Own Luck: 12 Practical Steps to Taking Smarter Risks in Business* (New York: Penguin Group, 2005), preface, Kindle.

Chapter 2

1. Ashley Stahl, "How to Find Your Purpose in Your Twenties," *Forbes*, August 26, 2015, https://www.forbes.com/sites/ashleystahl/2015/08/26/how-to-find-your-purpose-in-your-twenties.
2. Joseph Campbell and Bill Moyers, *The Power of Myth* (New York: Doubleday, 1988), 113.

3. John F. Demartini, *The Values Factor: The Secret to Creating an Inspired and Fulfilling Life* (New York: Berkley Publishing Group, 2013), chap. 5, Kindle.

4. John F. Demartini, "Our Values Determine What We Do," interview by Alan Hosking, *HR Future* (November 2008): 10–11.

Chapter 3

1. C. G. Jung, *Jung on Synchronicity and the Paranormal: Key Readings Selected and Introduced by Roderick Main* (London: Routledge, 1973), 176.

2. David Richo, *The Power of Coincidence: How Life Shows Us What We Need to Know* (Boston: Shambhala Publications, 2007), 8.

3. Robert H. Hopcke, *There Are No Accidents: Synchronicity and the Stories of Our Lives* (New York: Riverhead Books, 1997), 28.

4. Jung to Carl Seelig, February 25, 1953, in *C.G. Jung Letters*, ed. Gerhard Adler in collaboration with Aniela Jaffé, trans. R. F. C. Hull, vol. 2, 1951–1961 (Hove, UK: Routledge, 1990), 109.

5. Wolfgang Pauli, *Scientific Correspondence with Bohr, Einstein, Heisenberg, a.o.*, ed. Karl von Meyenn, vol. 4, part I, 1950–1952 (Berlin: Springer, 1996), 33.

Chapter 4

1. Napoleon Hill, *Think and Grow Rich* (New York: Random House, 1937), 182.

2. Willis Harman and Howard Rheingold, *Higher Creativity: Liberating the Unconscious for Breakthrough Insights* (New York: J.P. Tarcher, 1984), 64.

3. *The Collected Works of C. G. Jung*, ed. and trans. Gerhard Adler and R. F. C. Hull, 2nd ed., vol. 8, *The Structure and Dynamics of the Psyche* (Princeton: Princeton University Press, 1969), 376.

4. *The Collected Works of C. G. Jung*, ed. Gerhard Adler, trans. R. F. C. Hull, vol. 9, part 1, *The Archtypes and the Collective Unconscious* (Princeton, NJ: Princeton University Press, 1959), 3.
5. *The Collected Works of C. G. Jung*, ed. Herbert Read et al., trans. R. F. C. Hull, 2nd ed., vol. 11, *Psychology and Religion: West and East* (Princeton, NJ: Princeton University Press, 1969), 246.
6. *Collected Works of C. G. Jung*, 8:178.
7. Robert K. Merton, "The Role of Genius in Scientific Advance," *New Scientist* 12 no. 259 (November 2, 1961): 306.
8. Bob Proctor, *You Were Born Rich: Now You Can Discover and Develop Those Riches* (Scottsdale, AZ: LifeSuccess Productions, 1997), 191.

Chapter 5

1. David Eagleman, *Incognito: The Secret Lives of the Brain* (New York: Pantheon Books, 2011), 122.
2. Robert W. Firestone and Joyce Catlett, *Fear of Intimacy* (Washington, DC: American Psychological Association, 1999), 26.
3. Gary Klein, *The Power of Intuition: How to Use Your Gut Feelings to Make Better Decisions at Work* (New York: Currency, 2004), 24.
4. Gerd Gigerenzer, *Gut Feelings: The Intelligence of the Unconscious* (New York: Penguin Group, 2007), 153.
5. Blaise Pascal, *Pensées* (New York: Dover Publications, 1958), 212.

Chapter 6

1. *The Collected Works of C. G. Jung*, ed. Herbert Read et al., trans. R. F. C. Hull and H. G. Baynes, vol. 6, *Psychological Types* (Princeton, NJ: Princeton University Press, 1971), 282.
2. Caron Goode, "Intuitive Intelligence Comes of Age," SelfGrowth.com, February 1, 2010, https://www.selfgrowth.com/articles/intuitive_intelligence_comes_of_age.

3. William Hermanns, *Einstein and the Poet: In Search of the Cosmic Man* (Brookline Village, MA: Branden Press, 1983), 16.

4. R. Joseph, *The Right Brain and the Limbic Unconscious: Emotion, Forgotten Memories, Self-Deception, Bad Relationships* (University Press Science Publishers, 2012).

5. Goode, "Intuitive Intelligence Comes of Age."

6. Brigitte Stemmer and Harry A. Whitaker, eds., *Handbook of the Neuroscience of Language* (London/Burlington, MA: Academic Press, 2008), 205.

7. Thomas Lewis, Fari Amini, and Richard Lannon, *A General Theory of Love* (New York: Vintage Books, 2001), 32.

8. Cliff Saran, "Decision-Makers Rely on Intuition over Analytics," ComputerWeekly, June 5, 2014, https://www.computerweekly.com/news/2240221902/Decision-makers-rely-on-intuition-over-analytics.

9. Goode, "Intuitive Intelligence Comes of Age."

10. Lewis, Amini, and Lannon, *General Theory of Love*, 84.

11. Rick Beneteau, *Pearls of Success: Words to Succeed By* (self pub., n.d.), 5, PDF ebook.

12. Susan Jeffers, *Feel the Fear . . . and Do It Anyway* (New York: Random House, 1987), 94.

13. Adam Hadhazy, "Think Twice: How the Gut's 'Second Brain' Influences Mood and Well-Being," *Scientific American*, February 12, 2010, https://www.scientificamerican.com/article/gut-second-brain.

14. Malcolm Gladwell, *Blink: The Power of Thinking without Thinking* (New York: Little, Brown, 2005).

15. Edmund Jacobson, *Progressive Relaxation: A Physiological and Clinical Investigation of Muscular States and Their Significance in Psychology and Mecial Practice* (Chicago, IL: University of Chicago Press, 1938).

16. Meredith Marie Miller, *Freedom from the Story: From Trauma to Passion and Purpose* (Pasadena, CA: Best Seller Publishing, 2015), chap. 29, Kindle.

17. Francis P. Cholle, *The Intuitive Compass: Why the Best Decisions Balance Reason and Instinct* (San Francisco: Jossey-Bass, 2011), 8.
18. Cholle, *Intuitive Compass*, 98.
19. David Harp, *The Three-Minute Meditator* (Alcoa, TN: Fine Communications, 1999).

Chapter 7

1. *The Collected Works of C. G. Jung*, ed. Herbert Read et al., trans. R. F. C. Hull, vol. 8, *The Structure and Dynamics of the Psyche* (New York: Pantheon Books, 1960), 131.
2. Carl G. Jung, *Man and His Symbols* (London: Aldus Books, 1964), 87.
3. James Hillman, "Oedipus Revisited," in *Oedipus Variations: Studies in Literature and Psychoanalysis* (Washington, DC: Spring Publications, 1998), 90.
4. Joseph Campbell, *The Hero with a Thousand Faces* (Princeton, NJ: Princeton University Press, 1973).
5. Carl G. Jung, *The Red Book: Liber Novus; A Reader's Edition*, ed. Sonu Shamdasani, trans. Mark Kyburz and John Peck (London: W. W. Norton, 2009), 133.
6. Jung to Count Hermann Keyserling, April 23, 1931, in *C.G. Jung Letters*, ed. Gerhard Adler in collaboration with Aniela Jaffé, trans. R. F. C. Hull, vol. 1, *1906–1950*. (Princeton, NJ: Princeton University Press, 1992), 83.

Chapter 8

1. *The Collected Works of C.G. Jung*, ed. and trans. Gerhard Adler and R. F. C. Hull, 2nd ed., vol. 8, *The Structure and Dynamics of the Psyche* (Princeton, NJ: Princeton University Press, 1969), 452.
2. *Collected Works of C.G. Jung*, 8:451.
3. David Richo, *The Power of Coincidence: How Life Shows Us What We Need to Know* (Boston: Shambhala Publications, 2007), 152.

4. Molly Gilmour, "Steves: 'The Best Souvenir Is a Broader Perspective,'" *News Tribune*, January 22, 2015, https://www.thenewstribune.com/entertainment/article25920241.html.

Chapter 9

1. Graham Speechley, "Vision Is Not Enough," LeadershipQuote, last modified February 16, 2016, http://leadershipquote.org/vision-is-not-enough.
2. Daniel H. Pink, *When: The Scientific Secrets of Perfect Timing* (New York: Riverhead Books, 2018).
3. Hermann Hesse, *Siddhartha*, trans. Hilda Rosner (New York: New Directions Publishing, 1951).

Chapter 10

1. Malcolm Gladwell, *Outliers: The Story of Success* (New York: Little, Brown, 2008), chap. 2, Kindle.
2. Lao Tzu, Tao Te Ching, trans. Sam Hamill (Boston: Shambhala Publications, 2007), 122.

Chapter 11

1. Catherine Pulsifer, "What We Believe Becomes Who We Are," Inspirational Words of Wisdom, 1998, http://www.wow4u.com/what-we-believe.
2. Carol S. Dweck, *Mindset: The New Psychology of Success* (New York: Random House, 2007), 61.
3. Dweck, 61.
4. Bruce H. Lipton, *The Biology of Belief: Unleashing the Power of Consciousness, Matter, and Miracles*, 10th anniversary ed. (Carlsbad, CA: Hay House, 2016), xv.

5. Eileen C. Shapiro and Howard H. Stevenson, *Make Your Own Luck: 12 Practical Steps to Taking Smarter Risks in Business* (New York: Penguin Group, 2005), 38.
6. Robert H. Hopcke, *There Are No Accidents: Synchronicity and the Stories of Our Lives* (New York: The Berkley Publishing Group, 1997), 209.
7. David Richo, *The Power of Coincidence: How Life Shows Us What We Need to Know* (Boston: Shambhala Publications, 2007), 2.

Chapter 12

1. Marney K. Makridakis, *Creating Time: Using Creativity to Reinvent the Clock and Reclaim Your Life* (Novato, CA: New World Library, 2012), 92.
2. David Richo, *The Power of Coincidence: How Life Shows Us What We Need to Know* (Boston: Shambhala Publications, 2007), 31.
3. Richo, *Power of Coincidence*, 32.